浙江工业大学重点教材建设项目资助

实用跨文化交流教程

INTERCULTURAL COMMUNICATION: A PRACTICAL COURSE

主　编　　李果红

副主编　　郭亚莉

　　　　　姚冬莲

主　审　　刘绍龙

　　　　　楼荷英

ZHEJIANG UNIVERSITY PRESS
浙江大学出版社

前　　言

　　跨文化交际就是指不同国度、不同种族、不同文化背景下的人们借助于某种符号来传递信息、交流思想和感情并产生相应行为。这种不同文化间的交流源远流长，但是真正将文化交流上升到理论高度并发展成"跨文化交际学"，还只是近五十多年的事情。

　　美国是个移民国家，来自世界各个角落的移民都强调并维护自己的文化，因而形成了美国独特的多元文化格局。1959 年，以美国人类学家 Edward T. Hall 为代表的一些学者在前人研究的基础上提出了"跨文化交际"的理论，他的著作《无声的语言》(*The Silent Language, Anchor Books*, 1959) 因而也成为这一学科的奠基之作。1974 年，跨文化教育训练与研究学会(SIETAR，Society for Intercultural Education，Training and Research)在美国正式成立，学者们也开始把研究重点从对比和分析不同文化交际中的差异(Cross-cultural Communication)转向研究跨文化交际中动态变化的过程(Intercultural Communication)。理论的突破促进了该学科的快速发展，跨文化交际学所涉及的内容越来越多，方法也日臻完善。如今跨文化交际学已发展成为一门被全世界学者们充分重视的集人类学、语言学、心理学、传播学、社会学等为一体的综合性学科。

　　我国研究跨文化交际学起步较晚。20 世纪 80 年代，我国开始实行改革开放政策。一方面，海外归来的学者不断地把西方有关跨文化交际理论、研究方法、教学实践等引进到中国；另一方面，国内学者对语言学和文化的研究更趋于人文化，在学习与借鉴西方的同时结合我国的实际情况，从不同角度探索与发展我国跨文化交际的学科外延。

　　虽然跨文化交际学在我国的历史不算长，但是其发展速度相当快。1995 年在哈尔滨召开了我国第一届跨文化交际研讨会，并成立了全国性的跨文化交际研究组织——中国跨文化交际研究会。1997 年在北京又召开了第二届研讨会。参与跨文化交际研究的学者涉及外语界、对外汉语界、语言学界和心理学界等等。尽管学者们研究的角度有所不同，但是他们都对跨文化交际学在我国的确立和发展做出了自己的贡献。迄今为止，他们在学术杂志上发表的论文已达数千篇，专著也已有数十部。

　　纵观世界，"全球化"的浪潮已势不可当，跨文化交际正成为越来越普遍的现实。不同国家、不同文化、不同宗教、不同信仰的人们能否在"地球村"中和谐相处，共同解决人类生存的一系列问题，在很大程度上取决于我们能否有效地进行交往并达到相互理解、相互信任、相互促进。

　　作为外语教师，我们在长期的教学实践中已经充分认识到，跨文化交际能力的培养是外语教育的重要内容，外语教学必须与文化教育相结合。帮助学生拓宽视野，提高他们对异文化的宽容性和敏感度，这是我们义不容辞的责任。正是基于此目的，我们花费几年时间精心编写了《实用跨文化交流教程》，以满足广大师生及各方面读者的需要。

本书包括十二个单元，每个单元分四个部分：

第一部分为导入，对本单元涉及的话题作一个概括介绍。

第二部分提供一篇课内阅读、两篇课外阅读文章。课内阅读文章后列有词汇表（表中所列词汇在课文中用黑体显示）、难句解释，并且编有与课文相关的练习（阅读理解题、讨论题等）。两篇课外阅读文章后也有难句翻译、阅读理解练习。注释中还将包括**文化信息**的部分以**黑体**突出，以方便读者查看文化信息点。

第三部分设计了与话题相关的课堂活动，包括讨论、案例分析、角色扮演等，形式多样，内容翔实，如在课堂开展活动一定能活跃气氛，大大提高学生学习语言和文化的兴趣和效率。

第四部分提供背景知识，信息量大，知识面广，是学生自学或教师备课的有力帮手。

此外，每个单元后，编者还列出了相关网址和参考书目，可以为感兴趣的读者拓展学习提供方便。

本书既可作为高校跨文化交际学的教材，也可作为海外留学生的生活学习指南，它集语言学习和文化教育于一体，生动多样的案例分析等活动与练习更增添了它的实用性和独特性。

本书还配有精美教学课件（附练习答案），有需要的教师可到浙江大学出版社网站注册后下载或发邮件给责任编辑（zhugeq@126.com）索取。

本书由李果红任主编，郭亚莉、姚冬莲任副主编，刘绍龙教授、楼荷英教授审稿。各章节的编写人员为：价值观（章以华、张小霞、葛红霞），非语言交际（戴剑娥、刘百军、申屠玉君），海外求学（沈瑛、郭亚莉、邱明明），教育（何君、沈瑛、何艾莉），社会现象（许晓洁、吴娟红、方昉），社交礼仪（王晓霞、张小霞、方昉），社会福利（吴娟红、许晓洁、王晓霞），工作（刘百军、申屠玉君、戴剑娥），饮食（楼红燕、郑维南、章以华），影视（郭亚莉、何君、楼红燕），日常生活活动（郭亚莉、沈瑛、葛红霞），旅游与交通（郑维南、何艾莉、吴娟红、邱明明）。李昌祖、王健倩、赵宇、谭静等老师对本书编写的前期工作给予了大力支持与帮助，在此我们表示诚挚的谢意。书中的错误和不当之处，敬请广大同仁与读者指正。希望此书能为提高读者的跨文化交流的实用能力做出我们的一份贡献。

编　者

2014 年 7 月于杭州

Contents

Introduction

In *Broadening the Horizon of Linguistic Politeness*, Prof. Robin Lakoff says, "During the early twentieth century, anthropologists began to objectively examine the differences in interpersonal behavior among diverse cultures, noting that what one group considered polite or proper, another might find bizarre or rude. While all cultures seem to possess notions of what was appropriate or polite in specific contexts, there was no universal agreement about which behaviors fell under that rubric."

In the past, most people lived in a limited area, without any contact with people outside their own area. Today the world is undergoing rapid change. Trade barriers are collapsing around the globe, and companies are marketing their products and/or services worldwide. Consequently, business procedures and company structures are adapting to these challenges, too, and intercultural communication becomes more and more frequent. To meet these global challenges, according to M. Byram and many other scholars, language instruction needs to expand beyond verbal communication to include intercultural competence in its curriculum, because intercultural competence is the key to successful intercultural communication. It is said that studying a second language without learning the culture is like learning how to drive by studying a drivers' manual only and never getting behind the steering wheel. That's to say, acquiring a second language demands more than learning new words and another system of grammar. It involves developing sensitivity to aspects of language that are usually not taught in language textbooks, for instance, permissible degree, directness in speech, forms of politeness, etc.

Globalization enables people to get in touch with people of other cultural backgrounds very easily. The whole world has become one market open to all. Marshall McLuhan went a step further, calling today's world a global village "because of the rapid expansion of worldwide communication networks." These global communication networks allow individuals in industrialized nations to communicate with one another almost instantaneously. Parallel to the telecommunications revolution, global travel has become reality, too, allowing one to meet virtually anyone anywhere on the globe within a few hours. The advent of worldwide computer networks and satellite teleconferencing has shrunk distances even further. As a result, cooperation throughout the world can be found here and there now.

In today's world, intercultural communication competence can never be overemphasized. According to the Economist Intelligence Unit as well as the Ashbridge Management Research Group of England, the top five characteristics of an effective global manager are:

1. strategic awareness

2. adaptability to new situation

3. sensitivity to different cultures

4. ability to work in international teams

5. language skills

In other words, four of the five characteristics are intercultural communicative skills. In intercultural communication, even if we have mastered the target language well, we may still fail to understand and be understood. In order to minimize misunderstandings when we communicate with people from other cultures, a good knowledge of their cultures is of vital importance.

Yet, intercultural communication is not easy simply because culture is invisible. Culture influences us from our birth, but we are rarely conscious of cultural messages (perceptions, rules, and behavior) that we are receiving. We not only learn cultural behaviors unconsciously, but also perform them almost habitually and automatically. To reveal the secrets in intercultural communication scholars at home and abroad have done numerous studies in the field of intercultural communication, mainly theoretically of course. This textbook, as its title indicates, focuses on the practical aspects that are closely related to people's life and work. There are altogether twelve units. Besides the three reading articles and the relevant exercises in each unit, we also provide lots of topic-related information, lists of reference books and websites for further reading.

The publication of this textbook could not have been possible but for the materials we use in it. Therefore, the contribution of all the authors of these materials should not get unacknowledged. We find it a great pity that the lack of contact information prevents us from delivering our sincere thanks directly to all the authors. We would appreciate it if the authors could contact us.

Unit 1

Value

Part One

Lead-in

We may all be members of the same village, but we are sitting at our own campfires.

—Anonymous

也许我们都是地球村的一员，但是无疑我们都围坐在自己的篝火旁。

——无名氏

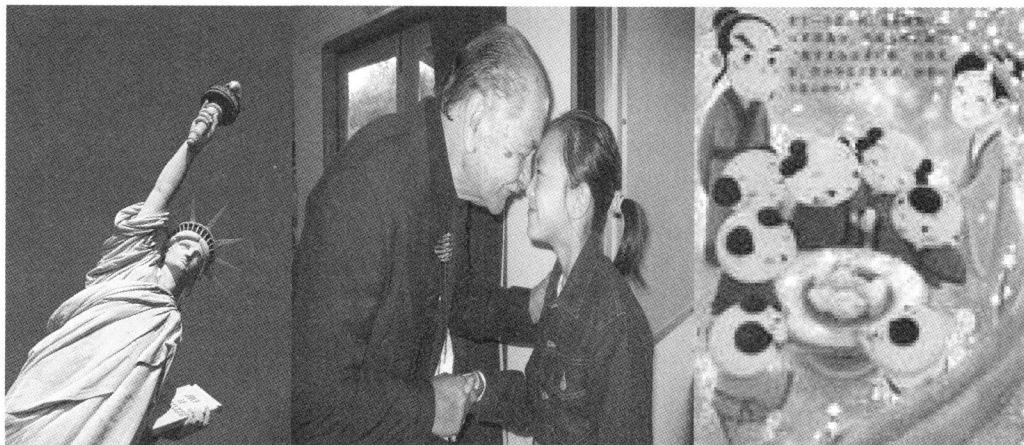

Values are deeply held beliefs—usually based on cultural traditions, long-held family, religious teachings and long-lasting memories of personal experiences. Given their sources, people's values seldom change, even when their more superficial desires are modified. "Asking someone to adjust his values is like asking him to alter his sense of reality," explain mediators Susan Carpenter and W.J.D. Kennedy. While this can happen, it doesn't happen often or easily. For this reason, values usually cannot be negotiated, nor can they be changed through persuasive arguments.

Part Two
Reading Passages

In-Class Reading

Warm-up questions:

1. What do you think is the most important in your life? Or what do you pursue in your life?
2. What do you know about cultural values in the U.S.?

The Greatest American Value

*If you ask most Americans what the cultural values in the U.S. are, you might get some blank stares, or a statement of some basic beliefs. The question may seem simple, but the answer is quite complex. In a society as highly diverse as the United States, there is likely to be a **multitude** of answers.*

*American culture has been enriched by the values and belief systems of virtually every part of the world. Consequently, it is impossible to be **comprehensive**. Now this author offers you his individual perspective on American values.*

1   This week I've realized something about America. In separate discussions over assisted suicide[1] and sex before marriage, I've found out that we've gone quite a way from the nation founded by men who **pledged** their lives, their fortunes, and their sacred honor to the **cause** of liberty. We've become a land where pleasure is king and pain for any reason is out.

2   There has always been this element in American life. After all, the South's avoidance of the uncomfortable task of **emancipation**[2] (which would have been a huge inconvenience) put our nation on the road to a war where half a million Americans died in senseless **slaughter**.

3   However, American life today is **overrunning** with the love of pleasure, like never before. In the debate over sex before marriage, the greatest argument encountered is that sex before marriage was necessary because without it, you could have a bad sex life.

4   The recent stories on women **aborting** their children so they could not have to delay school , not be too fat to fit into their wedding dress, and not be embarrassed are all part of the same trend. The most **heinous** case was a woman who aborted two of her triplets to avoid buying **jumbo jars** of **mayonnaise**.

5   In the Assisted Suicide debate, we want a quick way out. We can't wait for death to come; we must **hasten** its arrival, so as to avoid our pain. Issues of morality, **fidelity**, and truth are thrown out of the window for pleasure as our culture's greatest value.

6   Our love of pleasure leads us to make poor decisions in every area of life. For example, our need for instant **gratification** has driven our national savings rate to an all time low. Many marriages end each year because one partner is simply unhappy. Wisdom is less sought after than **despised**. Those who **dispense** advice that challenges us to do something other than what feels good such as Dr Laura, James Dobson, and Josh Harris of *I Kissed Dating Goodbye* are **ridiculed** and attacked, often without their ideas even being examined[3].

7   The impact it had on our nation's politics has been disheartening to say the least. The Clinton **Impeachment**[4] failed, not so much because people believed he was innocent but because:

   1) they didn't want to risk hurting a good economy;

   2) they were bored with the **scandal** and wanted to watch something else.

8   There are people (somewhere between 10%-20%) that care about issues on either side of the political fence, while the rest of the people are like **windsocks**, moving whichever way feels best at the moment. We wonder why we have **wishy-washy mealy-mouthed** two-faced **backstabbing** cheats in office. Well, folks, they REPRESENT us. If we don't like what we see in Washington, we'd better take a look in the mirror. We let them continue to represent us because our **patriotism** is shallow 4th of July stuff.[5]

9   It has **infected** our churches. Our hunger for God has been replaced by a desire for comfort. We ask **Pastors** to teach us only easy, light things and then walk away if they try and take us beyond our comfort zone. We choose or reject churches because of the style of music, not the guidance of the Holy Spirit,[6] not the eternal truths of God's Word, but our own passing fancies.

10   Now, I don't think we should become **masochists**, but we've gone beyond what is healthy in our quest for pleasure. We've become what the Apostle Paul[7] called, "Lovers of pleasure rather than lovers of God," lovers of pleasure rather than lovers of family, country, or morality. By choosing the path of least resistance time and time again, we're choosing to **forgo** those events in life that can build character and make us into better people and a better nation.

11   Is it any coincidence that what Tom Brokaw called the Greatest Generation[8] went through the Great Depression? Women did without nylons, people drove together, and **paid through the nose** to defeat Hitler because they knew how to do without.[9] They remembered the importance of sacrifice, honor, and love.

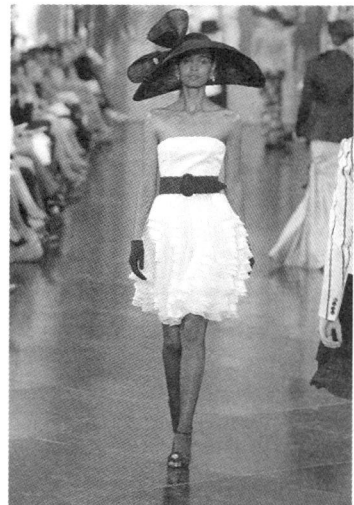

12   If we are to survive as a culture, we must also remember. We must find a calling higher than pleasure, a reason for existence greater than the next **fad** or cheap thrill.[10]

—Adam Graham

New Words and Expressions

abort	v.	terminate before completion, as of a computer process, a mission, etc. 异常中断，中途失败，夭折，流产
backstabbing	n.	hurting sb. at his back or without his knowing it by mean means (用诽谤或出卖等手段) 加害于人，卑鄙暗算
cause	n.	purpose for which efforts are being made 目标，理想，事业
comprehensive	a.	including all or everything 全面的，广泛的，包容的
despise	v.	look down on with disdain 轻视
dispense	v.	give up as not strictly needed 免除，省却，无须
emancipation	n.	freeing someone from the control of another 释放，解放
fad	n.	fashion, interest, preference, enthusiasm, unlikely to last 新奇的时尚；一时流行的嗜好或狂热
fidelity	n.	loyalty; faithfulness 忠实，诚实，忠诚
forgo	v.	give up 作罢，放弃
gratification	n.	state of being gratified; great satisfaction 满意
hasten	v.	act or move at high speed 催促，赶紧，促进，加速
heinous	a.	shockingly brutal or cruel 可憎的，极恶的
impeachment	n.	a formal document charging a public official with misconduct in office 弹劾，指摘
infect	v.	contaminate; give disease, (fig) feelings, ideas, to a person, his body or his mind 传染，感染
jar	n.	vessel, usu. round, with a wide mouth, with or without handle(s), of glass, stone or earthenware 罐，广口瓶
jumbo	a.	of great mass; huge and bulky 〈美〉巨大的
masochist	n.	someone who obtains pleasure from receiving punishment 性受虐狂者，受虐狂者
mayonnaise	n.	egg yolks and oil and vinegar 蛋黄酱
mealy-mouthed	a.	hesitant to state facts or opinions simply and directly 说话拐弯抹角的；说话委婉的
multitude	n.	a large indefinite number 多数，群众
overrun	v.	run over (a limit or brim) 溢出，超过限度
pastor	n.	minister of a church 牧师
patriotism	n.	love of country and willingness to sacrifice for it 爱国心，爱国精神

pledge	*v.*	promise solemnly 保证，使发誓
ridicule	*v.*	subject to laughter 嘲笑，奚落
scandal	*n.*	disgraceful gossip about the private lives of other people; a disgraceful event 丑行，丑闻，诽谤，耻辱，流言蜚语
slaughter	*n.*	the killing of animals (as for food); killing (animals, people) in large numbers 屠宰；残杀，屠杀
windsock	*n.*	a truncated cloth cone mounted on a mast used (e.g., at airports) to show the direction of the wind 风向袋
wishy-washy	*a.*	weak in willpower 缺乏力量或香味的，缺乏特点或决心的
pay through the nose		pay an expensive price 付出太多代价

Proper Names

Dr Laura	劳拉博士
James Dobson	詹姆士·杜布森
Josh Harris	约叔亚·哈里斯
Clinton (Bill Clinton)	克林顿 (美国前总统)

Notes

1. assisted suicide: suicide with the help of other people 受助自杀

2. **the South's avoidance of the uncomfortable task of emancipation:** In 1861, the American Civil War (1861-1865) began—a sectional conflict in the United States of America between the federal government (the "Union") and 11 Southern slave states that declared their secession and formed the Confederate States of America, led by President Jefferson Davis. The Union, led by President Abraham Lincoln and the Republican Party, which opposed expansion of slavery, rejected any right of secession. After the Battle of Antietam in September 1862, Lincoln's Emancipation Proclamation made the freeing of the slaves a war goal. The goal also allowed the Union to recruit African-Americans for reinforcements. This Emancipation Proclamation caused great opposition on the South side and hence put the two sides in bloody battles.

3. Those who dispense advice that challenges us to do something other than what feels good such as Dr Laura, James Dobson, and Josh Harris of *I Kissed Dating Goodbye* are ridiculed and attacked, often without their ideas even being examined: **Laura Catherine Schlessinger** is an American radio host, author, and conservative commentator who is an outspoken critic of practices that she considers immoral and have become too prevalent in contemporary American culture including sex outside of marriage. **James Dobson** is a radio psychologist and the founder of *Focus on the Family* (爱家协会), a Christian conservative organization. **Josh Harris** is the author of a book entitled *I Kissed Dating Goodbye*—A new attitude towards romance and relationships—dating. *I Kissed Dating Goodbye* suggests there is a better way to do with

romance than dating. It is reordering your romantic life in the light of God's Word and finding more fulfillment than a date could ever give—a life of sincere love, true purity and purposeful singleness. 整句话的大意是：如果有人做一些具有挑战性但不是为了享受的事情时不需要他人的忠告，如 Dr Laura, James Dobson，以及《我与约会吻别》的作者 Josh Harris 等，那么人们根本不会去考虑他们的想法如何就会去嘲笑他们、攻击他们。

4. **The Clinton Impeachment:** 克林顿弹劾案

The impeachment of President **Bill Clinton** arose from a series of events following the filing of a lawsuit on May 6, 1994, by **Paula Corbin Jones** in the United States District Court for the Eastern District of Arkansas. In her complaint initiating the suit, Ms. Jones alleged violations of her federal civil rights in 1991 by President Clinton when he was governor of Arkansas and she was an Arkansas state employee. According to the allegations, Governor Clinton invited Ms. Jones to his hotel room where he made a crude sexual advance that she rejected. The name of **Monica Lewinsky**, who had worked in the White House in 1995 as an intern, was first included on a list of potential witnesses prepared by the attorneys for Ms. Jones that was submitted to the President's legal team. Finally the Senate voted that the President was not guilty.

5. We let them continue to represent us because our patriotism is shallow **4th of July** stuff. 此句大意为：我们继续让他们来代表我们，因为我们没有足够的爱国情感。(人们只有在 7 月 4 日才爱国)

6. **Holy Spirit:** 圣灵

The Holy Spirit is one of the three persons of God: Father (圣父), Son (圣子) and Holy Spirit. The Bible declares that there is only one living God, yet we learn from scripture that He comprises three separate personages. The Holy Spirit, Father and Son all comprise a unified Godhead known in Christianity as the "Trinity (三位一体)." While each "personage" is distinct in function, each shares together in the same deity and each reflects the divine attributes of the one living God.

7. **Apostle Paul or Paul the apostle:** one of the most notable of early Christian missionaries, author of Fourteen epistles in the New Testament 使徒保罗

8. **The Greatest Generation:** The Greatest Generation is a term used to describe those U.S. citizens who fought in World War II, as well as those who kept the home front intact during it. Some of those who survived the war then went on to build and rebuild the United States' industries in the years following the war.

9. Women did without nylons, people drove together, and paid through the nose to defeat Hitler because they knew how to do without. 此句大意为：女人们没有尼龙面料的衣物 (因为第二次世界大战中很多尼龙被用来做降落伞了)，人们为了节省油拼车驾驶，付出很大的代价才击败了希特勒，这是因为他们知道如何应对匮乏。

10. We must find a calling higher than pleasure, a reason for existence greater than the next fad or

cheap thrill. 此句大意为：我们应当找到一种比享乐更高的生命的意义，一种比追求下一波时尚或廉价的刺激更伟大的存在理由。

● **Reading Comprehension**

1. Directions: *Discuss the following questions with your classmates.*

1) What did Americans pursue when the nation was founded?

2) What do they mainly pursue now according to the author?

3) What does the author say about American life today? Do you agree with him? Why or why not?

4) What impact does Americans' love of pleasure have on the nation?

5) What suggestion does the author give to solve the problem?

2. Directions: *Read the following statements carefully, and decide whether they are true (T) or false (F) according to the text.*

_____ 1) The author believes Americans now take pleasure as the first priority in their life.

_____ 2) The author supports the view that sex before marriage is necessary because without it, people could have a bad sex life.

_____ 3) Assisted suicide is reasonable in the author's opinion.

_____ 4) The author believes the love of pleasure has affected American economy adversely.

_____ 5) The author thinks Americans are not patriotic enough at present.

_____ 6) People choose different churches because they hold different faiths.

_____ 7) The author believes hardship can build character and make people into better people.

_____ 8) The author calls on people to find a higher goal in life in order to keep the culture.

● **Discussion**

1. People have very different views as to what Americans believe in or value. What opinions have you heard or read about it? If you have not, then try to seek relevant information from all the sources available and compare those views so as to draw your own conclusion. You can either submit a writing or give an oral presentation.

2. Based on your life experiences or those of others, talk about what many Chinese believe in or value, and give some examples to support your ideas.

After-Class Reading

Passage One

Warm-up questions:

1. What does "freedom" mean in your mind? Can you list some cases in which you can enjoy freedom and some other cases in which you can not?

2. Do you think there is any conflict between personal freedom and social loyalty? Illustrate your point with examples.

The Person between Personal Freedom and Social Loyalty

1   In traditional societies, an individual person's entire life was predetermined and regulated from the cradle to the grave.[1] Membership in families, castes, social strata, and a particular people determined the course of a person's life, with little room for personal decisions and development. One's personal name meant little, and in some societies daughters were simply numbered, since after their regulated marriage they acquired the family name of the husband. By contrast, one's family name meant everything. A "good family" ensured one's social status. One had to come "from a good house," as we used to say in Germany. In traditional societies, stability meant everything, while individuality meant little.

2   Modern societies place the values of personal freedom above the values of membership and belonging. Tradition no longer shapes life. We live in free choice societies, for we believe that only in its individual persons can a society become creative. This is why we may no longer accept anything as predetermined and prearranged. Every person must be able to determine everything himself or herself: free choice of schools, vocations, partners, domicile[2], politics, religion, and so on. We are even working on being able to determine freely our genetic composition as well. Nothing is permitted to be "destiny," not even gender; everything must be determinable. In half-traditional societies in Europe, a person is yet addressed by the family name; in completely modern societies, and among young people, the only name that applies is Jim and Joan, that is, a person's first or given name or the Christian name.

3   Modern big cities individualize and isolate persons. Only in villages or smaller towns can one live in an extended family. Modern apartments and cars are designed for at most four persons—father, mother, and two children. Free choice of vocation and free choice of domicile are tearing the older extended families apart. Ever since our own children have been living in Berlin, Hamburg, and New York, we rarely see our grandchildren. In the big cities of Berlin, Hamburg, Frankfurt, and Munich today, more than half of all households are single households.[3] More and more, family members are becoming single persons. This does not necessarily mean isolation, though this, too, is present to an unnerving degree, for example, among the aged; to a much higher degree than before, freely chosen friendships are replacing the predetermined family. The residential group is becoming the new life form, and "patchwork families" are emerging in which no one knows or cares anymore just who is descended from whom or who is related to whom, but rather only who cohabits with whom or who is living with whom.[4] The "reference person" is replacing relatives.[5]

4   In every living room, the public sphere is furnished by television. Persons merely sitting alone in front of the television set do participate in all the events of the city, nation, and world, or at least they think that this is the case, even if in truth they are participating merely in the "virtual world"

of previously selected information and entertainment. Certainly, a person can turn the television on and off, but this act does not constitute control of the media. Although people can indeed participate in everything insofar as they watch the news, they cannot participate in determining these things since they cannot broadcast anything themselves.[6] This distinguishes the television public from every human face-to-face discussion. Human beings are always rendered controllable through individualization: Divide et impera.[7]

5   Finally, there are indications that a new culture of death is emerging. In traditional societies, a person was in a religious sense "gathered to his fathers," and in an earthly sense interred in the family grave.[8] In the cult of ancestors[9], at the Christian All Souls' Day[10] or Totensonntag,[11] people visit and decorate the graves of their ancestors. In modern societies, personal care of graves is becoming increasingly difficult because people no longer live in the vicinity of the cemeteries. Religious interest in the family tradition is disappearing. This is why there are more and more "anonymous burials" in the secular spheres of modern human beings: the corpse is cremated and the ashes spread on a field or the sea.[12] "No one knows the place." The isolated, now merely self-determinative, person disappears into nothingness. Actually, this is quite consistent, since the family name already counted for nothing in life. Why should it now bind the children to the graves of the dead?

6   A series of excellent attempts has been made to balance out the deficits of the human person in modern society through a reflection on community values.[13] I am referring not to conservative and fundamentalist retrogressions, but rather to the communitarian idea of strengthening once again the sensibility of modern human beings for the notion of membership and belonging.[14] This includes the creation of local forms of community in overseeable circumstances; a reacquisition of the values of the common good; an enhanced appreciation of social consensus; and the development of a participatory economic democracy. All in all: the idea of the "good society," of a "civil society," actualized at every level, both large and small.[15]

7   I endorse such a balance between the values of personalism[16] and communitarianism[17], and will contribute no further vision here. I will restrict my consideration to personal freedom, a freedom that as a result of ever progressing individualism cannot be maintained. Neither can it be surrendered for the sake of belonging to a traditional society. In my opinion, it can be preserved only through dependability and loyalty.

8   The free human being is the being that can promise and that must also keep these promises. Through promises that I make, I in my multiplicity am making myself unequivocal both for others and for myself. In the act of promising, a person defines himself or herself and becomes dependable, acquires fixed contours, and can be addressed.[18] In keeping one's promises, a person acquires identity within time, since that person reminds himself of himself whenever he is reminded of his promises. Only within the nexus of promises made and fulfilled does the free person, the person not predetermined by traditions, first acquire continuity within time and thus

identity.[19]

9   A person who forgets his promises forgets himself; a person who remains true to his promises remains true to himself. If we keep our promises, then we gain trust; if we break our promises, we are mistrusted; we lose our identity and no longer know ourselves. This identity of the human person within a life history is designated by a person's name. Through my name, I identify myself with the person I was in the past, and anticipate myself as the person I want to be in the future. I can be addressed by my name; I sign contracts with my name and vouch for my promises. Free persons live together socially in a dense weave of promises made and kept, of agreements and trustworthiness; such coexistence cannot exist without trust. It is not predetermined membership, but rather covenant that is the paradigm of a free society; and this covenant is based on social consensus and responsibility.

10   The making and keeping of promises, the giving and receiving of trust—these are not restrictions on personal freedom, but rather the concrete actualization of that freedom. Where do I feel personally free? In a supermarket where I can buy whatever I want, but where no one knows me and not even the cashier looks into my eyes, or in a community in which I am accepted, and in which others know and thus affirm me as I am? The first is the reality of individual freedom of choice; the second the reality of communicative freedom. This first focuses on things; the second on persons. For me, true freedom is realized through mutual acknowledgment and reciprocal acceptance[20], that is: it is realized personally through friendship, and politically through covenant. The atmosphere of true freedom is trust.

Notes

1. In traditional societies, an individual person's entire life was predetermined and regulated from the cradle to the grave. 此句大意为：在传统社会中，一个人从出生到死亡的整个一生是早就注定的，并在控制范围之内。

2. domicile: 定居点

3. single household: 独立门户，自成一家

4. The residential group is becoming the new life form, and "patchwork families" are emerging in which no one knows or cares anymore just who is descended from whom or who is related to whom, but rather only who cohabits with whom or who is living with whom. 此句大意为：居民们的生活方式正在慢慢更新。在一个个"临时拼凑起来的家庭"组成的团体中，没有人会在乎谁来自哪个家族，有些什么亲戚，他们关注的只是谁与谁住在一起，或一起生活。

5. The "reference person" is replacing relatives. 此句大意为："证明人"或"与生活密切相关的人"正在逐渐代替"亲属"这一概念。

6. Although people can indeed participate in everything insofar as they watch the news, they cannot participate in determining these things since they cannot broadcast anything themselves. 此句大意为：虽然当人们在观看新闻的时候能够对目前为止发生的每一件事发表自己的看法，但

是他们不能自己去播出任何内容，因此他们也就不能参与决定那些事情。

7. Divide et impera: Divide and rule. 分区而治。

8. In traditional societies, a person was in a religious sense "gathered to his fathers," and in an earthly sense interred in the family grave. 此句大意为：在传统社会中，当一个人死亡时，从宗教意义上说，他是听从了天父的召唤，在人间则被埋入家族坟墓。

9. in the cult of ancestors: 在祭祀祖先的仪式上

10. **All Souls' Day:** 万灵之日

   All Soul' Day (sometimes called the "Day of the Dead") is November 2nd (November 3rd if the 2nd falls on a Sunday). It is a Roman Catholic day of remembrance for friends and loved ones who have passed away and are now in Purgatory, being cleansed of their venial sins and atoning before entering fully into Heaven.

11. **Totensonntag:** Sunday before Advent, on which the dead are commemorated 纪念亡灵星期日 (圣诞节前倒数第五个星期日，德国对第一次世界大战中殉难军民的纪念节)

12. This is why there are more and more 'anonymous burials' in the secular spheres of modern human beings: the corpse is cremated and the ashes spread on a field or the sea. 此句大意为：这就是为什么在现代世俗社会中有越来越多的匿名墓地：墓中的尸体被火化，骨灰被撒于大地或海洋。

13. A series of excellent attempts has been made to balance out the deficits of the human person in modern society through a reflection on community values. 此句大意为：人们需要通过思考团体价值来弥补现代社会中个人缺陷，在这一方面，已经有了一系列可贵的尝试。

14. I am referring not to conservative and fundamentalist retrogressions, but rather to the communitarian idea of strengthening once again the sensibility of modern human beings for the notion of membership and belonging. 在这里，我并不是说要退回到保守的完全基督教化的集体时代中去，我只是强调社区意识，即要加强现代人身份认同和归属感。

15. All in all: the idea of the "good society," of a "civil society," actualized at every level, both large and small. 此句大意为：总而言之，在各个层面，"良好的社会"或"文明的社会"这个想法都得到了实现。

16. **personalism:** 个人主义

17. **commmunitarianism:** 社区主义

   Communitarianism encourages the general public to participate in public affairs and to cultivate the sense of community through the promotion of altruism, fraternity, and service.

18. In the act of promising, a person defines himself or herself and becomes dependable, acquires fixed contours, and can be addressed. 此句大意为：通过许诺，人们可以界定自己，并使自己看起来可靠，获得一个固定的公众形象和一个恰当的称呼。

19. Only within the nexus of promises made and fulfilled does the free person, the person not predetermined by traditions, first acquire continuity within time and thus identity. 此句大意为：只有通过不断的承诺并实现承诺才使一个不受传统束缚的自由人随着时间的流逝先

慢慢稳定下来，从而获得一个身份。

20. mutual acknowledgment and reciprocal acceptance: 互相承认，互相接受

● Reading Comprehension

1. **Directions:** *Try to find out the differences in values between people in traditional societies and people in modern societies according to the passage. Discuss with your partners to see if you can find more differences and illustrate them with examples.*

2. **Directions:** *Complete the following passage by using the words in the box, based on the information from the text:*

discussion	dependability	membership	residential	given
anonymous	extended	family	freedom	ancestors

In traditional societies, an individual person's life was predetermined and regulated. At that time, a person's _____ name meant everything. A "good family" ensured one's social status. By contrast, modern societies place the values of personal _____ above the values of _____ and belonging. Among young people, the only name that applies is the _____ name or the Christian name.

In modern big cities, people are individualized and isolated. _____ families are replaced by nuclear families. The _____ group is becoming the new life form and "patchwork families" are emerging. People "participate in" all the events of the cities by watching television instead of face-to-face _____.

In traditional societies, dead people lived in the vicinity of the cemeteries. People gathered to visit and decorate the graves of their _____. In modern societies, there are more and more "_____ burials" on a field or in the sea.

Many excellent attempts has been made to keep the balance between the values of personalism and comunitarianism. The balance can be preserved only through _____ and loyalty.

Passage Two

Warm-up questions:

1. The famous British writer Robert Louis Stevenson ever said, "A friend is a present you give yourself." What does "a friend" mean to you? Discuss it with your partner and exchange your opinions with each other.

2. What do you value most in the friendship and how do you deal with the relationship with your friends?

On Friendship

1   Few Americans stay put for a lifetime.[1] We move from town to city to suburb, from high school to college in different states, from a job in one region to a better job elsewhere, from the home where we raise our children to the home where we plan to live in retirement. With each move we are forever making new friends, who become part of our new life at that time.

2   For many of us the summer is a special time for forming new friendships. Today millions of Americans vacation abroad, and they go not only to see new sights but also in those places where they do not feel too strange with the hope of meeting new people. No one really expects a vacation trip to produce a close friend. But surely the beginning of a friendship is possible? Surely in every country people value friendship?

3   They do. The difficulty when strangers from two countries meet is not a lack of appreciation of friendship, but different expectations about what constitutes friendship and how it comes into being. In those European countries that Americans are most likely to visit, friendship is quite sharply distinguished from other, more casual relations, and is differently related to family life. For a Frenchman, a German or an Englishman friendship is usually more special and carries a heavier burden of commitment.

4   But as we use the word, "friend" can be applied to a wide range of relationships—to someone one has known for a few weeks in a new place, to a close business associate, to a childhood playmate, to a man or woman, to a trusted confidant. There are real differences among these relations for Americans—a friendship may be superficial, casual, situational or deep and enduring. But to a European, who sees only our surface behavior, the differences are not clear.

5   As they see it, people known and accepted temporarily, casually, flow in and out of Americans' homes with little ceremony and often with little personal commitment.[2] They may be parents of the children's friends, house guests of neighbors, members of a committee, business associates from another town or even another country. Coming as a guest into an American home, the European visitor finds no visible landmarks.[3]

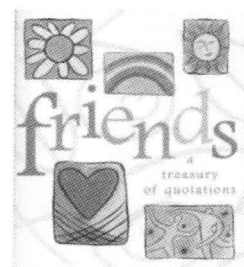

The atmosphere is relaxed. Most people, old and young, are called by first names.

6　Who then is a friend?

7　Even simple translation from one language to another is difficult. "You see," a Frenchman explains, "if I were to say to you in France, 'This is my good friend,' that person would not be as close to me as someone about whom I said only, 'This is my friend.' Anyone about whom I have to say more is really less."

8　In France, as in many European countries, friends generally are of the same sex, and friendship is seen as basically a relationship between men. French women laugh at the idea that "women can't be friends," but they also admit sometimes that for women "it's a different thing." And many French people doubt the possibility of a friendship between a man and a woman. There is also the kind of relationship within a group—men and women who have worked together for a long time, who may be very close, sharing great loyalty and warmth of feeling. They may call one another copains—a word that in English becomes "friends" but has more the feeling of "pals" or "buddies". In French eyes this is not friendship, although two members of such a group may well be friends.

9　For the French, friendship is a one-to-one relationship that demands a keen awareness of the other person's intellect, temperament and particular interests. A friend is someone who draws out your own best qualities, with whom you sparkle and become more of whatever the friendship draws upon.[4] Your political philosophy assures more depth, appreciation of a play becomes sharper, taste in food or wine is enhanced, enjoyment of a sport is intensified.[5]

10　And French friendships are divided into categories. A man may play chess with a friend for thirty years without knowing his political opinion, or he may talk politics with him for as long a time without knowing about his personal life. Different friends fill different niches in each person's life.[6] These friendships are not made part of family life. A friend is not expected to spend evenings being nice to children or courteous to a deaf grandmother. These duties, also serious and required, are primarily for relatives. Men who are friends may meet in a cafe. Intellectual friends may meet in larger groups for evenings of conversation. Working people may meet at the little bistro where they drink and talk, far from the family. Marriage does not affect such friendships; wives do not have to be taken into account.

11　In the past in France, friendships of this kind seldom were open to any but intellectual women. Since most women's lives centered on their homes, their warmest relations with other women often went back to their girlhood. The special relationship of friendship is based on what the French value most—on the mind, on having the same of outlook, on vivid awareness of some chosen area of life.[7]

12　In Germany, in contrast with France, friendship is much more clearly a matter of feeling, Adolescents, boys and girls, form deeply sentimental attachments, walk and talk together—not so much to polish their wits as to share their hopes and fears and dreams to form a common front against the world of school and family and to join in a kind of mutual discovery of each other's and their own inner life.[8] Within the family, the closest relationship over a lifetime is between brothers and sisters. Outside the family, men and women find in their closest friends of the same sex the devotion of a sister, the loyalty of a brother. Appropriately, in Germany friends usually are brought into the family. Children call their father's and their mother's friends "uncle" and "aunt". Between French friends, who have chosen each other for the similarity of their point of view, lively disagreement and sharpness of argument are the breath of life.[9] But for Germans, whose friendships are based on common feelings, deep disagreement on any subject that matters to both is regarded as a tragedy. Like ties of kinship, ties of friendship are meant to be absolutely binding. Young Germans who come to the United States have great difficulty in establishing such friendships with Americans. We view friendship more tentatively, subject to changes in intensity as people move, change their jobs, marry, or discover new interests.

13   English friendships follow still a different pattern. Their basis is shared activity. Activities at different stages of life may be of very different kinds—discovering a common interest in school, serving together in the armed forces, taking part in foreign missions, staying in the same country house during a crisis. In the midst of the activity, whatever it may be, people fall into step[10]—sometimes two men or two women, sometimes two couples, sometimes three people—and find that they walk or play a game or tell stories or serve on a committee with the same easy anticipation of what each will do day by day or in some critical situation. Americans who have made English friends comment that, even years later, "you can take up[11] just where you left off."[12] Meeting after a long interval, friends are like a couple who begin to dance again when the orchestra strikes up[13] after a pause. English friendships are formed outside the family circle, but they are not, as in Germany, relating to the family nor are they, as in France, separated from the family. And a break in English friendship comes not necessarily as a result of some irreconcilable difference of viewpoint or feeling but instead as a result of misjudgment, where one friend seriously misjudges how the other will think or feel or act, so that suddenly they are out of step.[14]

14   What, then, is friendship? Looking at these different styles, including our own, each of which is related to a whole way of life, are there common elements? There is recognition that friendships are formed, in contrast with kinship, through freedom of choice. A friend is someone who chooses and is chosen. Related to this is the sense each friend gives the other of being a special individual, on whatever grounds this recognition is based.[15] And between friends there is inevitably a kind of equality of give and take. These similarities make the bridge between societies possible, and the American's characteristic openness to different styles of relationship makes it possible for him to find new friends abroad with who he feels at home.

Notes

1. Few Americans stay put for a lifetime. 此句大意为：很少美国人一辈子待在一个地方。其中短语 stay put 意为 remain in a fixed or established position。

2. People known and accepted temporarily, casually, flow in and out of Americans' homes with little ceremony and often with little personal commitment. 此句大意为：早已熟悉的或是临时结交的朋友们随意进进出出美国家庭，很少有礼节，也甚少做出个人承诺。

3. finds no visible landmarks：身上没有明显的地缘印记

4. A friend is someone who draws out your own best qualities, with whom you sparkle and become more of whatever the friendship draws upon. 此句大意为：朋友们能引发出你最佳的特质，和朋友在一起你能得到启发，从而变得比原来更加优秀。

5. Your political philosophy assures more depth, appreciation of a play becomes sharper, taste in food or wine is enhanced, enjoyment of a sport is intensified. 此句大意为：你的政治哲理更加深邃，对戏剧的鉴赏力更加敏锐，品尝食物与葡萄酒的能力更强，从运动中得到的乐趣更多。

6. Different friends fill different niches in each person's life. 此句大意为：不同的朋友在每个人的生活中起不同的作用。

7. The special relationship of friendship is based on what the French value most—on the mind, on having the same of outlook, on vivid awareness of some chosen area of life. 此句大意为：友谊这一特殊关系以法国人最珍视的东西为基础——思想、观点的一致以及对生活中某一方面的具体感悟。

8. Adolescents, boys and girls, form deeply sentimental attachments, walk and talk together—not so much to polish their wits as to share their hopes and fears and dreams to form a common front against the world of school and family and to join in a kind of mutual discovery of each other's and their own inner life. 此句大意为：青年男女相互间建立了深情厚意，走在一起互相交谈——与其说是为了激发大家的聪明才智，不如说是为了倾诉各自的希望、忧虑和憧憬，为了团结一致共同对付学校和家庭事务，为了了解彼此以及各自的内心世界。

9. the breath of life: a thing that someone needs or depends on 生活中不可缺少的东西

10. fall into step: conform to what others are doing or thinking; walk in step with someone 步调一致

11. take up: continue 继续

12. leave off: break off; stop 停止

13. strike up: begin (a conversation, a piece of music, etc.) 开始(谈话、演奏等等)

14. And a break in an English friendship comes not necessarily as a result of some irreconcilable difference of viewpoint or feeling but instead as a result of misjudgment, where one friend seriously misjudges how the other will think or feel or act, so that suddenly they are out of step. 此句大意为：此外，英国人友谊的中断并不是由于见解不同或情感不和造成的，而是由于判断失误造成的，一个人可能会对另一个人的思维方式、感受或行为方式做出十分错误的

判断，于是彼此间突然变得不再默契。

15. Related to this is the sense each friend gives the other of being a special individual, on whatever grounds this recognition is based. 此句大意为：随之而来的是朋友之间对彼此的感受每个人都与他人不同，无论这种感受的依据是什么。

●Reading Comprehension

1. Directions: *Fill in the following table with the information from the text.*

	Definitions of friendship	Viewpoints of friendship	Basis of friendship
American		Friendship is superficial, casual, situational or deep and enduring.	
Englishman		2.	3.
Frenchman	1.		Friendship is based on the similarity of their point of view.
German	Friendship is much more clearly a matter of feeling.		4.

2. Directions: *Read the following statements carefully, and decide whether they are true (T) or false (F) according to the text.*

_____ 1) Americans seldom vacation abroad, and they go just to see new sights.

_____ 2) The difficulty strangers from two countries have when communicating with each other is a lack of appreciation of friendship.

_____ 3) For a Frenchman, the friend referred to in the sentence "This is my good friend" is more intimate than the friend referred to in the sentence "This is my friend".

_____ 4) In French people's eyes, although men and women have worked together for a long time and may be very close, there can't be any possibility of friendship between them.

_____ 5) English friendship is not made part of a family life. In France, friends usually are brought into the family.

_____ 6) German friendship is usually based on sharing the same feelings but Americans change their friends as they move from one place to another.

_____ 7) The basis of English and French friendship is shared activity.

_____ 8) A German may play chess with a friend for thirty years without knowing his political opinion, or he may talk politics with him for as long a time without knowing about his personal life.

Part Three

Topic-related Activities

1. Stories of Jesus and Buddha

Step One

Directions: *Divide the class into groups of 4-6.*

Step Two

Directions: *Each group role-plays the life stories of Jesus or Buddha.*

Step Three

Directions: *After one group finishes the performance, the other groups should figure out who is the person the group role-played.*

Step Four

Directions: *All the groups discuss the influences of Jesus and Buddha on different cultures and how they affect people's values in different cultures.*

2. National Characters: A Matching Game

Directions: *In your opinion, what general personality traits do you associate with the following: Chinese, Americans, English, French, Germans or Japanese? Tell the reasons. You can refer to the words in the next table.*

Adventurous	Dependable	Introverted	Responsible
Aggressive	Diligent	Liberal	Romantic
Ambitious	Dumb	Masculine	Rude
Bright	Energetic	Mean	Selfish
Carefree	Extroverted	Modest	Sloppy
Cautious	Feminine	Moody	Sociable
Cheerful	Generous	Nosy	Stingy
Clumsy	Gentlemanly	Opinionated	Strict
Confident	Honest	Optimistic	Submissive
Conservative	Humorous	Patriotic	Talkative
Cunning	Hypocritical	Pessimistic	Tolerant
Cynical	Innovative	Polite	Vain

　　1) Chinese:

　　2) Americans:

　　3) English:

　　4) French:

5) Germans:

6) Japanese:

3. Case Study

Steve and Yaser first met in their chemistry class at an American university. Yaser was an international student from Jordan. He was excited to get to know an American. He wanted to learn more about American culture. Yaser hoped that he and Steve would become good friends.

At first, Steve seemed very friendly. He always greeted Yaser warmly before class. Sometimes he offered to study with Yaser. He even invited Yaser to eat lunch with him. But after the semester was over, Steve seemed more distant. The two former classmates didn't see each other very much at school. One day Yaser decided to call Steve. Steve didn't seem very interested in talking to him. Yaser was hurt by Steve's change of attitude. "Steve said we were friends," Yaser complained. "And I thought friends were friends forever."

Yaser is a little confused. He is an outsider to American culture. He doesn't understand the way Americans view friendship. Americans use the word "friend" in a very general way. They may call both casual acquaintances and close companions "friends". Americans have school friends, work friends, sports friends and neighborhood friends. These friendships are based on common interests. When the shared activity ends, the friendship may fade. Now Steve and Yaser are no longer classmates. Their friendship has changed.

Questions

1. Why did Steve show little interest in talking with Yaser after they didn't attend the same class?
2. What can you infer about American friendship based on this case?

4. Writing

Directions: *Try to find out what cultural values the following proverbs from different countries suggest and then write a comment on one of them.*

1) Strike while the iron is hot.

2) God help those who help themselves.

3) Constant dropping wears the stone.

4) Actions speak louder than words.

5) From small beginnings come great things.

6) While there is life, there is hope.

7) Two heads are better than one.

8) He who stirs another's porridge often burns his own.

Part Four

Topic-related Information

1. Changing Conceptions of the American Dream

Traditionally, Americans have sought to realise the American dream of success, fame and wealth through thrift and hard work. However, the industrialisation of the 19th and 20th centuries began to erode the dream, replacing it with a philosophy of "get rich quick." A variety of seductive but elusive strategies have evolved, and today the three leading ways to instant wealth are large-prize television game shows, big-jackpot state lotteries and compensation lawsuits.

1) Who Wants to Be a Millionaire?

"Who Wants to Be a Millionaire," hosted by Regis Philbin, is a popular television game show. With an average of two hundred and forty thousand people per calling in on "Contest Day" attempting to become contestants, and a twenty-nine million per show viewing audience, it is safe to say that Americans are captivated by what many consider to be an easy avenue to achieving financial success. "Millionaire" was originally a British television show. However, the show achieved its greatest success in America. A contestant can win, combined with what at times seems to be amazingly easy questions, a large amount. Dozens have won upwards of $500,000. In the course of a play, every contestant has three "lifelines" designed as an aid in choosing the correct multiple-choice answer. The player can choose "Fifty-Fifty," in which the computer eliminates two incorrect responses, leaving only two possible answers; "Ask the Audience" allows the player to quiz the studio audience for the most likely correct answer; "Phone a Friend" enables the player to telephone one of five pre-arranged contacts who help to determine the correct response. All of these devices take the weight of knowledge off the contestant, and thus provide a real degree of luck.

2) State Lotteries (国家彩票)

More well known, and often more lucrative, are state run lotteries. All one needs is "A Buck and a Dream." Just as in the game shows, the lottery focuses on the hope of easy money with minimal effort. Whereas the payoffs for the big jackpot lotteries are significantly higher than the "Millionaire" games, a May 2000 Powerball game reached 350 million, the odds of winning are equally long. With an average 1 in 12 to 14 million chance of winning, and 1 in 80 million for the big prizes, the degree of luck needed is astronomical. Still, Americans flock to the lottery when the possibility of scoring big is most remote. But lotteries play both on the ethic of luck and attempt to fool one into believing that there is something more than luck—that skill is a component of winning. The National Gambling Impact Study Commission noted that lottery advertising specifically sought to persuade players that they could "influence their odds through the choices of numbers they pick." The implication is that through hard work one can develop the skill necessary to win the lottery, and thus the American Dream.

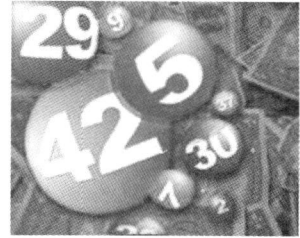

3) Compensation Lawsuits (赔偿案)

Litigation is as American as apple pie, though it does not leave so sweet a taste in the mouth of most Americans. If you have been involved in an accident, you may be entitled to compensation. Americans file tens of thousands of law suits each year, many in the hopes of cashing in on a personal injury or product liability case. Most crucial criteria for payment are largely controlled by chance: (1) whether one is "lucky" enough to be injured by someone whose product or conduct can be proved faulty; (2) whether the party's insurance limits or assets are sufficient to promise an award or settlement commensurate with losses and expenses; (3) whether one's own innocence of faulty conduct can be proved; and (4) whether one has the good fortune to retain a lawyer who can exploit all the variables before an impressionable jury, including graphically portraying whatever pain one has suffered. The similarity between game shows, lotteries, and tort litigation is not as farfetched as one might think. In all three situations the desired end is a trip to the bank with a fat check. In recent years a number of court cases have resulted in just such an outcome. If a plaintiff wins a lawsuit he will most likely receive not only compensatory damages (those that reimburse for medical expenses, lost wages, etc.), but may also be awarded punitive damages (those that punish the defendant for negligent or dangerous behavior). Moreover, in order to send a message to the offending company jury awards for punitive damages often far exceed compensatory damages. Thus like game shows and lotteries, injury and product liability lawsuits can be extremely lucrative.

2. The Value Orientations Method: A Tool to Help Understand Cultural Differences

One of the fundamental problems of working effectively with people of another culture is to understand basic differences in "world view." Without this understanding, it is difficult to provide appropriate services and easy to get into unnecessary conflict.

There is, however, a method to quickly help people understand cultural differences. This article introduces the Value Orientation Method (VOM), a tool that can help identify differences in core values across cultures. For those readers familiar with the Myers-Briggs Type Indicator (Keirsey, 1998) and how it describes types of individuals, the VOM provides a similar method for describing types of cultures.

The project team proposed that it is possible to distinguish cultures based on how they each addressed five common human concerns. They did not propose that these were the only five concerns but that they were useful in understanding cultural differences.

They also proposed from their study that cultures could respond to the problems in at least three ways and that all cultures would express each of the three responses. It was the rank order of responses that gave a culture its character. They called these responses to the five concerns "value orientations." Today we might call them "core values." Kohls (1981) provides a brief introduction to the five human problems and the three possible responses (Figure).

Figure

Description of Five Common Human Concerns and Three Possible Responses

(based on Kohls, 1981)

Concerns/Orientations	Possible Responses		
Human Nature: What is the basic nature of people?	**Evil.** Most people can't be trusted. People are basically bad and need to be controlled.	**Mixed.** There are both evil people and good people in the world, and you have to check people out to find out which they are. People can be changed with the right guidance.	**Good.** Most people are basically pretty good at heart; they are born good.
Man-Nature Relationship: What is the appropriate relationship to nature?	**Subordinate to Nature.** People really can't change nature. Life is largely determined by external forces, such as fate and genetics. What happens was meant to happen.	**Harmony with Nature.** Man should, in every way, live in harmony with nature.	**Dominant over Nature.** It is the great human challenge to conquer and control nature. Everything from air conditioning to the "green revolution" has resulted from having met this challenge.

Continued

Concerns/Orientations	Possible Responses		
Time Sense: How should we best think about time?	**Past.** People should learn from history, draw the values they live by from history, and strive to continue past traditions into the future.	**Present.** The present moment is everything. Let's make the most of it. Don't worry about tomorrow: enjoy today.	**Future.** Planning and goal setting make it possible for people to accomplish miracles, to change and grow. A little sacrifice today will bring a better tomorrow.
Activity: What is the best mode of activity?	**Being.** It's enough to just "be." It's not necessary to accomplish great things in life to feel your life has been worthwhile.	**Becoming.** The main purpose for being placed on this earth is for one's own inner development.	**Doing.** If people work hard and apply themselves fully, their efforts will be rewarded. What a person accomplishes is a measure of his or her worth.
Social Relations: What is the best form of social· organization?	**Hierarchical.** There is a natural order to relations. Some people are born to lead, and others are followers. Decisions should be made by those in charge.	**Collateral.** The best way to be organized is as a group, where everyone shares in the decision process. It is important not to make important decisions alone.	**Individual.** All people should have equal rights, and each should have complete control over one's own destiny. When we have to make a decision as a group it should be "one person one vote."

Most studies of the dominant Euro-American culture in the United States find that it is future oriented, focused on doing, emphasizes individualism, aspires to be dominant over nature, and believes that human nature is mixed, some people are good and some are bad (e.g., Carter, 1990). By contrast, most studies show that Native cultures are past oriented, focused on being, emphasize collateral (group) relations, aspire to be in harmony with nature, and believe that people are fundamentally good (e.g., Russo, 2000a).

It is important to note here that each culture will express all three possible responses at some time. For example, it is common for Euro-Americans to have a "doing" orientation during the workweek but to have a "being" orientation on weekends and while on vacation. The VOM theory recognizes that there is diversity within a culture—both among subgroups and individuals—and that degree of acculturation matters.

Hyperlinks

[1] http://www.jesuschrist.com/

[2] http://www.aboutbuddha.org/

[3] http://www.ouramericanvalues.org/

[4] http://americanvaluesnetwork.org/

[5] http://www.telegraph.co.uk/comment/telegraph-view/3618632/Ten-core-values-of-the-British-identity.html

[6] http://www.guardian.co.uk/commentisfree/2006/may/17/post97

References

[1] http://www.renewamerica.us/columns/graham/060119, January 19th, 2006

[2] http://www.ctinquiry.org/publications/reflections_volume_1/moltmann.htm

[3] http://www.zhuaxia.com/pre_channel/4880277/?logId=181

[4] http://www.for68.com/new/2006/8/ma45121438431328600213022-0.htm

[5] http://www.americansc.org.uk/online/American_Dream.htm

[6] http://joe.org/joe/2001december/tt1.html

Unit 2

Nonverbal Communication

Part One

Lead-in

Good communication is as stimulating as black coffee.

　　　　　　　　　—Anne Morrow Lindbergh (American author)

好的交流就如一杯纯咖啡，能激励你我。

　　　　　　　　　——安妮·莫洛·林伯格(美国作家)

Good communication skills can help you in both your personal and professional life. While verbal and written communication skills are important, research has shown that nonverbal behaviors make up a large percentage of our daily interpersonal communication. How can you improve your nonverbal communication skills? The following passages can help you learn to read the nonverbal signals of other people and enhance your own ability to communicate effectively.

Part Two

Reading Passages

In-Class Reading

Warm-up questions:

1. What else would you do in order to have a more effective communication apart from verbal communication?

2. Are you a very confident person? If not, do you know how to improve your confidence when you interact with other people?

Confident Nonverbal Communication

1   Your nonverbal communication which is more frequently but narrowly referred to as body language, is a universally overlooked area to improve your confidence in communication and general self-perception. The majority of people aim to build their confidence but rarely consider the power of communicating confidence nonverbally.

2   If you'd like to improve your confidence around women then you have even more reasons to read this article. Women love a confident man and they are extremely **adept** in picking up nonverbal signals. They will pick up your nonverbal signals that you wouldn't even have a clue about.

3   You need to have high self-awareness in order to be aware of your body language. It's a matter of knowing what you do in certain situations. When you have poor body language others can see fear in you.

4   Here are four examples of body language that is **counter-productive** in developing confidence and how you can solve them not only to communicate more powerfully but to **internalize** the confidence:

5   a. Moving eye contact—people with low confidence levels rarely make eye contact and when they do, as soon as the other person returns that eye contact the person looks away. You do not look silly looking the other person in the eyes. In fact, you look **weirder** and would be annoying the other person more so when you do not make eye contact.

6   Good eye contact will show the persons you are listening and that you are interested in what they have to say. However, you can have too much of a good thing.[1] Excessive eye contact is

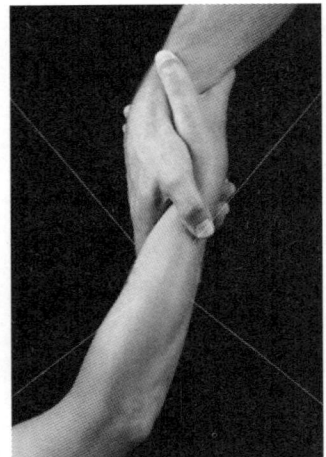

nonverbal aggression. Dr Peter Andersen, author of *The Complete Idiot's Guide to Body Language*, says you will make the other person feel comfortable with about 60% eye contact.

7   With practice I found that you will develop an intuition or "gut-feeling" when you make the other person uncomfortable. As an example when you make too much eye contact, they'll begin to not make eye contact with you or maybe **fidget**. At the moment, too much eye contact probably isn't your concern as you're trying to develop confident body language but you still should be aware of the problems with excessive eye contact.

8   b. Weak touch—it involves bodily contact. What bodily contact we are interested in to develop confident nonverbal communication is mostly the handshake. You will rarely use any other bodily contact other than a handshake in a normal social situation.

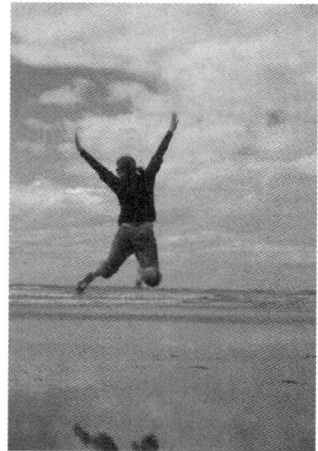

9   What did you feel when someone shook your hand with a soft handshake? I bet you wondered if they cared about you at all or if they lacked confidence to show this concern. This is a "girly touch". A good handshake depends on the receiving person. Most of the time you want a firm handshake but occasionally with, say, the elderly you don't want to be crushing their hand! When greeting ladies, be aware that they don't have gigantic and hard hands like many men so just go a little less firm. A firm handshake shows you care and is an **initial** way of communicating confidence when meeting someone.

10   c. Stay away—look at body positions relative to one another now otherwise known as proxemics.[2] What I mean by "relative to one another" is the distance between you and the other person. You are most comfortable with an intimate or well known person being close to you as opposed to someone you just met. However, people with low confidence will have a much wider **radius** of comfort. A more confident person will not show fear when someone "breaks" their comfortable proxemics. This doesn't mean they are comfortable with the closeness, it just means they don't show the uncomfortableness. They desire the other person to stay away but they cope with the situation.

11   An excellent example of this that I can remember is two Australian Politicians on October 8, the eve of the 2004 federal election. John Howard was greeted by opposition leader Mark Latham aggressively. While Mark Latham did pull John Howard towards him when shaking hands (aggressive haptics), Latham made his body position aggressive by being extremely close and **towering over** the shorter John Howard. Despite this, Mr. Howard nonverbally **stood his ground** in confidence by continuing the handshake and smiling towards the cameras. I'm sure John Howard would have felt uncomfortable but he still gave out signs of confidence.

12   It was said Latham attempted to get revenge for Howard squeezing his wife's hand too hard at

a press conference which I found to be funny! If only they were both able to read this!

13   d. Carry yourself—the last nonverbal communication technique that I feel is valuable in developing confidence is **kinesics**. It involves body movement. Possibly the most important kinesics in confidence is **posture**. A **slouched** posture has a physical and psychological effect on the person. The physical effect of slouching your shoulders forward is it causes your chest to compress inwards. Your chest compressing simulates **expelling** air causing you to breathe shallowly. This means if you have poor posture you will have poor breathing.

14   The psychological effect of poor posture is poorer confidence. Using the world's best golfer Tiger Woods as an example, he's taught to maintain good posture as he approaches each shot. By having good posture he is able to breathe correctly and physically get his body into the right state of confidence. From this his mind is able to focus on the shot ahead.

15   I know once golfers lose this state of confidence through poor posture, the effects are surprisingly strong. The golfer's chest begins to tighten and everything heightens. They then lose their state of control, calmness, and confidence, causing poor performance.

16   The same relates to everyday life. To practice a confident posture, roll your shoulders forward, upwards, and then back down to almost complete a circle. Watch your shoulders as you rotate them and if they are behind what they were prior to doing the activity and you are comfortable, you've done the activity correctly.[3]

17   Having learnt about these areas of nonverbal communication, all that's left to do is practice your new skills. Do not make the mistake of no action. Your self development will not progress forward until you move forward. Go out and practice your confident nonverbal communication skills.

—Joshua Uebergangs[4]

New Words and Expressions

adept	*a.*	skillful 熟练的，内行的
counter-productive	*a.*	having the opposite of the desired effect 适得其反的，事与愿违的
expel	*v.*	force out, eject 排出，喷出
fidget	*v.*	be or make uneasy (使)心神不宁，(使)烦躁
initial	*a.*	of or at the beginning 开始的，最初的
internalize	*v.*	make (attitudes, behaviour, etc.) part of one's nature by learning or unconscious assimilation 使(看法、行为等经吸收同化而)内在化
kinesics	*n.*	人体动作学
posture	*n.*	relative position of parts, esp. of the body; carriage, bearing (尤指身

体部位的)相对位置；姿势；举止

radius	*n.*	a line segment between any point on the circumference of a circle and its center/centre 半径；半径距离，半径范围
slouch	*v.*	stand, move, or sit in a drooping fashion 没精打采地站(走或坐)
weird	*a.*	queer, incomprehensible 奇怪的，不可思议的
stand one's ground		maintain or stick by an opinion or position 坚持立场
tower over		reach or be high or above; be superior 高于，胜过

Proper Names

John Howard	约翰·霍华德(澳大利亚前总理)
Mark Latham	马克·莱瑟姆(澳大利亚劳工党政治家)
Tiger Woods	泰格·伍兹(美国高尔夫球员)

Notes

1. However, you can have too much of a good thing. 此句意为：然而，一件好事做过头未必仍是件好事。

2. **proxemics**: Every culture has rules about the correct use of space. The "proxemics" (体距学) rules are very powerful and known to all members of the culture. The amount of distance we need and the amount of space we perceive as belonging to us is influenced by a number of factors including social norms, situational factors, personality characteristics, and level of familiarity.

3. Watch your shoulders as you rotate them and if they are behind to what they were prior to doing the activity and you are comfortable, you've done the activity correctly. 此句意为：当你在旋转你的肩膀的时候，注意观察。如果把你的肩膀放在你做活动之前的位置的后面，并且感到舒服，那么你的动作就做正确了。

4. Joshua Uebergangs: 佐斯华·乌尔贝刚斯(从事交际学的著名作家)

Joshua Uebergangs has been learning and teaching communication skills since he was just 19 years old! With his experience, and years of learning, he will give you skills that other "oldies" cannot give. You can get his free communication skills report by visiting his effective communication skills website and signing up to his newsletter at EarthlingCommunication.com.

● Reading Comprehension

1. **Directions:** *Discuss the following questions with your classmates.*

　1) What does the example of John Howard tell us in the passage?

　2) How does poor posture affect a person?

　3) What are the 4 examples of body language mentioned in the passage? What does the author want to tell us through the examples?

4) Suppose you are going to give a speech, what would you do in order to make it more successful and effective?

5) What can you learn from this article if you want to be a confident person?

2. Directions: *The following table is a list of the four examples of body language mentioned in the passage. Fill in the blanks with appropriate content based on the information given in the passage.*

Body Language	The consequence of too much or improper body language	The benefit of proper body language	Behavior of a confident person	Behavior of a person with less confidence
Eye Contact	Too much eye contact is 1) _____ while no eye contact will 2) _____.	Good eye contact will show the persons that 3) _____ _____ _____.		People with low confidence rarely 4) _____ _____ _____.
Handshake	A "girly touch" will make you wonder if others 5) _____ _____ _____.	A firm handshake shows 6) _____ _____ _____.	A good handshake depends on 7) _____ _____ _____.	
Proxemics (distance)	People will feel 8) _____ if a person they have just met is too close to them in communication.		A more confident person will not show 9) _____ when 10) _____ _____.	
Kinesics (posture)	A slouched posture not only 11) _____ _____, but it has 12) _____ _____ _____.	By having good posture, Tiger Woods is able to 13) _____ _____ _____.		

● **Discussion**

1. As is mentioned in the passage, men and women are different in their sensitivity to nonverbal signals. In fact, they behave quite differently in their body language. Discuss with your classmates about the gender differences in communication, especially in nonverbal communication.

2. As is known to all, sometimes the same gesture conveys different meanings in different cultures. Search the internet and list as many examples as possible.

After-Class Reading

Passage One

Warm-up questions:

1. Do you know the most common gestures in China?

2. Different meanings of the same gestures may cause communication problems, can you list some?

The Top Hand Gestures You'd Better Get Right

Does anybody remember that George H W Bush tried to signal "peace" during a visit to Australia in the 1990s by giving a huge crowd the time-honoured two-fingered salute? Though he didn't know it at the time, he was actually telling the whole crowd to go screw themselves—and all because he made the seemingly innocuous error that his palm was facing inwards instead of outwards.

Nacho highlighted the danger of using certain hand gestures when travelling in an earlier post, as some have very different meanings in some countries from what we as Westerners believe them to stand for. Let's take a look, shall we?

The "Thumbs-Up"

1　First of all, let's quash the urban legend of the "thumbs-up/thumbs-down" being used by the audience in the Roman coliseum to vote on the life or death of a defeated gladiator, as furthered by such movies as *Gladiator* and *Spartacus*. There's no evidence for this, and it's just massively unlikely.

2　While Western culture has become used to the thumbs-up as a positive, informal signal, generally indicating a job well done (probably stemming from World War II pilots using the signal to communicate that they were "good to go" with ground crews), there are cultures where a thumbs-up may land you in

trouble. In most of Latin America and West Africa, as well as Greece, Russia, Sardinia and the south of Italy, the thumbs-up basically means the same as the middle finger: "sit on it and swivel". Also, it's generally not recommended to use the thumbs-up around the Middle East as it's pretty much the biggest insult out there—and even worse if you pull off the emphatic version with both hands—so no Fonzie[1] impressions, please.

3   Rather more charming is a thumbs-up in Germany and in the less-Westernised areas of Japan —they just see it as the hand signal for the number one. Bless.

The "Moutza"[2]

4   Opening your palm to your target and stretching out your fingers seems harmless enough to most Westerners. Most of us would think you're waving. In Greece, however, the gesture is known as a moutza, and is one of their most traditional manual insults. With fingers slightly apart, you thrust your hand into your target's face, usually coupling the gesture with a brash "na!", meaning "here you go!". The basic suggestion is something like "eat shit[3]", implying that you're not particularly impressed and would rather the target of the moutza leave you alone—comparable to the American interpretation of the same signal as "talk to the hand, because the face isn't listening".

5   The gesture is also an insulting one in Pakistan and many parts of Africa. The Japanese use a very similar sign to insult their old enemies, the Koreans. Roughly translated as "animal", the signal is similar to the moutza in every way except they tuck the thumb into the palm.

6   Amusingly, Microsoft used to use a very similar-looking hand signal as an icon for warning dialogs in previous versions of Windows—what Greek users must have thought of that, I don't know… "This application has performed an illegal operation—now, eat shit!"

The "Dog Call"

7   Curling your index finger towards you in a summoning motion is a gesture generally linked with seductive temptresses in Hollywood movies, beckoning for their targeted men to follow them into another room.

8   Beware, however, of using this gesture in the Philippines—it's a method of communication considered worthy only to use on dogs, and is actually punishable by arrest. Worst of all, they'll break your index finger in order to prevent you from committing the same crime again!

The "A-OK"

9   Mainly used by scuba divers to mean "OK" (to prevent ambiguity with the thumbs-up sign, which means "ascend"), this hand gesture is generally called "A-OK", and in America and the UK is often used to tell somebody that they've made a great meal, as talking with your mouth full would just be impolite. Essentially the meaning comes out as *"great"*, or *"absolutely fine"*.

10   Not so, however, in a few countries in Europe, where the numerical interpretation gives the signal an insulting overtone—essentially you're telling them that you think they're a "zero".

11   Far worse, however, is the meaning in Brazil, Germany and a few Mediterranean countries: the circular shape of the gesture gives it the meaning of *"anus"*, and is therefore used to call somebody an "asshole", or, by extension, a homosexual.

The "V Sign"

12   The age-old "V sign" comes in two formats: one with the palm faced outwards, and one with the palm inwards. In America the two hand signals mean the same thing—"victory", as popularized by **Richard Nixon**, or "peace and love", which seemed to become the primary meaning after anti-Vietnam protesters used it during the 60s.

13   However, if the outside of your hand is facing your target, you're giving somebody a long-established insult in Great Britain and many English-speaking countries such as Australia, Ireland and New Zealand. **Winston Churchill** famously used the "incorrect" version of the V sign during the early years of the war, switching round later when he'd been told by his advisors that he wasn't exactly giving the lower social orders a positive message. The V sign is also considered rude in Italy, especially if you place your nose between the two fingers.

14   I myself have almost seen a fight start as a result of an American tourist ordering drinks in an English pub: when asked how many pints he wanted, he simply stuck two fingers up and looked straight into the eyes of the barman—perfectly normal on the other side of the Atlantic (it's actually the signal for the number 2 in American Sign Language), but it's fighting talk to the British.

The "Corna"

15   Consisting of a clenched fist with the second and fifth fingers straightened out, the *corna* ("horns") hand gesture has most recently been adopted by fans of rock and heavy metal music, first used by Black Sabbath[4] vocalist **Ronnie James Dio**[5]. The gesture carries only a vague meaning,

implying the presence of Satan, malevolence and loud guitar music, and is used in much the same way as head banging. The gesture was actually popularized as a Satanic salute during the 1960s, appearing in many editions of the Satanic Bible. Nowadays many Americans use the gesture simply to mean *"rock on"*, or in support of the University of Texas in Austin (known as the *"Hook' em Horns"*).

16   Occasionally used by baseball players to indicate "two outs", the *corna* is actually a positive hand gesture in Buddhism and Hinduism, known as the *Karana Mudra*[6] in such circles, and is used to dispel evil—an interestingly opposite meaning to its contemporary significance.

17   Historically, however, the symbol basically means *"cuckold"*[7] (or rather, *"your wife is cheating on you"*), and its origins are Mediterranean, possibly dating back to Ancient Greece. The *corna* is still popular in Spain, Portugal, Greece, Colombia, Brazil, Albania, Slovakia and the Czech Republic, and seems to be used most often to disagree with football referees—perhaps their wives are taking advantage of their husband's occupation to score with hunky football players—though only when the referees make an incorrect decision, of course…

"The Finger"

18   Most likely derived from Ancient Greece, "the finger" is one of the most widespread obscene gestures throughout the Western world. In a handful of Mediterranean and Arab countries the index finger is preferred to the middle, but the meaning remains crystal clear. There are a myriad of different stories for the origin of the finger (going back as far as 2500 years), making mention of Greek tragedies, perverse Roman emperors, and annoyed deaf people[8].

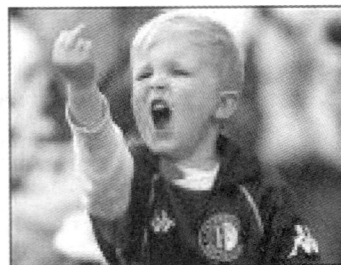

19   Also known as the "flip-off"[9], the "bird", the "highway salute", and the "One-Fingered Victory Salute" (thanks to President Bush's famous TV blooper[10]), the middle finger is probably the most universally-understood hand gesture in the world. This is owed mostly to its age and the sheer simplicity of the gesture.

—Adapted from Dave's blog

Proper Names

Richard Nixon	里查德·尼克松(美国前总统)
Ronnie James Dio	罗尼·詹姆斯·迪奥
Winston Churchill	温斯顿·丘吉尔(英国前首相)

Notes

1. Fonzie: Fonzie is a character in the film *Happy Day*. His snap has some irresistible, mystical power.

2. **Moutza:** or Mountza, is the most traditional gesture of insult among Greeks which consists of extending all fingers and presenting the palm towards the to-be-insulted person in a forward motion. It is often coupled with the expletives "να" (na), "παρ'τα" (par'ta) or "όρσε" (órse), meaning "here", "take these" and "there you go", respectively.

3. eat shit: It is used to express one's anger. The stronger one is "to eat my shit".

4. **Black Sabbath:** 黑色安息日(重金属的骨灰级老牌乐队)

   An English heavy metal band from Birmingham, England, formed in 1968 by Ozzy Osbourne (lead vocals), Tony Iommi (guitar), Geezer Butler (bass guitar), and Bill Ward (drums and percussion). The band has since experienced multiple lineup changes, with a total of twenty-two former members. Originally formed as a heavy blues-rock band named Earth, the band began incorporating occult-and horror-inspired lyrics with tuned-down guitars, changing their name to Black Sabbath and releasing multiple gold and platinum records in the 1970s.

5. Ronnie James Dio: born on July 10, 1942 in Portsmouth, New Hampshire, USA, is an American heavy metal vocalist who has performed with Elf, Rainbow, Black Sabbath, and his own band Dio. He is known for popularizing the sign of the horns in heavy metal. His Italian grandmother used it to ward off the evil eye (which is known as *malocchio* or *moloch*, Dio's term for the gesture). Dio began using the sign soon after joining (1979) the metal band Black Sabbath.

6. **Karana Mudra:** a sign of "Gesture of Banishing"(驱赶邪恶的手势) in Buddhism

7. cuckold: Cuckold has sometimes been written as "wearing the horns of a cuckold" or just "wearing the horns." This refers to the fact that the man being cuckolded is the last to know of his wife's infidelity. He is wearing horns that can be seen by everybody but him. This also refers to a tradition claiming that in villages of unknown European location, the community would gather to collectively humiliate a man whose wife gives birth to a child recognizably not his own. According to this legend, a parade was held in which the hapless husband is forced to wear antlers on his head as a symbol of his wife's infidelity. (通常是贬义) 指妻子与人通奸的人

8. There are a myriad of different stories for the origin of the finger (going back as far as 2500 years), making mention of Greek tragedies, perverse Roman emperors, and annoyed deaf people. 此句大意为：有一系列的关于手指手势起源说法(可以追溯到 2500 年以前)，主要提到了希腊悲剧，一意孤行的罗马皇帝，以及恼怒的失聪人士。

9. flip-off: 弹手指

10. Blooper: (美国口语) (可被对方利用的)政客的失言，在大庭广众面前犯的令人尴尬的错误

● **Reading Comprehension**

1. Directions: *In this passage seven top gestures are introduced about their different meanings in different cultures. Find out the positive and negative meanings of each gesture, and then discuss with your partners which meanings are used in your culture.*

2. Directions: *Read the following statements carefully, and decide whether they are true (T) or false (F) according to the text.*

_____ 1) In Roman coliseum, "thumbs-up/thumbs-down" was used to determine the life or death of a defeated gladiator.

_____ 2) "Thumbs-up" gestures are recommended to be used in Britain, Germany and the Middle East.

_____ 3) The Japanese use exactly the same gesture as "moutza" to insult their old enemies, the Koreans.

_____ 4) In Philippines, you are likely to be arrested if you use "dog call" gestures to other people.

_____ 5) Scuba divers use "OK" gestures to indicate that they have finished the job and want to ascend.

_____ 6) In Europe, if you use "OK" gestures, you are telling your counterparts that they are a "zero".

_____ 7) The "V sign", whether it is the one with the palm faced outwards or one with the palm inwards, means the same thing—"victory" in most countries.

_____ 8) The "finger" gesture is the most obscene gesture throughout the world.

Passage Two

Warm-up questions:

1. How many kinds of methods do you know about nonverbal communication?

2. How did the ancient people communicate with each other before the language appeared?

Nonverbal Communication: Fact and Fiction

1   Communication, one of the basic needs of human existence, can be defined as the transfer or exchange of information between entities. Sense deprivation experiments[1] have proved beyond

doubt that a person cut off from communication of any sort begins to go mad fast.

2   As soon as the word "communication" is mentioned, we immediately think of telephones, radios, television, comsats, books—in short, all the devices related to verbal communication.

3   Verbal communication requires a language. Language, defined in terms of semantics, is a group of labels used to represent approximations of space-time events and abstractions. The labels can be conveyed from one entity to another by a variety of means including vocalization, writing, etc.

4   Is verbal communication the only means of communication available to us? In fact, considering the importance of communication to us, is it fair to be gifted with only a single method of communication?

5   In view of the above given definition of verbal communication, nonverbal communication means a kind of communication which is independent of a formal language, whereby ideas and concepts can be expressed without the use of coherent labels. Do we have means of nonverbal communication versatile enough to qualify under the above definition?

6   The answer is, of course, a resounding "yes." Generations and generations of ancient tribes made do with nonverbal means of communication—animal-like guttural sounds, gestures, drawings—to fulfill their requirements before they latched on to a language.[2] Let us look around carefully, and we are sure to be surprised at the number of nonverbal communication methods we find at our disposal today.

7   One thing is certain. Whatever the means of nonverbal communication may be, it will have to be related to the senses of the communicators because, obviously, it is the senses which receive information. We, as humans, are aware of five senses (and perhaps a sixth?) suitable to be used in communicating. Communication for us can be related to any of these senses.

8   Let us first take nonverbal communication related to the sense of sight.

9   This kind of communication involves motion, color or shape. There are numerous examples of this kind of communication in nature. Let us begin with motion—the dance of the honey bees is the most obvious example. A worker bee makes intricate motions with its body, and these motions are seen and accurately interpreted by other worker bees. The dance of the bees is normally used to convey information to other bees about the location of a source of nectar, its direction and its distance.

10   What about us? Can we use such means of communication among us?

11   We can and we do.

12   What is an artist doing if he is not trying to communicate his thoughts, feelings, and ideas using colors and/or shapes?

13   As stated earlier, ancient man used pictures for communicating. Quite fascinating cave drawings, dating back some 20,000 years, have been discovered in the Franco-Cantabrian region[3] (Southwestern France and Northern Spain). The usage of drawings must have later developed into hieroglyphs or picture writing. Of the hieroglyphs[4] discovered, the oldest are from Egypt (c. 3100 B.C.)

and the latest, dated in the 4th century C.E., come from the island of Philae. Picture writings were also used by the ancient Cretans and Hittites.

14   Another means of communication at our disposal is the use of gestures. Gestures can be either ambiguous or unambiguous. Point at water and then point to your mouth. This is an example of an unambiguous gesture. Another person watching you is almost certain to understand that you want to drink water. There is hardly any chance of misinterpretation here.

15   In our everyday life, we frequently use a combination of words, gestures, and facial expressions to express our full meaning. Calling someone an "idiot" with an accompanying smile is different from saying it without a smile. In addition, gestures often have different meanings in different circumstances, depending upon various factors: cultural, geographical, social, etc.

16   For instance, if you nod by moving your head up and down, in India it means a concurrence, a "yes," whereas the same gesture in, say, Kuwait would mean the exact opposite, a dissent, a "no." In the Indian sub-continent, a woman sometimes uses the gesture of touching her forefinger to her nose to express astonishment. In the Middle East, the same gesture stands for "at your service," and can be employed by either sex, but is used predominantly by men. In Iran the gesture that stands for "at your service" is to put the palm of one's right hand over one's right eye.

17   A means of unconscious nonverbal communication is what is termed body language, or kinesics. Our bodies sometimes express our feelings and emotions better than words can. The body uses reflexive and non-reflexive movement, postures and positions to convey its message to anyone who would care to receive it. Our pupils dilate when we are excited. Our eyes narrow when we are concentrating. We slump when we are tired.

18   **Julius Fast**, in his famous book *Body Language*, writes that body language is also subject to cultural and environmental influences. A person familiar with the body language of, say, North America, may easily misinterpret the intentions of someone from, say, Spain. For example, a Spanish girl, secure in the knowledge of the strict code of behavior governing the males of her culture, may flaunt her sexuality without meaning it as a "come on" for the males.[5] The same behavior in an American girl would be interpreted as a pre-mating ritual and, in a statistically significant number of cases, this interpretation would be correct. The body language signals may also differ on the basis of gender.

19   Studies have shown the possibility that some components of body language may be universal and independent of culture, gender, or environment. However, the classification of body language into culturally dependent/independent components is still in its budding stages.[6]

20   The sense of hearing is fundamentally related to verbal communication, but can also be used as a means of nonverbal communication. It has been experimentally proved that feelings of calmness, lethargy, anger, depression, cheerfulness, etc. can be communicated to both animals and humans through the use of rhythmic sounds.

21   Communication can also be related to the sense of smell; many people claim that it's the most

evocative of all our senses. Let the scent of roses and jasmines penetrate into your nostrils, and suddenly there might appear on the screen of your mind the romantic image of a marriage bed. The musty smell of old books might bring forth images of H. Rider Haggard's mysterious Africa. Substances known as pheromones are used by certain insects and animals to communicate their sexual desire. Pheromones are also used to convey anger, fear, threat, danger, etc. Pheromones are used by humans, too, although to a lesser degree than by animals.

22　Even the sense of touch may be used as a means of communication. A kiss, a handshake, a hug, a pat on the back or on the head—all are examples of communication by touch. Also, if we are to believe accounts, there are people around who can hold your hand and divine your thoughts by the varying tensions of your muscles. I don't believe I have come across any example in nature of communication through the sense of taste, but that doesn't mean it isn't possible. "There are more things in heaven and earth..." [7]

23　Telepathy is one of the most talked about possibilities of communication without words, a possible "sixth sense." Again, if we are to believe certain accounts, instances of Extra Sensory Perception, including telepathy, have been observed among us. In 1921, three psychologists at the University of Groningen reported positive telepathic transmission in a rigidly controlled experiment.

24　The future might bring other novel modes of communication. One such mode is already in the offing, involving what can be called brain waves. We have learned, through scientific experimentation, that all mental processes, in both humans and animals, are accompanied by the production of a complex pattern of minute electric currents. Each mental process is associated with its own individual pattern of electric fluctuation. Experimenters have been able to record them. It was also discovered that by relaying back these electric currents, it is possible to recreate in the mind of the recipient the mental process associated with a particular set of patterns. [8] The effectiveness of this method has been spectacularly demonstrated by Dr Jose Delgado who, using equipment to relay minute electric currents, was able to control a bull charging at him in the ring. This method, when developed for human use, could be called artificial telepathy and it would come under the heading of extra-lingual transfer of information between entities, and so would classify as a means of nonverbal communication.

25　Reviewing all the data available about verbal and nonverbal communication, it should be clear that some means of nonverbal communication are already used by us; some means we can adapt; and some we can develop, such as the above-mentioned brain wave experiments. We also find that there are areas where the verbal and nonverbal means of communication overlap. Poetry is one such area.

26　A good poet uses words not only for their meaning, i.e. as a means of verbal communication, but also uses words for their sound, for the various rhythms that these sounds can produce, for images that these sounds can evoke in the mind. The form of a poem is as much an integral part of the poem as its substance. Another example where verbal and nonverbal means of communication overlap is the graphic story, the comic book, where words and pictures blend harmoniously to convey information.[9]

27   The means of communication discussed so far are related to the external senses that we use to communicate with others. But we have other, internal, senses that we can use and do use to communicate with ourselves. No, I am not venturing into the realms of metaphysics. My feet are still firmly planted on the turf of science. Let me ask a question. When we are hungry, how do we know it?

28   The answer is simple: the sensation of hunger originating somewhere within you is communicated to your consciousness. Communication involves senses, and this is exactly what I mean by "internal senses" and "self-communication."

29   How do we make the different members of our body move at our will? Self-communication, of course.

30   Ask a biologist, a physiologist, a neurologist, a psychologist, even a philosopher, and each one of them will give you many examples of self-communication, all of them nonverbal. Some of the examples that could be cited by the above-mentioned professionals could be, respectively: conveyance of the feeling of hunger, adrenalin secretion in states of fear and excitement, transfer of information between neurons, communication between ego and super ego, interaction of body and spirit.

31   In conclusion, I have one question: With all these means and methods of communication (verbal and nonverbal, internal and external) at our disposal, why is it that most of the time we misunderstand each other?

—Ahmed A. Khan

Proper Names

Julius Fast   朱利叶斯·法斯特(法国学者；代表作有《人体语言》)

H. Rider Haggard   瑞德·哈葛德(非洲作家；代表作有《所罗门宝藏》)

Dr Jose Delgado   何塞·德尔加多博士(西班牙科学家)

Notes

1. Sense deprivation experiments: 感觉剥夺试验

   A natural or experimentally arranged situation in which stimulation of a subject's senses is greatly reduced. Sensory deprivation experiments have demonstrated that humans need constant sensory contact with their environment in order to function.

2. Generations and generations of ancient tribes made do with nonverbal means of communication —animal-like guttural sounds, gestures, drawings—to fulfill their requirements before they latched on to a language. 此句大意为：一代又一代的古人在他们学会利用语言之前通过一

些非口头的交流手段——动物般的喉音、手势和画图来满足他们的需要。

3. **Franco-Cantabrian region:** The Franco-Cantabrian region (also Franco-Cantabric region) is a term applied in Archaeology and History to refer to an area that stretches from Asturias, in northern Spain, to Provence in SE France. It includes the southern half of France and the northern strip of Spain looking at the Bay of Biscay (known as Cantabrian Sea in Spanish, hence the name). Northern Catalonia is sometimes included as well. This region shows intense homogeneity in the prehistorical record and was possibly the most densely populated region of Europe in the Late Paleolithic. The inhabitants of the Franco-Cantabrian region produced some of the finest Paleolithic mural art.

4. **hieroglyph:** 象形文字

Egyptian hieroglyphs was a formal writing system used by the ancient Egyptians that contained a combination of logographic and alphabetic elements. Egyptians used cursive hieroglyphs for religious literature on papyrus and wood. Less formal variations of the script, called hieratic and demotic, are technically not hieroglyphs.

5. For example, a Spanish girl, secure in the knowledge of the strict code of behavior governing the males of her culture, may flaunt her sexuality without meaning it as a "come on" for the males. 此句大意为：比如一个西班牙女孩，她深知她们的文化中有一套严格的行为准则对男性进行约束，因此她可以安心地招摇她的性感而不会被男性理解为是一种"诱惑"。

6. However, the classification of body language into culturally dependent/independent components is still in its budding stages. 此句大意为：然而，对身体语言按照文化依存和无文化依存的元素进行分类还处在萌芽阶段。

7. "There are more things in heaven and earth..." It is one of the Quotations from Shakespeare. "There are more things between heaven and earth than are dreamt of in your philosophy." 在这天地间有许多事情(是人类哲学所无法解释的)。——莎士比亚

8. It was also discovered that by relaying back these electric currents, it is possible to recreate in the mind of the recipient the mental process associated with a particular set of patterns. 此句大意为：通过实验我们还发现如果中转回这些电流，接收者的大脑里就可能重新形成跟特定的一套图案有联系的心理过程。

9. Another example where verbal and nonverbal means of communication overlap is the graphic story, the comic book, where words and pictures blend harmoniously to convey information. 此句大意为：另外一个口头交流和非口头交流交迭的例子就是有插图的故事书和漫画本，在这些书中图片和文字和谐交融，共同传递信息。

● **Reading Comprehension**

1. Directions: *Choose the best answer for each of the following questions.*

1) According to the author, which of the following senses is the least possibly related to communication?

  A. taste   B. touch   C. smell   D. sight

2) If you nod by moving your head up and down, in some countries it means a concurrence, a "yes," whereas the same gesture in _____ would mean the exact opposite, a dissent, a "no."

  A. India   B. the Middle East   C. Kuwait   D. Spain

3) Substances known as pheromones are used by certain insects and animals to communicate the following feelings EXCEPT _____.

  A. sexual desire   B. fear   C. hunger   D. anger

4) According to the article, which of the following is true?

  A. Calling someone an "idiot" with an accompanying smile is an insult to somebody.

  B. Verbal communication enables us to avoid misunderstanding each other completely.

  C. The sense of hearing can not be used as a means of nonverbal communication.

  D. Pheromones are also used by humans, too, but to a lesser degree than by animals.

5) The newest mode of communication mentioned in the passage is _____.

  A. artificial telepathy   B. reflexive movement

  C. pheromones   D. neurons

2. Directions: *Read the following statements carefully, and decide whether they are true (T) or false (F) according to the text.*

_____ 1) Ancient people made use of nonverbal means of communication to fulfill their requirements before they latched on to a language.

_____ 2) A means of conscious nonverbal communication is what is termed body language, or kinesics.

_____ 3) Studies have shown that body language can sometimes be independent of culture, gender, or environment.

_____ 4) A kiss, a handshake, a smile, a pat on the back or on the head—all are examples of communication by touch.

_____ 5) The dance of the bees is only used to convey information to other bees about the location of a source of nectar.

_____ 6) If an American girl flaunts her sexuality, it would be interpreted as a "come on" for the males.

_____ 7) In the Indian sub-continent, a woman sometimes uses the gesture of touching her forefinger to her nose to express astonishment. In the Middle East, the same gesture stands for "at your service," and is only used by men.

_____ 8) Researchers have done little on the classification of body language into culturally dependent/independent components.

Part Three

Topic-related Activities

1. How to Make a Successful First Impression

Directions: *You make your first impression upon someone quickly—within seven to 30 seconds of meeting them. It is easier to make a good first impression than to correct a negative impression. A first impression is primarily dependent on your nonverbal signals. According to Albert Mehrabian, words are only 7 percent of your communication. The rest is your voice tonality (38 percent) and your body language at 55 percent. Work in groups and try to work out the ways to make a favorable first impression, especially by using your body language.*

2. How Do You Interpret the Following Celebrities' Poses?

Directions: *Suppose you are a group of editors of an entertainment magazine. You have just got some interesting photographs of some celebrity couples. Now you need to write an article to interpret the relationships of these celebrity couples. Remember the only purpose is to enlarge the circulation of your magazine. After you finish writing, read the article to the whole class. The class and the teacher should judge which article brings the greatest hit and is the most popular.*

3. To Be a Juryman

Step One

Directions: *Read the first part of the story. Discuss with your partner what kind of gestures the deaf man named Shaun Phuprate probably has made to bring offense.*

There is a crazy story evolving about a deaf man, by the name of Shaun Phuprate, who landed in jail for gesturing "fuck you" at the police. But did he really mean that?

"A DEAF man arrested after police mistook sign language for an obscene gesture has lost his court battle for compensation. Shaun Phuprate, of Town End Farm, was handcuffed and hauled before magistrates for making a two-finger salute at officers in Sunderland. The now 26-year-old insisted he was making the sign for 'I am deaf' and had not been rude."

Step Two

Directions: *Read the second part of the story. Suppose you are the members of a jury. Discuss in groups whether the deaf guy should be sentenced to prison.*

The policemen believed they saw a "palm-back v-sign", which is a cockney variant of giving the finger. As such it constituted an insult and, together with other misconduct, enough to land Phuprate (and his brother) in jail for the night. Initially when the case came before court in 2002 the defense claimed Phuprate was merely signing "I am deaf".

4. Case Study

Directions: *Read the story and then answer the question. Did Randy have any chance to date with beautiful Maya? Try to find clues in the body language Maya demonstrated.*

Randy held his breath as Maya passed by his locker. He wanted to breathe in all the air around her, but his life involuntarily stopped whenever Maya was near.

He watched as she and her best friend Michelle continued toward their English class. Maya moved in a blur of swinging blue jeans and thick brunette hair.

Maya stopped, spun around and caught Randy's eye before he could look away.

"Oh jeez." He sputtered (咕哝) lowly as he quickly turned his head, reached into his locker and began quickly re-arranging books.

In an instant she was leaning against the locker next to his.

"Hi Randy," she spoke, then suddenly smiled a wide smile directly at him.

"Oh, hi, Maya." He half choked then he glanced at her as if she had magically appeared in a whirl of fairy dust.

As he turned toward her, Maya twisted a long strand (股) of her brown hair behind her right ear into a ringlet (一绺).

"What's up?" Maya looked straight into his eyes with a calm gaze that could have taken his breath away, if he had any.

"Not," he could hear his heart as it struggled to crack his ribcage (胸腔), "not much."

"You know the project we're supposed to do?" She asked as she leaned toward him.

"Um, yea, um, the English one?" Randy could feel his face heating as he struggled for the right words.

"That would be the one." Maya, still smiling, raised her head and continued, "Would you like to work on it with Michelle and me?"

"Sure!" Randy blurted. "I'm sure that would be great!"

"Okay, good!" Maya turned as if to head back to her class, "We'll figure out exactly when we can all get together—maybe tomorrow?"

"Great." Randy answered as she started down the hall. "Good." He called after the scent of lilacs (紫丁香) that trailed behind her.

She turned back and flashed him a huge smile just before she disappeared through the classroom door.

"Wow." Randy inhaled (吸气) deeply as he gathered his books, "Wow."

He closed his locker and was halfway down the hall to English before he realized he was walking like John Wayne (美国西部牛仔明星约翰·韦恩).

Part Four

Topic-related Information

1. Types of Nonverbal Communication

According to experts, a substantial portion of our communication is nonverbal. Every day, we respond to thousands of nonverbal cues and behaviors including postures, facial expression, eye gaze, gestures, and tone of voice. From our handshakes to our hairstyles, nonverbal details reveal who we are and impact how we relate to other people.

Scientific research on nonverbal communication and behavior began with the 1872 publication of Charles Darwin's *The Expression of the Emotions in Man and Animals*. Since that time, there has been an abundance of research on the types, effects, and expression of unspoken communication and behavior. While these signals are often so subtle that we are not consciously aware of them, research has identified several different types of nonverbal communication.

1) Facial Expression

Facial expressions are responsible for a huge proportion of nonverbal communication. Consider how much information can be conveyed with a smile or a frown. While nonverbal communication and behavior can vary dramatically between cultures, the facial expressions for happiness, sadness, anger, and fear are similar throughout the world.

2) Gestures

Deliberate movements and signals are an important way to communicate meaning without words. Common gestures include waving, pointing, and using fingers to indicate number amounts. Other gestures are arbitrary and related to culture.

3) Paralinguistics

Paralinguistics refers to vocal communication that is separate from actual language. This includes factors such as tone of voice, loudness, inflection, and pitch. Consider the powerful effect that tone of voice can have on the meaning of a sentence. When said in a strong tone of voice, listeners might interpret approval and enthusiasm. The same words said in a hesitant tone of voice might convey disapproval and a lack of interest.

4) Posture

Posture and movement can also convey a great deal of information. Research on body language has grown significantly since the 1970's, but popular media have focused on the over-interpretation of defensive postures, arm-crossing, and leg-crossing, especially after the publication of Julius Fast's book *Body Language*. While these nonverbal behaviors can indicate feelings and attitudes, research suggests that body language is far more subtle and less definitive than previously believed.

5) Proxemics

People often refer to their need for "personal space," which is also an important type of nonverbal communication. The amount of distance we need and the amount of space we perceive as belonging to us is influenced by a number of factors including social norms, situational factors, personality characteristics, and level of familiarity. For example, the amount of personal space needed when having a casual conversation with another person usually varies between 18 inches to four feet. On the other hand, the personal distance needed when speaking to a crowd of people is around 10 to 12 feet.

6) Eye Contact

Looking, staring, and blinking can also be important nonverbal behaviors. When people encounter people or things that they like, the rate of blinking increases and pupils dilate. Looking at another person can indicate a range of emotions, including hostility, interest, and attraction.

7) Haptics

Haptic communication is communicating by touch. This is used in a number of contexts and also has dangers for the unwary as touching for example where another person can, in particular circumstances, be interpreted as assault. Touch is often intimate and can be used as an act of domination or friendship, depending on the context and who is touching who, how and when.

8) Appearance

Our choice of color, clothing, hairstyles, and other factors affecting appearance are also considered a means of nonverbal communication. Research on color psychology has demonstrated that different colors can invoke different moods. Appearance can also alter physiological reactions, judgment, and interpretations.

9) Time

The way a person treats time reveals something about that person. A person who is consistently late may not be well organized; the person who is kept waiting may feel that he or she is not highly regarded by the other person.

In some cultures, time is of less importance, but western business people tend to move by the clock—a two o'clock appointment usually means two o'clock or something within five or ten minutes of it.

2. Gender Differences in Communication

All of us have different styles of communicating with other people. Our style depends on a lot of things: where we're from, how and where we were brought up, our educational background, our age, and it also can depend on our gender. Generally speaking, men and women talk differently although there are varying degrees of masculine and feminine speech characteristics in each of us. But men and women speak in particular ways mostly because those ways are associated with their gender.

The styles that men and women use to communicate have been described as "debate vs. relate", "report vs. rapport", or "competitive vs. cooperative". Men often seek straightforward solutions to problems and useful advice whereas women tend to try and establish intimacy by discussing problems and showing concern and empathy in order to reinforce relationships.

Jennifer Coates, in her book *Women, Men and Language* (New York: Longman Inc., 1986) studied men-only and women-only discussion groups and found that when women talk to each other they reveal a lot about their private lives. They also stick to one topic for a long time, let all speakers finish their sentences and try to have everyone participate. Men, on the other hand, rarely talked about their personal relationships and feelings but "competed to prove themselves better informed about current affairs, travel, sport, etc." The topics changed often and men tried to "over time, establish a reasonably stable hierarchy, with some men dominating conversation and others talking very little".

Dr Lillian Glass' book *He Says, She Says: Closing the Communication Gap between the Sexes* (The Putnam Berkeley Group) details her findings on the many differences in the way men and women communicate, both verbally and nonverbally. She thinks differences can be found in body language, facial expression, speech patterns, and behavior.

Hyperlinks

[1] Resources for videos on body language

http://www.hodu.com/videosBL.shtml

http://www.youtube.com/watch?v=x9YTxff3pHU

http://www.howcast.com/videos/10608-How-To-Interpret-Body-Language

[2] Resources for body language across cultures

http://www.bodylanguageexpert.co.uk/BodyLanguageAcrossCultures.html

http://www.videojug.com/interview/manners-and-body-language-across-cultures-2

References

[1] http://www.ldrc.ca/contents/view_article/307/

[2] http://www.languagetrainers.co.uk/blog/2007/09/24/top-10-hand-gestures/

[3] http://www.strangehorizons.com/

[4] http://en.wikipedia.org/wiki/Main_Page

[5] http://louisville.bizjournals.com/louisville/stories/2002/05/13/editorial2.html

[6] http://www.thesun.co.uk/sol/homepage/woman/article1131967.ece

[7] http://jeroenarendsen.nl/2007/03/did-phuprate-sign-i-am-deaf-or-fuck-off/

[8] http://www.links2love.com/body_language_2.htm

[9] http://psychology.about.com/od/nonverbalcommunication/a/nonverbaltypes.htm

[10] http://my.24en.com/?110268/viewspace-12195

Unit 3

Studying Abroad

Part One

Lead-in

Study abroad is important for every college student to experience to help us prepare for work and life in today's globalized world.

—Lisa Burgelin (America)

对于每个大学生来说，出国留学很重要，不仅帮助我们为工作做准备，也为当今全球化世界而绸缪。

——丽莎·博格林(美国)

Studying abroad significantly enriches students' educational experience and prepares them to participate in the global knowledge economy. Students with overseas experience become more confident, self-reliant and adaptable. They are generally more creative in problem identification and solving because they bring back with them new and different perspectives. They also develop excellent cross-cultural communication skills. Essentially they develop into the type of employee employers require in a rapidly evolving global marketplace.

Part Two
Reading Passages

In-Class Reading

Warm-up questions:

1. What are the procedures of studying abroad?

2. Do you know the ways to contact home (China) if you study in the UK?

Study in the UK

1   Coming to study in the UK will be one of the most exciting adventures of your life, so be prepared! There are steps you can take before you leave that will help you feel right at home before you know it. Once you've arrived in the UK, we've provided some tips on settling in the UK and contacting home.

Before You Leave

Background reading

2   Once you've accepted a place on a course at a UK school, college or university, your institution may send you information to help you prepare for your arrival. Read this carefully—it may tell you more about the institution and the local area, and include practical information such as opening times of offices, local travel advice and important steps you need to take (such as applying for accommodation, or registering for your course).

Arranging your arrival

3   When booking your travel, try and make sure you arrive at a time that will enable you to get a transfer to your institution or accommodation. Aim to arrive on a weekday (Monday—Friday), rather than at the weekend (Saturday and Sunday) or on a public holiday, and try to arrive in the morning, as trains, coaches and taxis may not run throughout the night. This will give you time to reach your final destination and settle in during working hours when transportation links are most frequent and facilities such as banks and shops are open. This may mean that you travel through the night and arrive tired and slightly **jet-lagged** but it will help to make your onward journey easier.

Getting on Board

4   Before arriving in the UK, you must ensure you have the right documents and enough sterling[1] currency to cover any expenses when you arrive. Make sure you carry the following items with you in your hand luggage as you may need them before you collect your checked-in luggage: your valid passport, with visa or entry clearance[2] if you need it; your travel tickets; money—carry

cash, travellers' cheques and credit cards—preferably in a money belt[3] or a very secure inner pocket; health documents, if required; your letter of acceptance from your institution; documentation to show that you have enough money to pay your fees and meet your living costs for the duration of your course; originals (or **certified** copies) of any degree certificates or technical qualifications you have.

5   When you are leaving home, allow plenty of time to check in for your flight and to pass through security controls—there can be long queues at busy times, as security at international airports is very **stringent**. There are a number of items that are not permitted in hand luggage: sharp items, such as scissors and knives should be packed in your hold luggage[4] and there are restrictions on taking liquids and **gels** onto planes travelling to and from the UK. Your airline will be able to provide a full list of prohibited items when you book your tickets, although it may also be worth rechecking just before you depart, as hand luggage directives are currently being updated on a fairly frequent basis[5].

Reaching Your Destination

6   Your institution may operate a "meet and greet" service, where a representative from your school, college or university will collect you from the airport or nearest railway station and take you to the institution or your accommodation. If this is not the case and you need to make your own way, check with your institution as to the best way to get there. You should be able to access the timetables of onward travel services in advance on the web, to work out the best way to get to your institution.

Settling in

7   Many schools, colleges and universities run special introduction programmes for international students before term begins. A typical programme would involve a tour of the institution, an overview of the facilities available and help with registering for your course. It may also include a trip to the local supermarket and town centre, and an introduction to public transport links and local facilities, such as sports centres and libraries. These programmes are an excellent way to meet other students and staff and to settle in before your studies begin.

Contacting Home

8   The UK's excellent communications services make it easy for you to keep in contact with friends and family back at home. The UK's postal service and telecommunications network are fast and reliable and you will find that your school, college or university, and your local library and high street internet cafés, all provide easy access to e-mail and the internet.

Public telephones

9   You can operate public telephones in the UK by using coins, credit cards or pre-paid

phonecards. Phonecards come in a range of values including £5, £10 and £20 and you can buy them from newsagents, post offices and supermarkets.

Low-cost calling

10   You will soon discover that calling from a private phone is significantly cheaper than calling from a public phone. Calls from one part of the UK to another (inland calls) are cheapest from 6.00 p.m. to 8.00 a.m. and between midnight on Friday and midnight on Sunday. International calls are also cheapest between these times. Even if you are using a private phone, you can buy pre-paid phonecards or account-based cards from a number of different companies that aim their services specifically at people who need to make frequent international calls. Compare cards carefully as rates differ and, in some cases, making international calls using one of these cards could work out cheaper than using the main telephone service provider.

Mobile phones

11   Your best option may well be your own mobile (or cell) phone—they are widely used in the UK and can be particularly convenient for students. If you are buying a new one or switching to a new network, check details of the competing packages carefully. What appears to be a cheap phone may come with an expensive monthly **subscription** and high charges for individual calls. Typical mobile phone packages include: Pay-monthly plans[6]; Pre-paid plans[7]; Pay-as-you-go plans[8].

E-mail and the internet

12   Internet usage is widespread in the UK and most students will be familiar with its use. The majority of colleges and universities provide free e-mail accounts for their students; check with your Students' Union. At many colleges and universities, rooms in halls of residence[9] will have an internet connection provided at a set fee for the entire term or academic year.

13   If you have your own computer, you may also choose to sign up directly with one of the UK's internet service providers (ISP). Several now offer free access; all you will pay is the phone company's charges for your connection time.

14   If you do not have your own computer, sign up with one of the many web-based e-mail

services available (Hotmail, Yahoo, Tiscali[10] and so on) and then check your e-mail using online terminals at your institution, a public library or a friend's home. This option should cost you absolutely nothing. You will also find that most high streets have internet cafés, where you pay for use by the hour. If you have your own laptop, Wireless Hi Fi can be accessed for free in an increasing number of coffee shops and public places.

Postal services

15   If you prefer to write letters home, or want to post presents to your friends and family, post offices are usually open from 9.00 a.m. to 5.30 p.m. Monday to Friday, and from 9.00 a.m. to 12.30 p.m. on Saturday. You can also buy any stamps you need at newsagents, supermarkets and some other shops, and from special vending machines[11] which are usually located near a post office.

New Words and Expressions

certified	*a.*	proven to be right 经过鉴定的
gel	*n.*	a thick wet substance that is used in beauty or cleaning products 凝胶体
jet-lagged	*a.*	tired and confused after flying a very long distance, because of the difference in time between the place you left and the place you arrived at 时差失调的
stringent	*a.*	strict 严格的
subscription	*n.*	an amount of money you pay, usually once a year, to receive a service 订购费用

Notes

1. **sterling:** the standard unit of money in the United Kingdom, based on the pound 英国货币

2. **entry clearance:** a term under the UK Immigration legislation that refers to both visas and entry certificates issued to persons seeking to enter the UK 签证

3. money belt: a special belt that you can carry money in while you are traveling 可放钱的腰带

4. hold luggage: 托运行李

5. as hand luggage directives are currently being updated on a fairly frequent basis 该句大意为：对随身携带的行李的要求经常会有更新

6. **Pay-monthly plans**: You sign up with a mobile phone network and agree to use the network's service for a minimum period, usually 12 months. You choose a fee structure from a range of choices and the network will bill you monthly for your calls and services.

7. **Pre-paid plans:** You sign up with a network and pay a minimum of 12 months' service in advance, at a cheaper rate than for monthly plans. If you use the phone more than the agreed amount, network will bill you monthly for the extra time/calls.

8. **Pay-as-you-go plans:** You buy credit (talking time) in advance, either directly from the network or in the form of vouchers. You use the phone until the credit runs out and then you buy more

credit. No contracts or bills are involved.

9. hall of residence: sleeping quarters or entire buildings primarily providing sleeping and residential quarters for large numbers of people, often boarding school, college or university students (学校)公寓

10. Tiscali: Tiscali SpA is a European telecommunications company, based in Cagliari, Italy, and provides internet and telecommunications services to Italy, the United Kingdom. 欧洲一家电信公司

11. vending machine: a machine from which you can get cigarettes, chocolate, drinks, etc. by putting money in 自动售货机

● **Reading Comprehension**

1. Directions: *Fill in the blanks with appropriate content based on the information given in the passage.*

Study in the UK	
Before you leave (Para. 2—Para. 3)	1. Read the information about the _____ and the _____ and _____ information. 2. Make sure you arrive at a time that _____.
Getting on board (Para. 4—Para. 5)	1. Make sure you have the right _____ and enough _____. 2. Before leaving home, allow plenty of time to _____ for your flight and to pass through _____.
Reaching your destination (Para. 6—Para. 7)	1. _____ of onward travel services in advance on the web, to work out the best way to get to your institution. 2 Institutions may run _____ for international students.
Contacting home (Para. 8—Para. 15)	The communications services in the UK include _____ _____; _____; _____; _____.

2. Directions: *Read the following statements carefully, and decide whether they are true (T) or false (F) according to the text.*

_____ 1) Try to travel through the night and arrive in the morning in the international flight because it will help to make your onward journey easier.

_____ 2) Sharp items should be packed in your hand luggage and you are not allowed to take gels onto planes traveling to and from the UK.

_____ 3) You don't have to work out the best way to get to your institution because the institution will collect you and take you to your accommodation.

_____ 4) It is costly for overseas students to make the international calls by using public phones.

_____ 5) If you want to buy a cheap mobile phone, please check details of the competing packages carefully in order to avoid high charges.

●Discussion

1. What are the ways of contacting friends and family back at home in China while studying in the UK?

2. What are the procedures of studying abroad? Please put the following procedures of studying abroad in a right order.

1) Submit your studying abroad applications by the deadline

2) Select universities

Write down your priorities: academic atmosphere; location; cost; size; ranking;

Conduct research and rank universities which fit your priority factors

3) Select an academic level (graduate/4 yr Colleges/2 yr Colleges)

4) Pre-Departure Preparation

Collect details about the university environment, arrival information, registration, etc.

Register for housing: coed residence halls[1]; single-sex residence halls[2]; university apartments[3]; fraternity and sorority houses[4]; married student housing[5].

5) Determine financial aid options and complete a contractual agreement

6) Clarify your purpose of study

7) Getting to know the admission requirements/qualifications

required admission tests: TOEFL, SAT and ACT ;GRE and GMAT[6];

transcripts (GPA)[7] and recommendation letters

Clarify the Costs and ways of financing them[8]

8) Once accepted, apply for your passport and visa

The right order is: _____

Notes

1. **coed residence halls:** Coed dormitories have both men and women living in the same building. For some international students, this might be a new and very different concept, but it works very well on U.S. campuses. However, male and female students do not share rooms. Sometimes men and women live on different floors or in separate suites, which are small apartments that contain several sleeping rooms, a common living area, and one or two bathrooms.

2. **single-sex residence halls:** These dormitories are for those who prefer to live in an all-male or all-female environment. Universities may set aside a residence or at least part of a residence building that houses women and men separately.

3. university apartments: Some universities operate apartments on campus. Apartments are always

in high demand. Usually priority is given to upper-level undergraduate and graduate students and to students who are married.

4. **fraternity and sorority houses:** Fraternities (for men) and sororities (for women) are close-knit social organizations of undergraduate men and women who live in a house operated by the organization. Fraternity and sorority houses may be either on- or off-campus. There is emphasis on social activities in fraternities and sororities. New members are chosen through various means during a period called "rush week." Rush week is often held the week before classes begin. Living in a fraternity or sorority house may be restricted to upper-level students.

5. **married student housing:** At some universities certain apartments or houses are owned and operated by the university exclusively for married students and families. Usually, only a limited number of units are available. These houses and apartments are usually furnished. The demand for these units is very high. Married students should inquire as early as possible about the availability of these houses or apartments.

6. **TOEFL, SAT and ACT; GRE and GMAT:** Students register for the required admission tests such as TOEFL (Test of English as a Foreign Language), SAT (Scholastic Assessment Test) and ACT (American College Test, known in U.S only) for a Bachelor's programme or undergraduate study; and TOEFL, GRE (Graduate Record Examinations) or GMAT (Graduate Management Admission Test) for a master's or doctoral programme (graduate study and research.) The test takers can arrange with the testing agencies to send test scores directly to the colleges and universities they are applying to.

7. transcript: Transcripts are academic records including an official credential evaluation of the "marks card" (known in the USA). These records should include certificates of achievement in co-curricular and extra curricular activities.

8. ways of financing the costs: private funds; scholarships; assistantships; company sponsorship

After-Class Reading

Warm-up questions:

1. Do you want to go abroad for further study after graduation? Why or why not?

2. What do you know about financial aids when studying abroad?

Identifying Sources of Financial Assistance

1   "Be realistic about how much you need and what you can really afford."

—International studies and sociology student from Ghana[1].

2   All types of scholarships and financial aid for international students are highly competitive and require excellent academic records. You will often find the terms "scholarships" and "financial aid" used interchangeably, but technically speaking, a scholarship is a financial award based on merit, including outstanding academic performance, special talent in sports or performing arts, or perhaps community service or leadership. Financial aid is a "need-based" grant based on the student's financial need, as documented by family income, assets, and other factors. Below are the main types of financial assistance available for international students who want to study in the United States:

3   Home Country Funds: Conduct research at home to find possible funding from local government, corporate, or foundation sources. Although these sources are not found in all countries, you could reduce your educational cost with scholarships from local organizations.

4   Funding from Colleges: Meet with an educational adviser to learn how to research available financial aid for international students. Careful advance research and realistic expectations are more likely to result in success. Do not assume that all colleges award financial aid. In fact, less

than half of the institutions offering bachelor's degrees can provide financial assistance to students who are not citizens or permanent residents of the United States[2]. Keep in mind that financial aid for U.S. students is separate from financial aid for international students. Be sure to tell the admissions office your country of citizenship[3] and request information on financial aid available to non-U.S. citizens. If offered, financial aid is usually made up of a number of different types of assistance, including grants and scholarships and occasionally loans or part-time work programs[4].

5   You will discover that financial aid is very rare at state, or public, colleges and at colleges that offer professional courses such as engineering, business administration, and health professions. More financial aid may be available from the private liberal arts[5] colleges, which offer the arts and science subjects.

6   As you do your research, make a table listing the colleges you would like to attend. Write down annual costs, then enter the average financial aid award and the number of awards made by each of the colleges. Such information is available from resources in your information or advising center. This chart can quickly allow you to see where your best chances lie, and can help you eliminate from your list the colleges where your admission with the needed funding is not viable[6].

7   International students often ask advisers about full scholarships, which cover all the costs of education except for airfare. The total number of full scholarships available each year to incoming international students in the United States is about 1,000, offered by only about 100 colleges. To get a full scholarship, you must be one of the top students in your country, usually with "A"s (excellent) in almost every subject, high SAT and TOEFL scores, and distinguished performance in other areas such as leadership and community service. There are 20 top students from all over the world competing for each scholarship, so you must distinguish yourself among a pool of outstanding students.

8   Only a handful of wealthy colleges in the United States are able to meet the financial need of all the students they admit. (Please note that admission to these schools is usually very competitive.) Financial need is the difference between what you and your family can afford to contribute and the estimated cost of attending the college. The former is calculated on the basis of detailed information about your parents' financial circumstances, including supporting evidence such as bank statements, employers' letters, and other official documents and statements[7]. Other universities, which make more limited awards on the basis of your financial need, will also ask to see such evidence.

9   Financial assistance from colleges is awarded at the beginning of the academic year and is rarely available for students entering mid-year in January or at other times. More aid is available for freshman students than for those transferring in from other institutions. Students who have already proven themselves at a college may find it easier to obtain financial assistance from that college than new students.

10   Sports Scholarships: Some U.S. colleges offer opportunities for gifted student athletes to play

for the college team as a means of paying for their education.

11   International Awards: International students also ask about financial assistance from foundations, organizations, and the U.S. government. Very little aid exists through such sources, and it is usually earmarked[8] for advanced graduate students. Again, your educational adviser can tell you whether there are special funds available for students from your country.

12   Loans: In limited instances, you may be able to negotiate a loan to fund part of your educational costs. Your educational adviser may have information on loan programs for which you may be eligible. You must usually have a U.S. citizen co-signer to act as a guarantor for any loans from U.S. loan programs, and in most cases you must already be enrolled in a U.S. university before you apply[9]. Before taking a loan, make certain you know how you are going to repay it, and how a loan will affect your plans for graduate or other further study and for returning home.

13   Employment: Current immigration regulations permit international students to work only part-time—up to 20 hours per week—and only on campus during their first year of study. By working 10 to 15 hours a week, you could earn enough to pay for incidentals[10] such as books, clothing, and personal expenses, but your campus job cannot pay your major expenses, such as tuition or room and board. This income also cannot be used as a source of income for any official financial statements. Campus jobs may include working at the university's cafeteria, bookstore, library, or health club, or within the university's administrative offices.

14   After the first year, you can also apply for employment as a resident assistant (RA) in a university dormitory. RAs serve as the first point of contact for students needing assistance or who have queries regarding dorm life. In return, RAs receive free accommodation and sometimes a small salary and/or meal plan.

15   Under current regulations, after your first year of study, you may apply to the Immigration and Naturalization Service (INS)[11] for permission to work off campus for up to 20 hours a week. You should note, however, that there is no guarantee that this request will be granted. If you are married and are in the United States on an F-1 student visa[12], your spouse does not have permission to work. However, if you are in the United States on a J-1 student visa[13], your spouse is allowed to request a temporary work permit.

16   You should always check with your international student adviser before considering any form of employment.

Notes

1. **Ghana:** a republic in West Africa on the Gulf of Guinea 加纳

2. In fact, less than half of the institutions offering bachelor's degrees can provide financial assistance to students who are not citizens or permanent residents of the United States. 此句大意为：事实上，在开设学士课程的美国大学中，只有不到一半的学校能够给非美国学生提供经济资助。

3. **country of citizenship:** 国籍；比较：**country of residence** 居住国

4. If offered, financial aid is usually made up of a number of different types of assistance, including grants and scholarships and occasionally loans or part-time work programs. 此句大意为：如果提供经济资助的话，一般有几种不同的方式，其中包括助学金、奖学金，有时还有贷款或者提供兼职工作的机会。

5. liberal arts: 文科

6. This chart can quickly allow you to see where your best chances lie, and can help you eliminate from your list the colleges where your admission with the needed funding is not viable. 此句大意为：这张图表能帮你快速找出你最好的机会在哪里。它能帮你排除那些不能提供经济资助的学校。viable 在句中意为"可行的"。

7. The former is calculated on the basis of detailed information about your parents' financial circumstances, including supporting evidence such as bank statements, employers' letters, and other official documents and statements. 此句大意为：前者是根据你父母亲的具体经济状况来计算的，其中包括如银行账单、雇主推荐信等证明材料以及其他的正式文件。

8. earmark: reserve or set aside for a particular purpose 专为……设立

9. You must usually have a U.S. citizen co-signer to act as a guarantor for any loans from U.S. loan programs, and in most cases you must already be enrolled in a U.S. university before you apply. 此句大意为：你必须要有一位美国公民作为你从美国贷款项目中贷款的保证人与你一起签贷款合同。而且在多数情况下，在申请之前，必须要有美国的一所大学已经录取你。

10. incidentals：incidental costs 杂费

11. Immigration and Naturalization Service (INS)：移民局

12. **F-1 student visa:** An F-1 visa is issued to international students who are attending an academic program or English language program at a U.S. college or university. F-1 students must maintain the minimum course load for fulltime student status.

13. **J-1 student visa:** J-1 student visa is for people who want to participate in an exchange visitor program in the U.S. The J-1 visa is intended for students needing practical training that is not available in their home country to complete their academic program.

● **Reading Comprehension**

1. **Directions:** *Try to find out different types of financial assistance in the passage and then discuss with your partner which one(s) you think might be applicable to you if you want to study in the United States.*

2. **Directions:** *Discuss the following questions with your classmates.*

   1) "Scholarships" and "financial aid" are used interchangeably in many situations. Do you think they are the same? If not, what are the differences between them?

   2) How can one get informed about available financial assistance?

   3) What are the terms qualifying for a full scholarship?

4) Are scholarships only awarded to those top students according to the passage?

5) After graduation, if you want to pursue a master's degree in the United States, which type of visa should you apply for? Why?

6) What kinds of jobs are usually available to students on campus?

7) What is an RA? What is the main responsibility of an RA?

8) How can students make informed decisions about whether or not to study abroad?

Passage Two

Warm-up questions:

1. How much do you know about student societies and clubs both in China and in Western countries?

2. Are you a member of a student club in the university? What have you experienced and learned?

Guide to Student Societies and Clubs

Joining a uni society or club is sure to aid your social credentials[1].

—Marcus Jones

1　During the first week of each term, universities will almost certainly run an event with a catchy title like, "Freshers' fair" or "SocMart", where you will have the opportunity to sign yourself up to a plethora of societies and sport clubs[2]. Whatever university you are at, the choice you face will probably be huge, so it's always a good idea to try and get hold of a list of the options beforehand. You can then go through said list with a handy highlighter and work out a handful of groups that tickle your fancy[3]. That way you have some focus and direction before taking on what will probably be a packed hall, full of wild-eyed, sleep deprived first years each trying to sign random bits of paper that entitles them to membership of the Creative Writing society or Hockey club[4].

2　After the dust has settled, what will you end up with for your money[5] (and you will have to pay money to join 90% of the groups)? Firstly, sport clubs are often more expensive, but you arguably get more for your cash (or rather the student loan company's cash), as you often have to pay for some form of insurance and your money will probably go someway to providing for equipment and maybe even coaching.

3   The major sport clubs (football, rugby, hockey, cricket, tennis) are often the ones that are labelled for being arrogant, alcohol guzzling yobs and, as the old adage goes, there is often no smoke without fire[6]. There is a drinking culture connected to many of these sport clubs, with the traditional initiation ceremonies earning particular notoriety[7]. Evidently, for many members, this adds to their sense of enjoyment and camaraderie, but a well-run club should not be dependent upon beer and wine to fuel good times[8]. Indeed, it is probably written down in some constitution that provision[9] must be made for those who don't wish to drink. Cue paint-balling[10], group golfing and quiz nights. If you are quite clear in your desire not to join the drinking brigade[11] you should be met with respect and in no way ought it to detract from your sporting experience.

4   Your sporting experience could well be as productive as that experienced by Jemma Thake, an English Literature student who has been a member of the University of East Anglia's (UEA) athletic club for all of her three years. As well as a host of friends and the fitness benefits, she has learnt First Aid and how to drive a minibus—"and who doesn't need those sort of skills?" Quite true Jemma, quite true.

5   What societies (non-sporty clubs) don't exist at most universities are really probably not worth contemplating[12]. For example, UEA, a university of a little over 14,000 students, offers over 60 societies ranging from Debating and Deviant societies[13] to Pirate and Photo socs[14]. Many groups also offer fantastic opportunities to do volunteer and charity work, so if you join Make Poverty History[15] you can not only make lifelong friends and enjoy yourself, but do so safe in the knowledge[16] that you are really making a difference to people in need.

6   You can really make a difference to your CV as well with some shrewd societal choices. Joining the university paper or radio station, Nightline (student support helpline) or Links (the university branch of St. John's Ambulance) will all potentially give you that extra boost when employers start riffling through your application forms[17].

7   However, this does not mean that your choices should simply be made out of some crazed CV hoarding desire[18]. Whatever group you choose should be one you know you will enjoy and can contribute to in full. In fact, a future employer is likely to be as impressed by you organising trips and guest speakers for the History society, or being in charge of the squash club's[19] finances, as he will be by a few articles you've written for the uni magazine.

8   It isn't all sporting fun and society sweetness though; a natural side effect from all these groups being run by students (many of whom have little or no previous experience of such responsibility) is poor organisation and accusations of favouritism[20]. It is particularly in sport clubs, where team selections need to be made, that labels can be attached to those who only seem to pick their mates. While this sort of policy is not unheard of, it is by no means common. After all, those in charge of the basketball team achieve nothing by selecting their mates if they do not win games, so it is in their interests to choose the best players on offer. It is the law of averages that some

people get overlooked, but if you know you're good enough and show enough commitment, second trial days[21] often take place to give a chance to those that missed out first time round.

9   Sometimes clubs and societies are run poorly and in the short term, this is harder to rectify[22]. However, the hierarchy of most organisations changes rapidly each year as students move on, so you can always be patient and wait for that incompetent president to finish his degree. Alternatively, if you and enough others demonstrate your own organisational skills, you can probably set up your own group… or even conduct some sort of military coup to topple the corrupt leadership of a particular society[23]!

10   Personally, I don't think it is possible to have a true university experience if you are not involved in a club or society. You may have course friends and house-mates, but the individuals you meet in a group you have chosen to join will add a whole new dimension to your time at uni. The things you can achieve together, whether it be in the sporting arena, or raising money for a good cause, will bring a fantastic sense of achievement and fulfillment and provide you with memories and experiences that will last for many a year.

—Marcus Jones

Notes

1. Joining a uni society or club is sure to aid your social credentials. 此句大意是：加入大学中的社团无疑能增加你的社会资历。credentials 在句中意为个人能力的证明，如 academic credentials 意为学历，学术造诣。uni 是 university 的缩写。

2. During the first week of each term, universities will almost certainly run an event with a catchy title like, "Freshers' fair" or "SocMart", where you will have the opportunity to sign yourself up to a plethora of societies and sport clubs. 此句大意是：在开学的第一周，几乎所有的大学都会有一个招募新生的活动。这些活动往往有着诱人的名称，如 "新生见面会"、"社团纳新" 等。在那里你有机会加入各种社团和体育俱乐部。catchy 在句中意为诱人的。SocMart 是 society mart 的缩写。a plethora of 原意为过多的，极多的，句中意为各种各样的。

3. You can then go through said list with a handy highlighter and work out a handful of groups that tickle your fancy. 此句大意是：你在看一览表时可以随手用荧光笔划出少数几个你感兴趣的社团。

4. That way you have some focus and direction before taking on what will probably be a packed hall, full of wild-eyed, sleep deprived first years each trying to sign random bits of paper that entitles them to membership of the Creative Writing society or Hockey club. 此句大意是：那样做使你(对加入什么样的社团)有重点和方向。而不会像其他人一样直接冲进挤满两眼发直、缺乏睡眠的大一新生的大厅，随意在申请加入各种社团，如创意写作社团或曲棍球俱乐部的文件上签字。wild-eyed 在句中意为眼球充血的。

5. After the dust has settled, what will you end up with for your money? 此句大意是：当一切尘埃落定，你口袋里的钱还剩下多少？

6. The major sport clubs are often the ones that are labelled for being arrogant, alcohol guzzling yobs and, as the old adage goes, there is often no smoke without fire. 此句大意是：主要的几个体育俱乐部的成员往往被人们看成是傲慢的酗酒的一帮年轻人。老话说无风不起浪。alcohol guzzling yobs 在句中意为酗酒的年轻人。

7. notoriety: 恶名

8. Evidently, for many members, this adds to their sense of enjoyment and camaraderie, but a well run-club should not be dependent upon beer and wine to fuel good times. 此句大意是：显然饮酒能使队员们更加高兴，并能增进他们之间的友谊。但是一个好的俱乐部不应该依靠酒精来增加欢乐气氛，欢度好时光。camaraderie 在句中意为"友情"。

9. provision: 规定

10. cue paint-balling: 彩弹军事游戏

11. brigade: 队，组

12. what societies (non-sporty clubs) don't exist at most universities are really probably not worth contemplating. 此句大意是：你不必考虑那些在绝大部分高校都不存在的社团(非体育俱乐部)。contemplate 在句中意为"思量"。

13. deviant society: 另类社团

14. Pirate and Photo socs: 盗版和影像社团

15. Make Poverty History: an organization that fights against extreme poverty and global disease 使贫穷成为历史(一个扶贫的社团)

16. safe in the knowledge: 确切地知道

17. …will all potentially give you that extra boost when employers start riffling through your application forms. 此句大意是：当雇主在快速翻阅你的申请表时，你(之前的经历)将大大提升你的竞争力。

18. However, this does not mean that your choices should simply be made out of some crazed CV hoarding desire. 此句大意是：然而这并不意味着你对社团的选择只能由你将来疯狂的简历需求所决定。hoarding 在句中意为"囤积"。

19. squash club: 壁球俱乐部

20. accusations of favouritism: 对于徇私的指责

21. trial days: 试用期

22. rectify: 改正，调整

23. or even conduct some sort of military coup to topple the corrupt leadership of a particular society: 甚至以类似发动军事政变的方式来颠覆那个社团的腐败领导

● **Reading Comprehension**

1. Directions: *After reading the whole passage, could you tell your partner what can be expected from clubs and societies at university?*

2. Directions: *Read the following statements carefully, and decide whether they are true (T) or*

false (F) according to the text.

_____ 1) As a freshman, you have a lot of opportunities to become a member of societies and clubs at the university during the first week.

_____ 2) It is a good idea to rush into a packed hall and sign random bits of paper that entitles you to a membership of a club.

_____ 3) Creative Writing Society is more expensive than Hockey Club.

_____ 4) Usually the major sport clubs are connected to a drinking culture.

_____ 5) If you don't drink beer or wine, you can not join the sports club at university.

_____ 6) Jemma thought that people don't need to learn First Aid or how to drive a minibus.

_____ 7) To make one's CV more competitive is the only criterion for a student to choose clubs and societies at university.

_____ 8) The author discourages students from joining different clubs and societies at university.

Part Three

Topic-related Activities

1. Writing a Personal Statement

Step One

Directions: *Read the following guide about how to write a personal statement.*

A good personal statement is important. It is your chance to tell the universities and colleges you have chosen the reason why you are applying, and why they should want you as a student. Admissions officers will want to know why you are interested in your chosen subjects. And it could help to persuade an admissions officer to offer you a place. Meanwhile, writing a personal statement is probably one of the most difficult parts in your application.

We've produced this short guide to help you write a personal statement. Before you start, remember, this is a "personal" statement—i.e. it's about you, and there is no real right or wrong way to do it. What we've written below is just a guide, and should not be stuck to rigidly. You may find by choosing your own structure, and writing what you want to write about, you give a better picture of yourself to the reader than anyone else can.

In most cases, your personal statement should be no longer than an A4 paper. Your statement must be clear, and your writing should not be too small. If you are using a word processor, you can use size 12. It is up to you how you write your statement but we suggest you include some or all of the following points.

The reason why you have chosen the courses you have listed.

Things that interest you about your chosen subject. Include details of what you have read about the subject.

Particular interests you have in your current studies.

Any job, work experience, placement or voluntary work you have done, particularly if it is relevant to your subject. Details of key skills you have gained.

Other achievements, such as the scholarships from your university.

Your future plans.

Any sponsorship or placements you have or have applied for.

Your social, sports or leisure interests.

Step Two

Directions: *Suppose you are applying to the University of Cambridge for graduate study. Write a personal statement based on your own situation.*

Step Three

Directions: *After your first draft is complete, read through what you've written slowly and try to read it from someone else's point of view. Make sure it's easy to read and not confusing. Make sure you've said everything you want to say and not under—or oversold yourself. Then change your statement with your partner and modify each other's statement based on the guide until you are happy with it.*

2. Writing a Résumé

Step One

Directions: *Résumés summarize our education, work experience, and other accomplishments for prospective universities and employers. Discuss with your partner and try to find out what must be included in a résumé.*

Step Two

Directions: *The following five elements are usually presented in a résumé when one applies to a university. Discuss with your partner and put them in the right order.*

1. _____   A. contact information

2. _____   B. work experience

3. _____   C. social and volunteer activities

4. _____   D. interests and abilities

5. _____   E. education

Step Three

Directions: *Look at the following sample résumé and try to make your own one.*

Résumé

Samuel Ruff

Address

2232 Chicago Street

Valparaiso, IN 46383

Phone: 464-555-2640

E-mail: samuel08@webmail.com

Education

B.A. in Psychology, Minor in East Asian Studies, Warwick University, Sept. 2004-June 2008

Work Experience

Research Assistant, December 2005-June 2008

Warwick University, Warwick, UK

Data collection from research participants through interviews

Assistant Swim Coach, Summer 2003

Valparaiso Student Club, Valparaiso, IN

Instructor of children between 6 and 19 in competitive swimming techniques and rules

Honors

Community Service Scholarship, Warwick University, 2005

Activities

Make Poverty History Fund-raiser

Skills

Microsoft Office; SPSS for windows; Fluency in English and Chinese language

---

3. Application to Study Abroad

Step One

Directions: *Suppose you are thinking of going abroad to further your studies. You go online and searche for some information about an English-medium university that you are interested in. Take note of the application requirements (including GPA, language proficiency tests such as TOEFL or ETS, other tests including GRE or GMAT, etc.), application stuff (including résumé, personal statement, recommendation letters, etc.)*

and deadline for that university.

Suggested criteria: *Different students prefer different universities on the grounds of various factors. The factors might be as follows: 1) the quality of its professors; the quality and diversity of the students; 2) the level of competition at entry; 3) the quality and influence of the research done; 4) the reputation of the university; 5) the programmes and the faculties and how easy it is for graduates to get jobs when they finish their programmes; 6) the number and quality of publications; 7) the number and quality of the patents produced in research related to the university; 8) the number of Nobel prizes won and 10) other very well reputed people related with the universities.*

Step Two

Directions: *The whole class gather together to: 1) report the university you are interested in; 2) discuss the reasons why you are interested in the university; 3) share the notes you take about the university you are interested in concerning the information about application requirements, application stuff and application deadlines.*

Step Three

Directions: *A brief survey is to be made to see how many of the students are interested in American universities, British universities and other English-speaking universities. Divide those students into several groups, several groups who prefer American universities, several who are in favor of British ones, and others. Each group recommends a representative. The representative will give a report in class about the reasons why he/she prefers this university and also the important dates and application stuff in applying.*

4. Case Study

The Price of Admission
How America's Ruling Class Buys Its Way into Elite Colleges
and Who Gets Left Outside the Gates

Every year thousands of middle- and low-income high school seniors learn they've been rejected by America's top universities. What they may never learn is that candidates like themselves have been passed over for wealthy students with lesser credentials—children of alumni, big donors or celebrities.

- At least half of the children of 425 big Harvard donors who applied to the school were accepted, By contrast, Harvard only admits 10% of applicants overall. Separately, Harvard provides a special entrée known as the "Z-list" for well-connected but under-qualified students; they are quietly admitted on the condition that they wait a year to enroll.

- Princeton admitted Senate Majority Leader Bill Frist's son even though it gave him the lowest ranking on its academic scale. Sen. Frist is an alumnus, an ex-trustee and prominent politician—and his family has donated $25 million to the school.

- Brown University sought to expand its Hollywood connections by admitting the son of powerbroker Michael Ovitz. Chris Ovitz was a mediocre student who'd been suspended in middle school for swinging a baseball bat at a female classmate. Even though he dropped out in less than a year, Brown still reaped the benefits: it snagged Ovitz pals and A-list celebrities Martin Scorsese and Dustin Hoffman at university events.

- At most colleges, the president and fundraisers funnel a "development list" of applicants from rich families to the admissions office for priority treatment. In addition, college presidents often have a powerbroker, a right-hand man to the president, whose responsibility is to usher children of the rich and famous through the admissions process.

- Children of key alumni and donors enjoy advantages every step of the way, such as extended application deadlines, personal interviews with admissions deans, "special student" status and deferred admissions.

Questions

1. What American values have been reflected in the case?

2. Does admission system in China favor the students of the rich and powerful families over those poor ones? What kind of students will have privilege when admitted by the university? Can you give some examples?

Part Four
Topic-related Information

1. Introduction to the World's Most Popular English Language Examinations

1) TOEFL IBT (TOEFL Internet-based Test)

For more than 40 years the Test of English as a Foreign Language (TOEFL) has been the leading academic English proficiency test in the world. TOEFL is organized by a non-profit organization of ETS (English Testing Service)[1] in Princeton University in the United States of America.

The Test of English as a Foreign Language (TOEFL) measures the ability of non-native speakers of English to combine the listening, reading, speaking and writing skills to perform academic tasks. Nowadays TOEFL is offered on computer in most regions of the world. In areas where access to computer-based testing is limited, a paper-and-pencil version of the test is administered. Each test taker will receive four scaled section scores (ranging from 0 to 30) and a total score (ranging from 0 to 120) and the scores are valid for two years after the test date.

Most people who take the TOEFL test are planning to study at colleges and universities where instruction is in English. In addition, many government agencies, scholarship programs, and licensing/certification agencies use TOEFL scores to evaluate English proficiency.

Currently more than 4,400 two- and four-year colleges and universities, professional schools, and sponsoring institutions accept TOEFL scores.

2) IELTS

IELTS is the International English Language Testing System. It measures ability to communicate in English across all four language skills—listening, reading, writing and speaking —for people who intend to study or work where English is the language of communication.

Since 1989, IELTS has been measuring life ability to communicate in English. More than 6,000 education institutions, faculties, government agencies and professional organisations around the world recognise IELTS scores as a trusted and valid indicator of ability to communicate in English.

Over 1,000,000 people a year are now using IELTS to open doors throughout the English-speaking world and beyond. The test is taken every year across 120 countries, and is one of the fastest growing English language tests in the world, and sets the standard in integrity, research and innovation.

The IELTS test has two forms: the Academic test (or module) and the General Training test (or module). The module that you take depends on the reason that you are taking it for. Generally speaking, the Academic Module is for those people who are trying to gain entry onto undergraduate or postgraduate education courses or for professional reasons. The General Training Module is for those people who wish to join some kinds of vocational or training courses, secondary schools or for immigration purposes.

The IELTS test (both Academic and General Training modules) is divided into four parts: reading, writing, listening and speaking. The listening and speaking tests are exactly the same for the Academic and General Training modules but the reading and writing tests are different.

IELTS is jointly managed by British Council[2], IDP: IELTS Australia[3] and the University of Cambridge ESOL Examinations (Cambridge ESOL)[4] through more than 500 locations in 120 countries.

2. Introduction to Some Other University Entrance Tests

1) GRE

The GRE (Graduate Record Examination) measures a variety of skills that are thought to predict success in graduate school across a wide variety of disciplines. Actually, there are several GRE tests. Most often when an applicant, professor, or admissions director mentions the GRE, he or she is referring to the GRE General Test. Depending upon your discipline, you may be required to take a GRE Subject Test or the GRE Written Test in addition to the GRE General Test.

The GRE General Test measures the skills that you've acquired over the high school and college years. It is an aptitude test because it is meant to measure your potential to succeed in graduate school. While the GRE is only one of several criteria that graduate schools use to evaluate your application, it is one of the most important. This is particularly true if your college GPA (Grade Point Average) is not as high as you'd like. Exceptional GRE scores can open up new opportunities for grad school.

The GRE General Test contains sections that measure verbal, quantitative, and analytical writing skills.

The verbal section tests your ability to understand and analyze written material through the use of analogies, antonyms, sentence completions, and reading comprehension questions.

The quantitative section tests basic math skills and your ability to understand and apply quantitative skills to solve problems. Types of questions include quantitative comparisons, problem solving, and data interpretation.

The analytical writing section tests your ability to articulate complex ideas clearly and effectively, examine claims and accompanying evidence, support ideas with relevant reasons and examples, sustain a well-focused, coherent discussion, and control the elements of standard written English. It consists of two written essays: 45-minute "Present Your Perspective on an Issue" task and a 30-minute "Analyze an Argument" task.

GRE test scores are valid for five years after the testing year in which you tested. The revised verbal and quantitative subtests introduced in August 2011, yield scores ranging from 130 to 170.

2) GMAT

The Graduate Management Admission Test (GMAT) is a standardized test which has been widely used as part of the assessment process for admission to MBA (Master of Business Administration) programs in Business Schools for many years. Initially used in admissions by 54 schools, the GMAT is now used by more than 1,500 schools and 1,800 programs.

The GMAT measures basic verbal, mathematical, and analytical writing skills that you have developed over a long period of time in your education and work.

Over the 50 years of its use, the GMAT has been repeatedly studied, tested, and modified to ensure that it continues to help predict performance in the first year or midway through a graduate management program.

The Graduate Management Admission Test (GMAT) is designed for the applicants who wish to enter business schools. Therefore, the GMAT measures a variety of skills that are thought to predict success in business school. It measures skills that you've acquired over the high school and college years.

The GMAT contains sections that measure verbal reasoning, quantitative reasoning, and analytical writing skills. Total GMAT scores range from 200 to 800. Scores for the analytical writing range from 0 to 6.

The official organization that offers the GMAT, the Graduate Management Admission Council[5], is a leading advocate and resource for quality graduate schools of business worldwide. They provide information that helps business schools and students succeed.

3) SAT

SAT (Scholastic Assessment Test) and SAT Subject Tests are admission exams for entry to the colleges of America for undergraduate courses. SAT is conducted by the college board.

The College Board is a non-profit organisation and committed to the principles of excellence and equity. The commitment of college board embodifies in all of its programs, services, activities and concerns.

SAT scores are reported on a scale from 200 to 800, with additional subscores reported for the essay (2-12) and for multiple-choice writing questions (20-80).

Notes

1. **ETS** is a nonprofit, non-stock corporation organized under the education laws of the State of New York. Its work is supported through revenue from their products and services, as well as contracts and grants with government agencies, private foundations, universities and corporations. Their mission is to help advance quality and equity in education by providing fair and valid assessments, research and related services.

2. **British Council** connects people worldwide with the learning opportunities and creative ideas from the UK and builds lasting relationships between the UK and other countries. British Council is the UK's international organisation for educational opportunity and cultural relations and is represented in 109 countries worldwide.

3. **IDP: IELTS Australia** is Australia's international education organisation. It undertakes a broad range of activities from student advisory services and educational publications to project consultancy and English language teaching and testing.

4. **University of Cambridge ESOL Examinations (Cambridge ESOL)** is the world's leading provider of exams for learners of English. Each year the exams are taken by around 1.5 million people, in 135 countries.

5. **The Graduate Management Admission Council (GMAC)** is the association of leading graduate business schools around the world. GMAC meets the needs of business schools and students through a wide array of products, services, and programs and serves as a primary resource of research and information about quality graduate management education.

3. Introduction to the Hottest Schools in the United States

College Guide: It's that time of year again, when high-school seniors and their parents gear up for the admissions game. In excerpts from our annual newsstand issue, here's what you need to know about the newest trends.

● **Hottest Ivy:** Cornell University, Ithaca, N.Y.

Unlike the other Ivies, Cornell is a land-grant college emphasizing problem solving as well as scholarly debate. The university boasts a world-class engineering college and top-flight liberal arts, science and fine arts. Cornellians, proud of the variety on campus, point to the president, David Skorton, a cardiologist, jazz musician and computer scientist who is the first in his family to have a college education.

● **Hottest for Sports Fans:** University of Florida, Gainesville, Fla.

Winning the national football championship, as well as two consecutive basketball titles, is clearly a draw. Applications to Gatorland are up 15 percent in the last two years, nearly twice the national average. But high-school counselors are discovering it has more to offer its 35,000 undergraduates than just a great excuse to hit the sports bars. The university attracts more students from the International Baccalaureate program—the most challenging courses in American high schools—than any other college. The average Gator freshman had a 3.99 GPA in high school. Freshman Robin Prywes, a Maryland resident, says the only thing those sports championships taught her was that Florida had great school spirit. She says she liked the school's "academic reputation, student involvement, great weather and friendly atmosphere." But her mother says it was mostly the weather.

● **Hottest for No SAT or ACT Needed:** Bates College, Lewiston, Maine

Many colleges are SAT- or ACT-optional only for students with very good grades. But at Bates, applicants never have to submit their test scores, and half do not. The liberal-arts school, with about 1,700 students in central Maine, gets high marks on various college rankings. Students like Alex Chou, valedictorian at his Old Orchard Beach, Maine, high school, love the no-test-score option. "My high school did not prepare us for the SATs," he says. When Chou applied, he thought his 1220 score would hurt him, so he didn't submit it. He got in, and graduated this spring summa cum-laude. Once at Bates, students say they like that professors are hired particularly for their teaching ability, the relaxed social atmosphere free of fraternities and sororities, and the international atmosphere—70 percent of students study abroad.

● **Hottest for Science and Engineering:** California Institute of Technology, Pasadena, Calif.

Caltech students think of themselves as geeks with power tools. On a beach weekend they may get sand kicked in their faces, but their assailant will soon find his car disassembled and reassembled on top of a lifeguard station, with the engine still running. There are only 900 undergraduates, and admission is very competitive: 17 percent get in. The lucky ones go on to reap the wealth and fame that come to them in an era in which so many of our troubles—global warming, rush-hour traffic, male-pattern baldness—are thought to be solvable if we just give scientists enough money. Even female teachers say they have fun once they get used to attending one of the last colleges in America where women are still a distinct minority (30 percent). All students look forward to Ditch Day, when automobiles are sometimes found reassembled in side dorm rooms—with the engines still running.

- **Hottest for Rejecting You:** Harvard University, Cambridge, Mass.

This was a close one. Harvard rejected 91.03 percent of its applicants to the class of 2011. It seemed likely, once again, to win the trophy for Stingiest Admissions. But wait: Columbia College, part of Columbia University, rejected 91.05 of applicants. Its student newspaper declared it the winner. Some Columbia freshmen, however, attend the School of Engineering and Applied Science or the School of General Studies, which means that only 89.6 percent of applicants felt the pain. Not that any of the people who send out all those thin envelopes are happy about it. The über-selective Ivies know their admission process is a dreary march toward disappointment. The Harvard admissions office, the prime offender, particularly feels the strain. Its top officials recently coauthored an essay in The Harvard Crimson, saying they hoped the elimination of Early Decision (along with Princeton's and the University of Virginia's) will give students more time to consider where to apply. That may reduce autumn-application pressure, but nine out of 10 of those candidates will still likely be getting bad news.

- **Hottest for Free Tuition:** Cooper Union for the Advancement of Science and Art, N.Y.

This collection of 1,000 undergrads in the East Village of Manhattan is one of the oddest, and most selective, colleges in the country. Tuition is free, even for millionaires' kids, but the Cooper Union mantra is they all pay for it in sweat and blood because of demanding courses and tough grading. There are just three majors—architecture, art and engineering. That produces an unusual mix of computer engineers and introspective painters. The big excitement on campus, particularly for the architecture majors, is the new nine-story academic building, the city's first green college laboratory building with a cogeneration plant, radiant ceiling heating and cooling panels, and photovoltaic panels.

- **Hottest Big State School:** University of Wisconsin-Madison, Madison, Wis.

Growing up in Wisconsin, Laura Sullivan was raised on Badger mania. But she was initially afraid that she would get lost in Madison amid 41,000 students, 140 undergraduate majors and nearly 700 student organizations. So when her high-school German class visited, Sullivan says she was shocked to find that she immediately felt at home. The tree-filled campus of nearly 1,000 acres looked to her exactly like what a college should. It occurred to her that its enormity actually meant "endless opportunities," she says. It is the old traditions graduates remember most, including Picnic Point, declared by one newspaper to be "the kissing-est spot in North America."

- **Hottest for International Studies:** University of Richmond, Richmond, VA.

Seventy percent of the class of 2007 studied abroad, attending universities in Oxford, Edinburgh, Prague, Milan, Buenos Aires, Hong Kong, Bangkok and other cosmopolitan spots. The 3,000-student university has exchange agreements with more than 50 schools around the world and ensures that time spent abroad costs no more than time on campus. The faculty is strong in many areas, particularly business, science and leadership studies, but all students are urged to see the world.

- **Hottest for Business:** Babson College, Babson Park, Mass.

Just as violinists know why they're at Juilliard, and physicists at Caltech, the 1,700 students attending Babson understand what made them choose this small campus. They are entrepreneurs, and no school does a better job than Babson in teaching how to start businesses. Jason Reuben grew up in Los Angeles and by fourth grade was selling ketchup packets at his elementary school's Friday barbecues. He started a Web design firm in high school. He knew Babson was for him when, during a campus visit, he saw all the people in one lecture hall pull out their laptops to look up business data.

Hyperlinks

[1] Resources for financial assistance

　　http://www.scholarships.com/

　　http://www.internationalscholarships.com/

[2] Resources for visa application

　　http://shanghai.usembassy-china.org.cn/general_information.html

　　http://ukinchina.fco.gov.uk/en/visas/

[3] Resources for tests

　　http://www.taisha.org/

　　http://51ielts.com/

[4] Resources for general information (applications, tests, scholarships)

　　http://www.infozee.com/

　　http://tigtag.com

[5] www.educationusa.state.gov (美国留学网站)

[6] www.vco-edusa.net (美国教育在线咨询)

[7] www.educationuk.org (英国留学网站)

References

[1] http://www. ets.org

[2] http://www.ielts.org

[3] http://www.gmac.com/gmac/aboutus/

[4] http://www.collegeboard.com/

[5] http://www.educationuk.org/pls/hot_bc/page_pls_user_article?x=933991611803&y=0&a= 0&d=4050

[6] Jay Mathews. 25 hottest schools[J]. *Newsweek*, 2007(8).

[7] http://www.educationusa.state.gov/finaid.htm

[8] http://www.timesonline.co.uk/tol/life_and_style/education/student/article2071591.ece

[9] http:// www.mostblessedsacrament.com

[10] http://www.studential.com/personalstatements

Unit 4

Education

Part One

Lead-in

The roots of education are bitter, but the fruit is sweet.

—Aristotle (Ancient Greek philosopher)

教育的根是苦的，但其果实是甜的。

——亚里士多德（古希腊哲学家）

Education is the transmission of civilization, the chief defense of nations; Education is a progressive discovery of ignorance. Education is not the filling of a pail, but the lighting of a fire. Education does not mean teaching people to know what they do not know. It means teaching them to behave as they do not behave.

Part Two

Reading Passages

In-Class Reading

Warm-up questions:

1. What do you know about the higher education in the Great Britain? Can you name some famous universities in Britain?

2. Do you know how one can apply for the entrance to Oxford or Cambridge University?

A Guide to Higher Education in Britain

Entrance Procedures

1   A bachelor degree (BA, BSc[1], etc.) can be obtained by a minimum of three years' study at one of the more than 200 universities or institutions of higher education in the UK offering degree courses. Some degree courses last four years, the extra year being spent in practical training, as in many "sandwich" degrees[2] such as engineering, or as a year abroad if studying a modern language. Only about the top 7% of the age cohort[3] in the UK studies for a degree; consequently entry to universities or similar institutions is highly competitive. Typical entry requirements would be at least 3 C grades[4] at A Level[5] for university courses and perhaps 3 grade Ds for entry to other institutions of higher education.

2   In the third term of Year 12 students prepare their applications to university. Applications are then made in the first term of the Year 13 through one centralised organisation known as UCAS (Universities and Colleges Admissions Service).

3   The applications are made on a UCAS form, electronically through the EAS (Electronic Applications Systems). Students can apply to a maximum of six universities/institutions. As well as the student's personal details and a paragraph on their extra-curricular interests, the UCAS form will carry details of their (I) GCSE[6] grades and AS grades[7] so far and an academic/character reference from the school which will include a prediction of the grades that the applicant is likely to obtain at A Level. It is therefore vital that students impress upon their teachers the quality of their work throughout the entire sixth form course and that they do not think of Year 12 as an "easy" year. If a university or institution is impressed by the student's UCAS form they will send an offer of a place conditional upon obtaining certain stated A Level grades. Applicants are allowed to **provisionally** accept and hold a maximum of two offers. The final decision on which institution the student will actually attend will be taken when the A Level results are published in mid-August. Degree courses start in late September or early October.

4   There are special procedures for application for art courses or teacher training.

Financial Considerations

5   A student who is a European Citizen (or if one of their parents is a EU[8] citizen) AND if they have been fully resident in the Union for the last three years will have to pay up to approximately £1,000 per academic year towards their tuition fees. The remainder of the tuition costs should be covered by the **competent** authority. If the student is not **eligible** for the Home Student status they will be charged as an Overseas Student and these range from about £6,000 per year for non-science courses up to about £10,000 per year for medicine and related courses. The universities estimate that living and travelling expenses are about £5-6,000 per year for a student in the UK depending on the individual's life-style and most importantly, whether or not he/she lives in London.

6   Very few **sponsorships** or scholarships are available to help students to finance their stay at a British university. Most are only available to British citizens and those that are open to a wider range of students are highly sought after. It is unrealistic for students to assume that they will be able to find financial help or to think that they can work their way through university by doing part-time jobs.

7   There are some web sites which give information about the possibilities of obtaining grants or scholarships. Students should consider asking the universities which they are interested in about financial support.

Studies

8   It should be noted that a degree from any one British university or institution of higher education is considered to be academically **equivalent** to a degree from any other British university or institution of higher education. However, certain British universities carry, for historical reasons, extra prestige. Oxford and Cambridge are obvious examples, and competition for entry to these universities is so great that applicants typically require three A grades at A Level to earn a place. In the case of Cambridge applicants may be asked to obtain a good mark in an extra exam (called the STEP[9]), which they can sit just after the A Level exams. Applications through UCAS to Oxford and Cambridge also have to be sent by a special early deadline accompanied by a special extra form.

9   Many students and their parents ask the question, "What is the difference between a university and an institution of higher education and, above all which is best?" The answer is that the "best" institution is the one that most clearly matches the individual student's aspirations and abilities. So there is no set answer to this question. Nevertheless certain remarks are worth making although these are generalisations, not "truths".

  1) The universities concentrate on bachelor degree courses or higher degrees (masters, doctorates) whereas other institutions offer bachelor degrees and lower level courses (2 year HND[10], Dip Ed[11], etc.).

2) The universities tend to enjoy higher prestige in the mind of the general (uninformed?) public, but this is very subjective and may be totally unjustified in the case of certain courses. (See next point).

3) Other institutions of higher education offer courses which are more directly **orientated** towards preparing students for the world of work than is the case for universities. These institutions often have closer links than universities with industry and commerce. For both these reasons the degree courses involving engineering, business studies, and modern languages for use in the work place may well be superior to the corresponding university course.

10   The above statements about the differences between universities and other institutions are generalisations but they will help students in the decision making.

11   Some British degrees are one-subject in style, eg BSc in Chemistry, but many dual-subject degrees and, increasingly, special combinations such as sciences or business administration with a modern language are offered. An increasing number of degrees involving study in Britain and another EU country are now available particularly, but not exclusively, in the area of business studies. Many are sponsored by the European Union's "Socrates-Erasmus" programme[12]. Some degree courses with links to non-EU countries, eg the USA, also exist.

12   Class sizes at British universities and other similar institutions are typically small and a mixture of lectures and tutorials are commonly given, plus practical work where relevant. Many language, engineering and certain other degree courses also involve practical experience outside the university itself which may extend the length of the course from the normal three years to four. Take note that courses in medicine and certain other subjects will be even longer.

13   Assessment is mainly by examinations held either at the end of the three year course (the dreaded "Finals") or perhaps two years through the course (Part I examinations) and at the end of the course (Part II examinations). Some courses at some universities have a certain amount of continuous assessment. Bachelor degrees are usually classified or graded as follows:

>   First Class Honours (a "First")
>
>   Second Class Honours Division One (a "2-1")
>
>   Second Class Honours Division Two (a "2-2")
>
>   Third Class Honours (a "Third")
>
>   Pass Degree

14   Repeating a year of study or transferring from one institution to another are both comparatively rare. Some universities are changing their attitudes about these possibilities but generally if students are working badly they simply lose their place.

15   A special mention should be made of Scottish universities. In Scotland, pupils leave school after the equivalent of Year 12 and so they spend four years at university (equivalent to Year 13 plus the three years, which is normal at other universities) in order to obtain a degree. As a result of

this Scottish universities may require relatively lower grades at A Level for students who have completed two years of sixth form study and who are willing to spend four years getting their degree. Students obtaining very good grades at A Level go into the second year of certain courses at some Scottish universities. Furthermore, Scottish university curricula usually offer more opportunities for combining the study of several subjects than commonly exist when taking a typical single-subject English university course.

16　Most British universities have their own optional "Halls" or student residences. For a student coming from overseas to have a room in a hall is probably an ideal way to meet people and make new friends in the first year. Students may then prefer to make their own living arrangements for their other years of study. Whether students live in a university residence or outside, they will find life at a British university very rich in terms of social, sporting, cultural events and political clubs and societies.

New Words and Expressions

provisionally	*ad.*	providing for immediate needs only, temporarily 暂时地，临时地
eligible	*a.*	fit or entitled to be chosen (for office, award, etc.); desirable or suitable, esp. for marriage 符合条件的，合格的
competent	*a.*	properly or sufficiently qualified or capable or efficient 有能力的，胜任的
sponsorship	*n.*	the act of sponsoring　赞助者的地位，任务等
equivalent	*a.*	equal in amount or value 相等的，相当的，同意义的
orientate	*v.*	adjust or establish oneself in relation to surroundings; place (building, etc.) to 使适应环境，朝向

Notes

1. **BA:** Bachelor of Arts 文学士; **BSc：** Bachelor of Science 理学士

2. **sandwich degree:** This takes place between Level 2 and Level 3 of formal study. The Sandwich Year comprises about 48 weeks of employment, and during this period you are not just left to your own devices. You will have both a University and an "industrial" supervisor, will be visited on occasions during your placement, and you are also assessed through your performance in the workplace and through formal reports that you will write.

3. age cohort: 年龄段（的人）

4. **C grades:** The European Credit Transfer and Accumulation System (ECTS) is a standard for comparing the study attainment and performance of students of higher education across the European Union. For successfully completed studies, ECTS credits are awarded. One academic year corresponds to 60 ECTS-credits in all countries, irrespective of standard or qualification type, and is used to facilitate transfer and progression throughout the Union.

ECTS also includes a standard grading scale:

Grade Percentile of passed students			
A 10%	B 25%	C 30%	D 25%
E 10%	FX —	F —	

The grade FX indicates that "some more work required before the credit can be awarded." The grade F indicates "considerable further work required."

5. **A Level:** The A level, short for Advanced Level, is a General Certificate of Education qualification in England, Northern Ireland and Wales, usually taken by students during the optional final two years of secondary school [Years 12 & 13 (usually ages 16-18), commonly called the Sixth Form except for Scotland], or at a separate sixth form college or further education college, after they have completed GCSE or IGCSE exams (refer to Note 6 below). The qualification is recognized around the world and is used as a sort of entrance exam for some universities.

6. **(I) GCSE:** The General Certificate of Secondary Education (GCSE) is the name of a set of English qualifications, generally taken by secondary school students at age of 14-16 in England, Wales, and Northern Ireland (in Scotland, the equivalent is the Standard Grade). It is usually taken between these ages although some students may have the opportunity to take one or more GCSEs early. The International "version" of GCSE is IGCSE, which can be applied to the whole world and which includes some more options, such as coursework options, language options, etc. GCSEs are often a requirement for taking A-levels, a common type of university entrance requirement.

7. **AS grades:** The exams people who are sitting A Levels take between GCSE and A Level, the summer before they start to apply to university, at the end of the English Year 12. They refer to the first half of the course, which is examined after one year, and will then lead onto the full A Level in the second year. They can be counted as a qualification individually, worth half an A Level if the person decides they don't want to continue with their AS into a second year.

8. **EU:** The European Union is a political and economic union of twenty-seven member states, located primarily in Europe. It was established in 1993 as a result of the signing of the Treaty on European Union, adding new areas of policy to the existing European Community. 欧共体

9. **STEP:** Achievement in the Sixth Term Examination Papers (STEP). It normally forms part of a conditional offer to read mathematics at Cambridge. The examinations are administered by Cambridge Assessment (which is the parent company of the OCR examination board) and are taken in late June.

10. **HND:** Higher National Diploma 英国的国家高等教育文凭，类似于中国的大专

11. **Dip Ed:** Diploma Education 文凭教育

12. **"Socrates-Erasmus" programme:** The **ERASMUS programme**, also known as *European*

Community Action Scheme for the Mobility of University Students, was established in 1987 and forms a major part of the European Union Lifelong Learning Programme 2007-2013. It is the operational framework for the European Commission's initiatives in higher education.

● **Reading Comprehension**

1. Directions: *Discuss the following questions with your classmates.*

1) How long does one need to study for a Bachelor's degree in the UK?

2) Why is the entry to universities and institutions in the UK highly competitive?

3) What organization helps in application to universities and institutions in the UK?

4) What should applicants do to apply for the entry to universities and institutions?

5) What is the difference between a university and an institution of higher education?

2. Directions: *Read the following statements carefully, and decide whether they are true (T) or false (F) according to the text.*

_____ 1) Most bachelor degrees in the UK take three to four years.

_____ 2) The entry to universities is higher than that to other institutions of higher education.

_____ 3) Applicants usually make their application to universities first in the second term of Year 13.

_____ 4) The applicants first need to apply online through UCAS.

_____ 5) A non-England European citizen needs to pay from £6,000 to £10,000 per year.

_____ 6) A European citizen needs to reside in the Union for at least three years before they can be allowed to pay £1,000 per academic year.

_____ 7) To apply to Cambridge University, the candidates need to take STEP, an extra exam.

_____ 8) In Scotland, the school system is the same as that in England.

● **Discussion**

1. After reading the text, can you compare the difference in application to universities in China and in the UK?

2. If one Chinese student is applying for the entry to Oxford University, what should he/she do? And what should a European Union citizen do to apply for university admission?

After-Class Reading

Passage One

Warm-up questions:

1. How did you spend your days in high school?

2. What are the differences between life in high school and college life?

Changes to Come in U.S. Education

1　The biggest "infrastructure"[1] challenge for the United States in the next decade is not the billions needed for railroads, highways and energy. It is the American school system, from kindergarten through the Ph.D. program and the postgraduate education of adults. And it requires something far scarcer than money—thinking and risk-taking.

2　The challenge is not one of expansion. On the contrary, the rapid growth in enrollment over the last 40 years has come to an end. By 1978, more than 93 percent of young people entering the labor force had at least an eighth-grade education.[2] So even if the birthrate should rise somewhat, little expansion is possible for elementary and secondary school enrollments.

3　The last 30 years' social upheavals are also over.[3] Busing will continue to be highly emotional issue in a good many large cities.[4] And there will still be efforts to use schools to bring women into fields such as engineering that have traditionally been considered "male." But this shift has already been accomplished in many fields: half or more of the accounting students in graduate schools of business, for example, are now women. As for most other social issues, the country will no longer try to use schools to bring about social reform. It's becoming increasingly clear to policy makers that schools cannot solve all the problems of the larger community.

4　Instead, the battle cry for the 1990s will be the demand for performance and accountability.[5] For 30 years, employers have been hiring graduates for their degrees rather than their abilities; employment, pay and often even promotion have depended on one's diploma. Now many major employers are beginning to demand more than the completion of school. Some of the major banks, for example, are studying the possibility of entrance examinations that would test the knowledge and abilities of graduates applying for jobs.

5　Students and parents, too, will demand greater accountability from schools, on all levels. It will be increasingly common to go to law against school districts and colleges for awarding degrees without imparting the skills

that are supposed to go along with them.[6] And many young people are already switching to practical "hard" subjects.[7] Caring little about the so-called "youth culture" and the media, they have been shifting from psychology into medicine, from sociology into accounting and from black studies[8] into computer programming.

6   Demand for education is actually going up, not down. What is going down, and fairly fast, is demand for traditional education in traditional schools.

7   Indeed, the fastest growing industry in America today may be the continuing professional education of highly schooled adults. Much of it takes place outside the education establishment—through companies, hospitals and government departments that run courses for managerial and professional employees; or through management associations and trade associations. In the meantime, a number of private enterprises are organizing courses, producing training films and tapes and otherwise taking advantage of growth opportunities that universities shy away from.[9]

8   The demand for continuing education does not take the form that most observers, including this writer, originally expected—namely, "Great Books" classes for adults wanting to learn about the humanities, the arts, the "life of the mind."[10] We face instead a growing demand for advanced professional education: in engineering and medicine, in accounting and journalism, in law and in administration and management.

9   Yet the adults who come back for such studies also demand what teachers of professional subjects are so rarely able to supply: a humanistic perspective that can integrate advanced professional and technical knowledge into a broader universe of experience and learning.[11] Since these new students also need unconventional hours—evenings, weekends or high-intensity courses that stuff a term's work into two weeks—their demands for learning bring a vague but real threat to the school establishment.[12]

10   The greatest challenge to education is likely to come from our new opportunities for diversity. We now have the chance to apply the basic findings of psychological, developmental and educational research over the last 100 years: namely, that no one educational method fits all children.

11   Almost all children are capable of attaining the same standards within a reasonable period of time. All but a few babies, for instance, learn to walk by the age of two and to talk by the age of three, but no two get there quite the same way.

12   So too at higher levels. Some children learn best by rote, in structured environments with high certainty and strict discipline. Others gain success in the less structured "permissive" atmosphere of a "progressive" school. Some adults learn out of books, some learn by doing, some learn best by

listening. Some students need prescribed daily doses of information; others need challenge and a high degree of responsibility for the design of their own work.[13] But for too long, teachers have insisted that there is one best way to teach and learn, even though they have disagreed about what that way is.

13   A century ago, the greatest majority of Americans lived in communities so small that only one one-room schoolhouse was within walking distance of small children. Then there had to be "one right method" for everybody to learn.

14   Today the great majority of pupils in the United States (and all developed countries) live in big cities with such density that there can easily be three or four elementary schools—as well as secondary schools within each child's walking or bicycling distance. This enables students and their parents to choose between alternative routes to learning offered by competing schools.

15   Indeed, competition and choice are already beginning to infiltrate[14] the school system. Private schools and colleges have shown an unusual ability to survive and develop during a period of rising costs and dropping enrollments elsewhere. All this presents, of course, a true threat to the public school establishment. But economics, student needs and our new understanding of how people learn are bound to break the traditional education monopoly just as trucks and airplanes broke the monopoly of the railroads, and computers and "chips" are breaking the telephone monopoly.[15]

16   In the next 10 or 15 years we will almost certainly see strong pressures to make schools responsible for thinking through what kind of learning methods are appropriate for each child. We will almost certainly see great pressure, from parents and students alike, for result-focused education and for accountability in meeting objectives set for individual students. The continuing professional education of highly educated adults will become a third tier in addition to undergraduate and professional or graduate work.[16] Above all, attention will shift back to schools and education as the central capital investment and infrastructure of a "knowledge society."

Notes

1. infrastructure: 基础；基础结构(设施) (尤指社会、国家赖以生存和发展的，如道路、学校、电厂、交通、通讯系统等) (此处作者借用了马克思主义理论的一个关键术语，因而加引号。

2. By 1978, more than 93 percent of young people entering the labor force had at least an eighth-grade education. 此句大意为：到 1978 年，加入劳动大军的 93%以上的年轻人至少受过 8 年教育。Children generally go through elementary schools (kindergarten to 5th or 6th grade), middle school (grades 6-8) or junior high schools (grades 7-9), and high schools (grades 9-12 or 10-12).

3. The last 30 years' social upheavals are also over. 此句大意为：过去 30 年的社会动荡也要结束了。(此处的"社会动荡"主要是指美国 19 世纪 70 年代以来发生的一系列社会重大变革及其引起的争议，其中包括下文将提到的校车接送学生问题和妇女争取在教育和择业等方面平等权益的问题。)

4. **Busing will continue to be highly emotional issue in a good many large cities.** 此句大意为：在许多大城市，校车接送学生仍将是个极富感情色彩的问题。这里指的是美国上个世纪 70 年代引起全国大争论的用校车接送学生的规定，即为了消除种族隔离(desegregation)，要求黑白学生混校，规定用校车将孩子送到较远的学校去上学。

5. Instead, the battle cry for the 1990s will be the demand for performance and accountability. 此句大意为：相反，20 世纪 90 年代的强烈呼声将是要求工作表现和能够承担责任。

6. It will be increasingly common to go to law against school districts and colleges for awarding degrees without imparting the skills that are supposed to go along with them. 此句大意为：因为学区和学院只授予学位而不传授必要技术而诉诸法律的事将越来越普遍。

7. practical "hard" subjects: 实用的、"过硬的"学科

8. **black studies:** 黑人研究

9. In the meantime, a number of private enterprises are organizing courses, producing training films and tapes and otherwise taking advantage of growth opportunities that universities shy away from. 此句大意为：与此同时，有些私人企业也在组织课程，制作用于培训的影片和磁带并且以其他方式利用各种大学避而不用的增长机会。shy away from: 躲避，离开；羞于

10. The demand for continuing education does not take the form that most observers, including this writer, originally expected—namely, "Great Books" classes for adults wanting to learn about the humanities, the arts, the "life of the mind." 此句大意为：对继续教育的要求不采用包括本文作者在内的大多数观察者原先所想象的形式——即给那些想了解人文学科、艺术以及心智活动的成年人用"大部头书"上课。

11. Yet the adults who come back for such studies also demand what teachers of professional subjects are so rarely able to supply: a humanistic perspective that can integrate advanced professional and technical knowledge into a broader universe of experience and learning. 此句大意为：然而回来进行这类学习的成年人还要求专业课程的老师很少能提供的东西：一种从人文主义的角度，将先进的专业技术知识融会到经验和常识的更广阔的普遍体系中的观点。

12. Since these new students also need unconventional hours—evenings, weekends or high-intensity courses that stuff a term's work into two weeks—their demands for learning bring a vague but real threat to the school establishment. 此句大意为：由于这些新学生还需要非常规的时间——晚上、周末或者说把一个学期的任务挤到两周的强化课程——他们的学习要求给学校的体制带来一种模糊而又实实在在的威胁。

13. Some students need prescribed daily doses of information; others need challenge and a high degree of responsibility for the design of their own work. 此句大意为：有的学生每天需要定

量的信息；有的需要挑战，要赋予他们一定的责任，让他们自己安排工作。prescribed daily doses of...原意为"医生所开的每日的用药剂量"，此处为比喻的用法。

14. infiltrate:(常与 into, through 连用)渗透

15. But economics, student needs and our new understanding of how people learn are bound to break the traditional education monopoly just as trucks and airplanes broke the monopoly of the railroads, and computers and "chips" are breaking the telephone monopoly. 此句大意为：但是经济情况、学生的需要以及我们对人们如何学习的理解肯定会打破传统的教育垄断，就像卡车和飞机打破铁路的垄断、计算机和芯片正在打破电话的垄断一样。

16. The continuing professional education of highly educated adults will become a third tier in addition to undergraduate and professional or graduate work. 此句大意为：对受过高层次教育的成年人的继续职业教育将是除本科生以及职业或研究生教育之后的第三种教育。

●Reading Comprehension

1. Directions: *Try to summarize the challenges facing the United States described in the passage. What suggestions can you offer to settle the problem?*

2. Directions: *Discuss the following questions with your classmates.*

1) What is the biggest challenge for the United States in the next decade according to the author?

2) What does the challenge call for if it is to be tackled successfully?

3) What are the fields that have traditionally been considered "male"?

4) In the past 30 years what have employers valued most when hiring people? What about now?

5) What subjects are now more popular with young people?

6) What is the author's attitude towards the future of school education?

Passage Two

Warm-up questions:

1. Do you know any Ph.D. or Ph.D. candidate? What do you think of a person with a doctor's degree?

2. Do you want to pursue a doctoral program? Why or why not?

Exploring Ways to Shorten the Ascent to a Ph.D.

1   Many of us have known this scholar: The hair is well-streaked with gray, the chin has begun to sag, but still our tortured friend slaves away at a masterwork intended to change the course of civilization that everyone else just hopes will finally get a career under way.[1]

2   We even have a name for this sometimes pitied species—the A.B.D.—All But Dissertation. But in academia these days, that person is less a subject of ridicule than of soul-searching about what can be done to shorten the time, sometimes much of a lifetime, it takes for so many graduate students to,

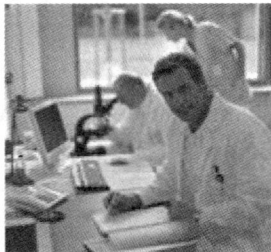

well, graduate.[2] The Council of Graduate Schools[3], representing 480 universities in the United States and Canada, is halfway through a seven-year project to explore ways of speeding up the ordeal.

3   For those who attempt it, the doctoral dissertation can loom on the horizon like Everest, gleaming invitingly as a challenge but often turning into a masochistic exercise once the ascent is begun.[4] The average student takes 8.2 years to get a Ph.D.; in education, that figure surpasses 13 years. Fifty percent of students drop out along the way, with dissertations the major stumbling block. At commencement[5], the typical doctoral holder is 33, an age when peers are well along in their professions, and 12 percent of graduates are saddled with more than $50,000 in debt.

4   These statistics, compiled by the National Science Foundation[6] and other government agencies by studying the 43,354 doctoral recipients of 2005, were even worse a few years ago. Now, universities are setting stricter timelines and demanding that faculty advisers meet regularly with protégés[7]. Most science programs allow students to submit three research papers rather than a single grand work. More universities find ways to ease financial burdens, providing better paid teaching assistantships as well as tuition waivers[8]. And more universities are setting up writing groups so that students feel less alone cobbling together[9] a thesis.

5   Fighting these trends, and stretching out the process, is the increased competition for jobs and research grants; in fields like English where faculty vacancies are scarce, students realize they must come up with original, significant topics. Nevertheless, education researchers like Barbara E. Lovitts, who has written a new book urging professors to clarify what they expect in dissertations; for example, point out that professors "view the dissertation as a training exercise" and that students should stop trying for "a degree of perfection that's unnecessary and unobtainable."

6   There are probably few universities that nudge students out the door as rapidly as Princeton, where a humanities student now averages 6.4 years compared with 7.5 in 2003. That is largely because Princeton guarantees financial support for its more than 2,000 scholars for five years, including free tuition and stipends that range up to $30,000 a year. That means students need no more than two courses during their schooling and can focus on research.

7   "Princeton since the 1930s has felt that a Ph.D. should be an education, not a career, and has valued a tight program," said William B. Russel, dean of the graduate school.

8   And students are grateful. "Every morning I wake up and remind myself the university is paying me to do nothing but write the dissertation," said Kellam Conover, 26, a classicist who expects to complete his course of study in five years next May when he finishes his dissertation on bribery in Athens. "It's a tremendous advantage compared to having to work during the day and complete the dissertation part time."

9   But fewer than a dozen universities have endowments or sources of financing large enough to afford five-year packages. The rest require students to teach regularly. Compare Princetonians with Brian Gatten, 28, an English scholar at the University of Texas in Austin. He has either been

teaching or assisting in two courses every semester for five years.

10　"Universities need us as cheap labor to teach their undergraduates, and frankly we need to be needed because there isn't another way for us to fund our education," he said.

11　That raises a question that state legislatures and trustees[10] might ponder: Would it be more cost effective to provide financing to speed graduate students into careers rather than having them drag out their apprenticeships?

12　But money is not the only reason Princeton does well. It has developed a culture where professors keep after students. Students talk of frequent meetings with advisers, not a semiannual review. For example, Ning Wu, 30, a father of two, works in Dr Russel's chemical engineering lab and said Dr Russel comes by every Friday to discuss Mr. Wu's work on polymer films used in computer chips. He aims to get his Ph.D. next year, his fifth.

13　While Dr Russel values "the critical thinking and independent digging students have to do, either in their mind for an original concept or in the archives," others question the necessity of book-length works. Some universities have established what they call professional doctorates for students who plan careers more as practitioners than scholars. Since the 1970s, Yeshiva University has not only offered a Ph.D. in psychology but also a separate doctor of psychology degree, or Psy.D.[11], for those more interested in clinical work than research; that program requires a more modest research paper.

14　Other institutions are reviving master's degree programs for, say, aspiring scientists who plan careers in development of products rather than research.

15　Those who insist on dissertations are aware that they must reduce the loneliness that defeats so many scholars. Gregory Nicholson, completing his sixth and final year at Michigan State, was able to finish a 270-page dissertation on spatial environments in novels like Kerouac's *On the Road*[12] with relative efficiency because of a writing group where he thrashed[13] out his work with other thesis writers.

16　"It's easy, especially in our field, to feel isolated, and that tends to slow people down," he said. "There's no sense of belonging to an academic community."

17　Some common sense would also hasten the process. The dissertation is a hurdle that must be cleared, not a *magnum opus*[14], the capstone of a career. Princeton's Mr. Wu has made that calculation.

18　"You do not want to stay forever," Mr. Wu said. "It's a training process."

—Joseph Berger

Proper Names

the Council of Graduate Schools　　　研究生院委员会(美国)

the National Science Foundation	国家科学基金会(美国)
Princeton	普林斯顿(大学)(美国著名高等学府)
University of Texas at Austin	得克萨斯大学奥斯汀分校
Yeshiva University	犹太大学/叶史瓦大学(美国最古老，最具综合性的著名犹太人教育机构)
Michigan State University	密歇根州立大学
Everest	珠穆朗玛(峰)
Athens	雅典(希腊首都)

Notes

1. our tortured friend slaves away at a masterwork intended to change the course of civilization that everyone else just hopes will finally get a career under way. 此句意为：我们这位备受折磨的朋友心怀改变文明进程的宏愿辛辛苦苦地撰写大部头的论著，而其他人仅仅指望完成学业，最终获得一份工作而已。slave away: work continuously like a slave; to drudge.

2. But in academia these days, that person is less a subject of ridicule than of soul-searching about what can be done to shorten the time, sometimes much of a lifetime, it takes for so many graduate students to, well, graduate. 此句意为: 可是那样的人在如今的学术界与其说会受人嘲笑，不如说他们促使人们去反省如何让众多研究生缩短修学时间，节约宝贵时光。soul-searching: 反省，内省

3. **The Council of Graduate Schools' (CGS):** Its mission is to improve and advance graduate education in order to ensure the vitality of intellectual discovery. CGS accomplishes its mission through advocacy, innovative research, and the development and dissemination of best practices. Supporting graduate education is critical to achieving the highly skilled workforce needed for the U.S. to compete effectively in the 21st century global economy. More can be found at http://www.cgsnet.org/.

   ACGS: Association of Chinese Graduate Schools 中国研究生院院长联席会

4. For those who attempt it, the doctoral dissertation can loom on the horizon like Everest, gleaming invitingly as a challenge but often turning into a masochistic exercise once the ascent is begun. 此句的大意为：对那些敢于尝试的人来说，博士论文像远处地平线上若隐若现的珠穆拉玛峰，闪耀着诱人的光芒，吸引他们去挑战极限，然而攀登一旦真正开始，挑战往往就变成了一件受虐狂式的事情。loom: 隐隐呈现，朦胧出现

5. commencement: 毕业典礼；[美]授奖典礼日，学位授予典礼

6. **The National Science Foundation (NSF):** It is an independent federal agency created by Congress in 1950 "to promote the progress of science; to advance the national health, prosperity, and welfare; to secure the national defense…" With an annual budget of about $6.06 billion, they are the funding source for approximately 20 percent of all federally supported basic research conducted by America's colleges and universities. In many fields such as mathematics,

computer science and the social sciences, NSF is the major source of federal backing.

7. protégés: 被保护者；门徒

8. tuition waiver: 免学费

9. cobble together: 修，拙劣地修补；粗制滥造

10. trustee: (大学等的)评议员，理事

11. **Psy.D.:** The Psy.D. or Doctor of Psychology is a professional doctorate in Clinical Psychology. There are two models through which a student can be trained in Clinical Psychology—one is the Psy.D doctorate which places more emphasis on clinical practice, the other is the Ph.D. (Doctor of Philosophy) which places more emphasis on research. 心理学博士

12. Kerouac's *On the Road*: 凯鲁亚克(美国作家)的著作《在路上》(1957)

13. thrash: 反复进行；仔细研究，推敲，研讨

14. *magnum opus*: [拉]巨著，杰作；代表作，主要作品

● **Reading Comprehension**

1. Directions: *Choose the best answer for each of the following questions.*

1) What does "the ordeal" (Lines 6-7, Para. 2,) refer to according to the author?

  A. An experience from which people suffer a lot.

  B. The process of applying for a Ph.D. program.

  C. A seven-year project.

  D. The whole period of pursuing a Ph.D. program.

2) What is the primary reason for 50 percent of students dropping out?

  A. The students cannot afford the huge amount of tuition fee.

  B. The students are too old to finish their study successfully.

  C. It is difficult for the candidates to fulfill the requirement of writing a dissertation.

  D. The students are not patient enough to accomplish the whole program.

3) Which of the following is NOT included in the measures taken by universities to improve the situation?

  A. Universities are now setting stricter timelines and demanding that faculty advisers meet regularly with protégés.

  B. Some science programs allow students not to submit research papers.

  C. More universities provide better paid teaching assistantships as well as tuition waivers to ease the financial burdens on students.

  D. Writing groups are being set up so that students feel less alone cobbling together a thesis.

4) Which of the following is true about Barbara E. Lovitts?

  A. She views the dissertation as anything but a training exercise.

  B. She believes that professors should make it clear what they expect in dissertations.

  C. She advocates that it is necessary for students to obtain perfection in their studies.

D. She makes the students realize they must come up with original, significant topics.

5) Universities have done all the following to shorten the ascent to a Ph.D. EXCEPT _____.

    A. holding frequent meetings between advisers and students

    B. providing a variety of degrees for different students

    C. reviving master's degree programs

    D. organizing writing groups within an academic community

2. Directions: *Read the following statements carefully, and decide whether they are true (T) or false (F) according to the text.*

_____ 1) When a typical doctoral holder gets his degree, his peers are still struggling on their way to the primary professional achievement.

_____ 2) Few universities require faculty advisers to meet regularly with protégés.

_____ 3) Princeton seems more efficient in cultivating its students because it offers short-term programs.

_____ 4) Humanities students now spend less than 7.5 years on average in Princeton to get their Ph.D.

_____ 5) Students' attitudes towards being needed as cheap labor by universities are ambivalent.

_____ 6) Princeton supports each of its scholars financially for five years, including free tuition and a $30,000 stipend a year.

_____ 7) Students applying for a Psy.D. in Yeshiva University do not have to write a research paper.

_____ 8) Apart from financial burden, psychological stress also serves as a cause for Ph.D. candidates' dropping-out.

Part Three

Topic-related Activities

1. Speech Contest

Title: "If I were the president of our college…"

Step One

Directions: *Work in groups of 4 or 5, discussing what reforms you would make if you were the president of our college.*

Step Two

Directions: *Choose one of the students from each group as the speaker to represent the whole group to give a speech.*

Step Three

Directions: *Choose one of the students from each group as the judge and evaluate the performance* *of speakers from each group based on the criteria provided by the teacher. The speaker who has got most points will be awarded the "best speaker" and the group the "best group".*

Suggested criteria: 1) Cooperation of the group members (2 points)

2) Language (fluency and correctness) (3 points)

3) Content (creativity/ feasibility/ wholeness) (3 points)

4) Interaction with the audience (1 point)

5) Voice (1 point)

Total points: (10 points)

2. Talking about Ways of Classroom Education

Directions: *Work in groups to discuss the difference between Chinese and American education, their advantages and disadvantages. The following pictures may give you some hints.*

1)

2)

3. Case Study

Darin Yokel is an art teacher from one primary school in Cincinnati, America; she is also a current student of Miami University. As one of the exchange teachers with Chinese, she came to Kunming, Yunan to have an academic interchange. Her objective was split into 3 parts, teaching Chinese students, communicating with Chinese teachers and independent training.

In Kunming, Darin found out that the painting skills of Chinese students are very good. One day, she gave out one topic "Happy Festival" to her students, but all the students were drawing the same Christmas tree. At first she thought that Chinese students are friendly so when they met a western teacher, they drew the Christmas tree for her. But later she found that every Christmas tree those children drew was with the same pattern. She looked closer, and discovered that all the students were looking toward the same direction—one of the classroom walls. Then she realized that there was one Christmas tree painting on the wall which was prepared by the school so as to create a suitable painting atmosphere for students.

Darin covered the painting on the wall and asked the students to create their own picture. To her surprise, she found once she covered the wall painting, the students could not draw a "happy festival". Some students were scratching the head, some biting the pencil, some staring at each other, but no one knew how to start their work.

There is another case in America: one professor mentioned in his article that his son did some research when he was in primary school. One day he came back from school and asked his father to go to the library. He said he was doing one research on whales so he needed some information. The professor took his son to two libraries and borrowed more than ten books about whales. The little boy finished his first research in his whole life on the topic of whales. It contained 3 pages and one cover with a picture of whales in the sea. There were 4 tittles inside the report: introduction, what whales eat, how whales eat and the features of whales.

Questions

1. What differences are reflected in the two cases about Chinese and American education?
2. What can we learn from American way of education?

Part Four

Topic-related Information

1. UNESCO (联合国教科文组织)

United Nations Educational, Scientific and Cultural Organization (UNESCO) is a specialized agency of the United Nations established on November 16, 1945. Its stated purpose is to contribute to peace and security by promoting international collaboration through education, science, and culture in order to further universal respect for justice, the rule of law, and the human rights and fundamental freedoms proclaimed in the UN Charter. It is the heir of the League of Nations' International Commission on Intellectual Cooperation.

UNESCO has 193 Member States and 6 Associate Members. The organization is based in Paris, with over 50 field offices and many specialized institutes and centers throughout the world. Most of the field offices are "cluster" offices covering three or more countries; there are also national and regional offices. UNESCO pursues its objectives through five major programmes: education, natural sciences, social and human sciences, culture, and communication and information. Projects sponsored by UNESCO include literacy, technical, and teacher-training programmes; international science programmes; the promotion of independent media and freedom of the press; regional and cultural history projects, the promotion of cultural diversity; international cooperation agreements to secure the world cultural and natural heritage (World Heritage Sites) and to preserve human rights; and attempts to bridge the world-wide digital divide.

2. Education Systems

1) China

China's basic education involves pre-school, nine-year compulsory education from elementary to junior high school, standard senior high school education, special education for disabled children, and education for illiterate people.

National examinations to select students for higher education (and positions of leadership) are an important part of China's culture, and, traditionally, entrance to a higher education institution was considered prestigious.

2) The United States

Most children enter the public education system around ages five or six. The American school year traditionally begins in August or September, after the traditional summer recess. Children generally go through elementary schools (kindergarten to 5th or 6th grade), middle school (grades 6-8) or junior high schools (grades 7-9), and high schools (grades 9-12 or 10-12). Children customarily advance together from one grade to the next as a single cohort or "class" upon reaching the end of each school year in May or June, although developmentally disabled children may be held back a grade and gifted children may skip ahead early to the next grade.

Students traditionally apply to receive admission into college, with varying difficulties of entrance. Schools differ in their competitiveness and reputation; generally, the most prestigious schools are private, rather than public. Admissions criteria involve the rigor and grades earned in high school courses taken, the students' GPA, class ranking, and standardized test scores (Such as the SAT or the ACT tests). Most colleges also consider more subjective factors such as a commitment to extracurricular activities, a personal essay, and an interview. While numerical factors rarely ever are absolute required values, each college usually has a rough threshold, below which admission is unlikely.

3) England

Full-time education is compulsory for all children aged between 5 and 16 (inclusive). Students may then continue their secondary studies for a further two years (sixth form), leading most typically to an A level qualification, although other qualifications and courses exist, including GNVQ and the International Baccalaureate. The leaving age for compulsory education is raised to 18 by the Education and Skills Act 2008. The change takes effect in 2013 for 17 year olds and 2015 for 18 year olds.

Students normally need 3 A-levels, which are the exams taken by people leaving school at 18, in order to enter an undergraduate degree course. Students also need an IELTS score of at least 5.5, but many universities offer foundation or access courses to prepare students for their studies.

4) Germany

Optional kindergarten education is provided for all children between three and six years old, after which school attendance is compulsory for mostly 11 to 12 years. In the first nine years all students attend school from age six to fifteen or sixteen. Each group of students born in the same year forms one grade or class, which remains the same for elementary school (years 1 to 4), orientation school (if there's orientation school in the state) or orientation phase (years 5 to 6), and secondary school (years 5 to 10 or years 5 to 11). Upon leaving school, students may choose to go on to university; however, most male students will have to serve nine months of military or alternative service beforehand.

The high school graduation opens the way to any university; there are no entrance examinations. Something similar to GPA in the U.S., or A-Level results in the UK is the deciding factor in granting university places; an institution may quote an entry requirement for a particular course.

5) Canada

Education is compulsory up to the age of 16 in every province in Canada, except for Ontario and New Brunswick, where the compulsory age is 18. Elementary, secondary, and post-secondary education in Canada is a provincial responsibility and there are many variations between the provinces.

Most Canadian education systems continue up to grade twelve (age seventeen to eighteen). In Quebec, the typical high school term ends after Secondary V/Grade eleven (age sixteen to seventeen); following this, students who wish to pursue their studies to the university level have to attend CEGEP (Collèges d'Enseignement Général Et Professionnel).

6) Australia

Generally, education in Australia follows the three-tier model which includes primary education (primary schools), followed by secondary education (secondary schools/high schools) and tertiary education (universities and/or TAFE Colleges). Education is compulsory up to an age specified by legislation; this age varies from state to state but is generally 15-17, that is prior to completing secondary education.

The Australian government operates the Higher Education Contribution Scheme for undergraduate students, so admission is rarely limited by prospective students' ability to pay up-front. All states use a system that awards the recipient with an Equivalent National Tertiary Entrance Rank, or ENTER, and the award of an International Baccalaureate meets the minimum requirements for admission in every state. The Special Tertiary Admissions Test is the standard test for non-school-leavers nationwide.

3. Suggested Films about Education

1) *Dead Poets Society* (《春风化雨》)

2) *Accepted* (《录取通知》)

3) *The Scent of a Woman* (《女人香》)

4) *Mona Lisa Smile* (《蒙娜丽莎的微笑》)

Hyperlinks

[1] http://www.dcsf.gov.uk/index.htm

[2] http://www.newswise.com/articles/view/525884/

[3] http://www.enfang.com/english/2008-04/14205.htm

[4] http://blog.sina.com.cn/s/blog_4bb207ab010009e8.html

References

[1] http://www.exue.com/zt/2006-05-29/131_8941.shtml

[2] http://www.cobisec.org/highered.htm

[3] http://www.doudoubar.com/Article/nengli/shenghuo/200606/2012.html

[4] http://en.wikipedia.org/wiki/Education_in_the_People's_Republic_of_China

[5] http://en.wikipedia.org/wiki/Education_in_the_United_States

[6] http://en.wikipedia.org/wiki/Education_in_England

[7] http://en.wikipedia.org/wiki/Education_in_Germany

[8] http://en.wikipedia.org/wiki/Education_in_Canada

[9] http://en.wikipedia.org/wiki/Education_in_Australia

Unit 5

Social Phenomena

Part One

Lead-in

It is better to fight for justice than to rail at the ill.

—Alfred Tennyson (Britain)

与其责骂罪恶，不如伸张正义。

——艾尔弗雷德·丁尼生（英国）

Social phenomena include all behavior which influences or is influenced by organisms sufficiently alive to respond to one another. They are events or facts brought about by human beings: it is their passions which stimulate their great political, religious and cultural creations.

Part Two
Reading Passages

In-Class Reading

Warm-up questions:

1. Who raised you up? What do you think of your relationship with your parents?

2. Do you know any campus violence in America or in China? Can you say something about it?

Who Is Raising Our Children?

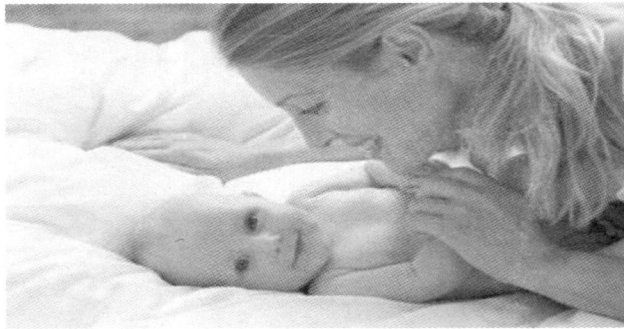

1   Tuesday Morning, April 20th: two teenagers entered a high school with intent to destroy. Between them they had a **sawed-off** shotgun, a rifle, a semi-automatic handgun, and countless **explosives.** That day in that school fifteen people lost their lives. While we could look at this as an isolated incident, we can't hide the fact that our society is **permeated** with violence and violent tendencies. Within two days nearly every news reporting service published a list of "…some of the warning signs that someone may be considering violence," part of a brochure created in response to the many school shootings in the last few years.[1] In the past thirty years, violence has increased an **astounding** 500%(American Family Institute[2]). Compare the top seven school problems in California for 1940 and today:

Top Seven School Problems—1940:	Top Seven School Problems—Today:
1. Talking out of turn	1. Drug Abuse
2. Chewing gum	2. Alcohol abuse
3. Making noise	3. Pregnancy
4. Running in the halls	4. Suicide
5. Cutting in line	5. Rape
6. Dress code violations	6. Robbery
7. Littering	7. **Assault**

2   We, as a society, have allowed our level of acceptable behavior to rise to incredible heights. Who is to blame? Where did the failure occur? Astonishingly, the failure has occurred in our own homes.

The Webster's Dictionary[3] defines a parent as follows:

Parent   *n:* a father or mother; one who begets or one who gives birth to or nurtures and raises
              a child; a relative who plays the role of ***guardian***

         v: bring up; "raise a family"; "bring up children" [syn: {rear}, {raise}, {bring up},
              {nurture}]

A parent is a person who "nurtures and raises a child…a relative who plays the role of guardian." Our society has "progressed" to the point where we do not see parenting as a noble and good contribution to society. When one answers the question "What do you do for a living?" with "I am a homemaker", that person is often looked on as an **oddity**. It is thought that the person is lazy, or could not secure employment. In our society the definition for a parent has been shortened to, "a father or mother; one who **beget**s or one who gives birth to" a child. Sixty-six percent of all American families with children under eighteen are families where both parents are employed. Since 1960 the average income of Americans has doubled in **inflation**-adjusted dollars. The median income for two-income families is $63,772, while the median income for single-income families is only $18,078 less at $45,694. While one cannot say that there are no families which must have both incomes to survive, one also has to admit that there are many people who will put their wants and perceived needs ahead of their children's need to be nurtured.

3   The family structure remained virtually intact— weathering[4] disease, famine, natural disaster and war—until the 1960's. That **tumultuous** decade attacked authority and institutions and society's long-accepted rules and norms. Personal freedoms **overrode** personal responsibility. As personal responsibility gave way to personal freedom, many parenting skills were lost. Divorce **skyrocket**ed. As each generation progressed, more skills were lost. People are playing out these parenting roles in the same way they saw their parents play out these roles. The roles have changed, but the need for security and safety within the family structure still exists. The average couple today spends only four minutes of uninterrupted time together a day (American Family Institute).

4   Where does this place our children? We send them to day care[5] centers, to school, and to their friends. Only 34% of America's families eat one meal together each day. The average father spends 8-10 minutes a day with his children, including TV and meal times (American Family Institute). As we place our children in other institutions, what values and

morals do they gain? Certainly not those of their parents. We are leaving them to learn, on their own, the principles that will guide their life. What principles are they learning? "The plain truth is that I wouldn't even want my children in a day care center that I myself directed, simply because of the number of children that they would have to compete with for attention. I have learned that if they can't get the attention they need, they will seek it in other ways." (**Anonymous**)

5   The lists published of warning signs of **impending** violence were created from the **profile** of individuals who were crying out for individual attention. There is no possible way that any institution can give that attention to each individual. As we neglect our children, sending them to others to be raised, we send the message that they are not individually important. "It tells children that no one loves them specifically for their unique traits and is willing to sacrifice to meet their needs. And we wonder why children are growing up to be selfish and hard to handle. The message that they are special and important gets lost, so they seek for identity in other ways—sometimes in scary ways." (Anonymous)

6   We must give our attention to the nurturing of our children. A family who is close together will not need a list of warning signs. They will know if a member is unhappy. This closeness must start with the parent(s). There is no other **substitute** for the family, and there is no one who will take the responsibility of the parent.

7   It has been said that within the family exist the greatest joys that can be felt by the human soul. Often left out is the fact that within the same family can be felt the greatest pain.[6] This pain is the pain of a child who does not feel loved. It is the pain of the parent who has lost his/her child, either physically or emotionally. Only through our own sacrifice can we, as parents, experience the joy that children can bring. It really **boils down to** the knowledge and **commitment** on the part of a parent with a child, or more children. It's in that give and take that we are defining what the next generation in this country is going to be like and what our country is going to look like.

8   Unfortunately many of the skills parents need have been lost. We don't know how to nurture each other. Someone who is able to accept the responsibility for being a parent, which means setting aside one's personal goals, setting aside career **pursuit**s, not completely, can establish priorities that place family and children at the

top, and everything else comes after that. If you have that, then you have people who are comfortable in the parenting role. The responsibility for making this happen lies with us. We have to make our families our first priority. We can't let other things get in the way of our children's future. We need to teach commitment and responsibility to our children, so they can be better parents.

9   "Husband and wife have a **solemn** responsibility to love and care for each other and for their children…Parents have a sacred duty to rear their children in love and **righteousness**, to provide for their physical and spiritual needs, to teach them to love and serve one another, to observe the **commandment**s of God and to be **law-abiding** citizens wherever they live." (LDS Church[7]) We can only blame ourselves for the tragedies that are occurring in our society. But we can do something about them. We must teach our children to be better parents than we are. We can only do that by being better parents ourselves.

—M. Adam Davis

New Words and Expressions

anonymous	*a.*	written or given by sb. who does not reveal his name 匿名的，不具名的
assault	*n.*	a threat or attempt to inflict offensive physical contact or bodily harm on a person that puts the person in immediate danger of or in apprehension of such harm or contact 攻击，袭击
astounding	*a.*	amazing 使人震惊的
beget	*v.*	be the father of (sb.) 为(某人)之父
commandment	*n.*	command; order 戒律；命令
commitment	*n.*	something one has promised to do; pledge; undertaking 承诺，允诺，保证
explosive	*n.*	substance that is likely or able to explode 爆炸物，炸药
guardian	*n.*	person who is legally responsible for sb. who cannot manage his own affairs, e.g. an orphaned child 保护人，监护人
impending	*a.*	about to happen; imminent 即将发生的，迫在眉睫的，行将到来的
inflation	*n.*	rise in prices resulting from an increase in the supply of money, credit, etc. 通货膨胀，物价上涨
law-abiding	*a.*	obeying the law 遵守法律的
oddity	*n.*	unusual act, event, person or thing 异常的行为、事情、人或东西
override	*v.*	(overrode, overridden) be more important than (sth.) 比(某事物)更重要
permeate	*v.*	enter sth. and spread to every part 弥漫，散布；充满，遍布
profile	*n.*	brief biography of sb. or description of sth. in a newspaper article,

		broadcast program, etc. (报刊文章、广播节目等中的)人或事之简介，概况
pursuit	*n.*	action of pursuing sth. 追求，寻求；从事，进行
righteousness	*n.*	action in accord with divine or moral law 正义，正当
sawed-off	*a.*	having an end sawed off 锯短的，截短的
skyrocket	*v.*	(cause to) rise or increase abruptly and rapidly(使)暴涨,猛涨；迅速、突然地升高
solemn	*a.*	done, said, etc. in a serious and committed way, after deep thought 庄重的，郑重的；深思熟虑的
substitute	*n.*	person or thing taking the place of, acting for or serving for another 代替者，代用品
tumultuous	*a.*	marked by violent or overwhelming turbulence or upheaval 骚乱的，狂暴的
boil down to		constitute the equivalent of sth. in summary 简单地归结为

Notes

1. Within two days nearly every news reporting service published a list of "…some of the warning signs that someone may be considering violence", part of a brochure created in response to the many school shootings in the last few years. 此句中 "part of a brochure… in the last few years"是前半句引号中内容的同位语，意思是：过去几年为应对许多校园枪击事件而制作的手册内容的一部分。

2. **American Family Institute:** 美国家庭协会

3. Webster's Dictionary: Webster's Dictionary is the title given for the common type of English language dictionaries in the United States. It is derived from American lexicographer Noah Webster and in the United States, the phrase Webster's has become a genericized trademark for dictionaries. Although Merriam-Webster dictionaries are descended from those of the original purchasers of Noah Webster's work, many other dictionaries bear his name, such as those published by Random House and John Wiley & Sons. 韦氏词典

4. weather: come safely through a difficult period or experience 经受住，平安地度过(困难等)

5. **day care:** 日间幼托

   Day care or **child care** is care of a child during the day by a person other than the child's parents or legal guardians, typically someone outside the child's immediate family. The service is known as *child care* in the United Kingdom and Australia and *day care* in North America. Child care or day care is provided in nurseries or crèches or by childminders caring for children in their own homes.

6. Often left out is the fact that within the same family can be felt the greatest pain. 此句采用了倒装语序，以使句子前后平衡。

7. **LDS Church:** 后期圣徒教会或摩门教会

The Church of Jesus Christ of Latter-day Saints, widely known as the **LDS Church** or the **Mormon Church**, is the fourth largest Christian denomination in the United States and the largest and most well-known denomination originating from the Latter Day Saint movement founded by Joseph Smith, Jr. in 1830. The church is headquartered in Salt Lake City, Utah, and has established congregations and temples worldwide, reporting approximately 13 million members on its rolls.

● **Reading Comprehension**

1. Directions: *Discuss the following questions with your classmates.*

1) What is the fact we can find from the incident that 15 persons were shot to death in a high school?

2) Why is a person often regarded as an oddity when he or she is a homemaker?

3) According to this article, what is the definition of a parent in the present society?

4) What is the message sent by parents when their children are sent to be raised by others?

5) What can people get from their family?

6) In this article, what does "accepting the responsibility for being a parent" mean?

2. Directions: *Take for reference the top seven school problems in this article. Discuss within a group. List the possible top seven school problems in China nowadays. One student from each group should present the list in public and state the reasons appropriately.*

> **Top Seven School Problems in China—Today:**
> 1._____
> 2._____
> 3._____
> 4._____
> 5._____
> 6._____
> 7._____

● **Discussion**

1. Who is to blame for the increasing violence of teenagers, and why?

2. What is the advice from the author?

After-Class Reading

Passage One

Warm-up questions:

1. Do you think it is preferable to allow everyone to carry a gun for self-defense?

2. What gun laws do you think are effective in decreasing the level of violence?

Wouldn't You Feel Safer with a Gun?
—British attitudes are supercilious and misguided

1   Despite the recent spate of shootings on our streets, we pride ourselves on our strict gun laws. Every time an American gunman goes on a killing spree, we shake our heads in righteous disbelief at our poor benighted colonial cousins.[1] Why is it, even after the Virginia Tech massacre[2], that Americans still resist calls for more gun controls?

2   The short answer is that "gun controls" do not work: they are indeed generally perverse in their effects.[3] Virginia Tech, where 32 students were shot in April, had a strict gun ban policy and only last year successfully resisted a legal challenge that would have allowed the carrying of licensed defensive weapons on campus. It is with a measure of bitter irony that we recall Thomas Jefferson, founder of the University of Virginia, recording the words of Cesare Beccaria[4]: "Laws that forbid the carrying of arms... disarm only those who are neither inclined nor determined to commit crimes... Such laws make things worse for the assaulted and better for the assailants; they serve rather to encourage than to prevent homicides, for an unarmed man may be attacked with greater confidence than an armed man."

3   One might contrast the Virginia Tech massacre with the assault on Virginia's Appalachian Law School[5] in 2002, where three lives were lost before a student fetched a pistol from his car and apprehended the gunman.

4   Virginia Tech reinforced the lesson that gun controls are obeyed only by the law-abiding. New York has "banned" pistols since 1911, and its fellow murder capitals, Washington DC and Chicago, have similar bans. One can draw a map of the U.S., showing the inverse relationship of the strictness of its gun laws, and levels of violence: all the way down to Vermont, with no gun laws at all, and the lowest level of armed violence (one thirteenth that of Britain).

5   America's disenchantment with "gun control" is based on experience: whereas in the 1960s and 1970s armed crime rose in the face of more restrictive gun laws (in much of the U.S., it was illegal to possess a firearm away from the home or workplace), over the past 20 years all violent crime has dropped dramatically, in lockstep with the spread of laws allowing the carrying of

concealed weapons by law-abiding citizens. Florida set this trend in 1987, and within five years the states that had followed its example showed an 8 percent reduction in murders, 7 percent reduction in aggravated assaults, and 5 percent reduction in rapes. Today 40 states have such laws, and by 2004 the U.S. Bureau of Justice[6] reported that "firearms-related crime has plummeted".

6   In Britain, however, the image of violent America remains unassailably entrenched.[7] Never mind the findings of the International Crime Victims Survey (published by the Home Office in 2003), indicating that we now suffer three times the level of violent crime committed in the United States; never mind the doubling of handgun crime in Britain over the past decade, since we banned pistols outright and confiscated all the legal ones.

7   We are so self-congratulatory about our officially disarmed society, and so dismissive of colonial rednecks[8], that we have forgotten that within living memory British citizens could buy any gun—rifle, pistol, or machinegun—without any license. When Dr Watson[9] walked the streets of London with a revolver in his pocket, he was a perfectly ordinary Victorian or Edwardian. Charlotte Brontë[10] recalled that her curate father fastened his watch and pocketed his pistol every morning when he got dressed; Beatrix Potter[11] remarked on a Yorkshire[12] country hotel where only one of the eight or nine guests was not carrying a revolver; in 1909, policemen in Tottenham[13] borrowed at least four pistols from passers-by (and were joined by other armed citizens) when they set off in pursuit of two anarchists unwise enough to attempt an armed robbery. We now are shocked that so many ordinary people should have been carrying guns in the street; the Edwardians were shocked rather by the idea of an armed robbery.[14]

8   If armed crime in London in the years before the First World War amounted to less than 2 percent of that we suffer today, it was not simply because society then was more stable. Edwardian Britain was rocked by a series of massive strikes in which lives were lost and troops deployed, and suffragette incendiaries, anarchist bombers, Fenians, and the spectre of a revolutionary general strike made Britain then arguably a much more turbulent place than it is today.[15] In that unstable society the impact of the widespread carrying of arms was not inflammatory, it was deterrent of violence.

9   As late as 1951, self-defense was the justification of three quarters of all applications for pistol licenses. And in the years 1946-1951 armed robbery, the most significant measure of gun crime, ran at less than two dozen incidents a year in London; today, in our disarmed society, we suffer as many every week.

10   Gun controls disarm only the law-abiding, and leave predators with a freer hand. Nearly two and a half million people now fall victim to crimes of violence in Britain every year, more than four every minute: crimes that may devastate lives. It is perhaps a privilege of those who have

never had to confront violence to disparage the power to resist.[16]

—Richard Munday

Notes

1. **Every time an American gunman goes on a killing spree, we shake our heads in righteous disbelief at our poor benighted colonial cousins.** 此句大意为：每一次，当一个美国人持枪肆意杀人的时候，我们就摇头，显示我们的正义感，表示难以相信我们的殖民表亲会有这种愚昧的行为。

2. **Virginia Tech massacre:** 弗吉尼亚理工大学枪击案

   The Virginia Tech massacre was a school shooting consisting of two separate attacks approximately two hours apart on April 16, 2007, which took place on the campus of Virginia Polytechnic Institute and State University (Virginia Tech) in Blacksburg, Virginia. The perpetrator, Seung-Hui Cho, killed 32 people and wounded many others before committing suicide, making it not just the deadliest school shooting, but the deadliest shooting rampage by a single gunman in U.S. history.

3. **The short answer is that "gun controls" do not work: they are indeed generally perverse in their effects.** 此句大意为：答案很简单，就是"枪械管制"不起作用：实际上这种管制的作用与人们想象的完全相反。

4. **Cesare Beccaria:** 意大利刑法学家，1763 年 3 月到 1764 年 1 月，以 10 个月时间写成了《论犯罪与刑罚》一书，一鸣惊人。Cesare Beccaria 明确提出了后来为现代刑法制度所确认的三大刑法原则：(1)罪刑法定原则；(2)罪刑相适应原则；(3)刑罚人道化原则。

5. **the assault on Virginia's Appalachian Law School:** 弗吉尼亚阿巴拉契亚法律学院枪击事件

   On Jan. 16, 2002, graduate student Peter Odighizuwa, 42, dismissed from Virginia's Appalachian School of Law not long ago, returned to campus and killed the dean, a professor and a student before being tackled by students. The attack also wounds three female students.

6. **the U.S. Bureau of Justice:** 美国司法局

7. **In Britain, however, the image of violent America remains unassailably entrenched.** 此句大意为：然而在英国，美国是个暴力国家这一形象在人们心里根深蒂固，不可磨灭。

8. **rednecks:** 红脖子。这个词有两个含义，一是对农村劳动阶层(特别是美国南方这一阶层)白人的贬称，还可以指狭隘保守、持有社会政治偏见的人。文中作者指美国人，用这个词体现了英国人对美国人的蔑视。

9. **Dr Watson:** 华生医生，《福尔摩斯探案》里一个人物。《福尔摩斯探案》作者柯南·道尔(1859—1930)被誉为"英国侦探小说之父"，迄今为止仍是全世界最畅销侦探小说作家之一。

10. **Charlotte Brontë:** 夏洛蒂·勃朗特(1816—1855)，英国小说家，生于贫苦的牧师家庭，曾在寄宿学校学习，后任教师和家庭教师。1847 年，夏洛蒂·勃朗特出版著名的长篇小说《简·爱》，轰动文坛。

11. **Beatrix Potter:** 比阿特丽克斯·波特(1866—1943)，生于维多利亚时代的一个英国贵族家庭，从小受到良好的绘画教育，喜爱将身边的小动物拟人化，用绘画来表达自己对周围世界的观察和想象。英格兰湖区是她灵感特殊的来源，她对大自然的热爱使她创作出著名的"小书"系列。

12. Yorkshire: 约克郡(英国英格兰北部的旧郡，原为英国最大的郡，1974 年分为北约克、南约克和西约克三个郡)

13. Tottenham: 托特纳姆热刺队，英国一足球俱乐部名字，该俱乐部成立于 1882 年，是英国五大俱乐部之一。

14. We now are shocked that so many ordinary people should have been carrying guns in the street; the Edwardians were shocked rather by the idea of an armed robbery. 此句大意为：我们现在很震惊，原来那么多普通人都是可以持枪在街上走的；而爱德华七世时期的英国人一定认为持枪抢劫不可思议。这里作者旨在说明：普通人持枪没什么，在爱德华七世时代人们都有枪，人们之间互相牵制，持枪犯罪也就少见了。

15. **Edwardian Britain** was rocked by a series of massive strikes in which lives were lost and troops deployed, and suffragette incendiaries, anarchist bombers, Fenians, and the spectre of a revolutionary general strike made Britain then arguably a much more turbulent place than it is today. 此句大意为：爱德华七世时代(1901—1910)的英国遭受着一系列重创，许多人失去生命，大量军队被部署。妇女参政论者的煽动、无政府主义者的扔炸弹、芬尼亚会会员的反英活动以及 1926 年全英国革命性大罢工前夕的恐慌，所有这些都使得当时的英国无可争议地成为比现在动乱得多的时代。(芬尼亚会是 1858 年在美国创建的爱尔兰爱国组织。)

16. "It is perhaps a privilege of those who have never had to confront violence to disparage the power to resist." 大概只有那些从来都不用抵抗暴力侵袭的人才可以对"抵抗能力"这一说法不屑一顾，嗤之以鼻吧。

●Reading Comprehension

1. Directions: *Choose the best answer for each of the following questions.*

1) Which of the following statements is NOT true according to Para. 1?

A. British people think non-strict gun laws in America facilitate its citizens' killing with guns.

B. British people attribute their less shootings to their strict gun laws.

C. British people think it's urgent for America to put more gun controls into effect.

D. British people know what's wrong with their own gun laws because of the shootings on their streets.

2) From the words of Cesare Beccaria (Para. 2) we can infer that _____.

A. laws that forbid the carrying of arms are effective to prevent homicides

B. the law-abiding become more dangerous in attacks because of the laws that forbid the carrying of arms

C. because of the laws that forbid the carrying of guns, it is more difficult for the assailants to attack others

D. Cesare Beccaria thinks highly of the laws that forbid the carrying of arms

3) In Para.5, the author lists a few facts and figures in order to emphasize that _____.

A. more restrictive gun laws don't necessarily bring about lower level of violence

B. in the past 20 years the making of gun laws has progressed rapidly

C. the spread of laws allowing the carrying of guns helped reduce the crimes

D. the more strict the gun laws are, the more armed crimes there are

4) According to the article, which of the following statements about Britain is NOT true?

A. People in Britain suffer no less violent crimes than people in America.

B. It's groundless for British people to feel proud of their disarmed society.

C. British people will be safer if they are allowed to be armed with guns.

D. Before World War I, Britain was a more stable place.

5) Which of the following words can best describe the author's attitude toward America's gun laws?

A. Critical.   B. Indifferent.   C. Appreciative.   d. Joyous.

2. Directions: *Read the following statements carefully, and decide whether they are true (T) or false (F) according to the text.*

_____ 1) The writer would rather that Virginia Tech had adopted the legal challenge that would have allowed the carrying of defensive weapons.

_____ 2) There are no gun laws in Vermont (佛蒙特州), while the level of armed violence there is the lowest.

_____ 3) The level of violent crimes in Britain is lower than that in America, and that's why British people think America is violent.

_____ 4) The ban of pistols and the confiscation of legal guns have helped a lot to reduce the handgun crimes in Britain over the past 10 years.

_____ 5) Though the Victorians and Edwardians were allowed to carry guns with them, there were not so many armed crimes at that time.

_____ 6) In an unstable society, the carrying of guns will worsen the situation of turbulence.

_____ 7) People in Britain are now much safer because Britain is now an officially disarmed society.

_____ 8) British attitudes toward gun controls are not wise.

_____ 9) In the author's opinion, the carrying of guns can strengthen people's power to protect themselves when they are confronting violent crimes and it is also deterrent of violence.

_____ 10) Nobody will ignore his power to resist violence so long as he is in a world of possible violent crimes.

Passage Two

Warm-up questions:

1. Which way do you prefer, living in the dorm with your classmates, or renting an apartment outside the campus? Please explain the reasons.

2. If you are going to buy a house in the future, will you buy a big one? Why or why not?

Big Homes, Big Problems
—How the size of our houses inflated the housing crisis

1   Down the block from my home, workmen are finishing a new house. It replaces a bungalow that had measured about 1,500 square feet. The new home has a covered front porch, two fireplaces and a finished basement. It comes in at just under 5,700 square feet. What is it with Americans and their homes?

2   Everyone knows the direct causes of the present housing collapse: low interest rates, lax mortgage lending, rampant speculation. But the larger force lies in Americans' devotion to homeownership. It explains why government officials, politicians and journalists (including this one) overlooked abuses in "subprime" lending[1]. The homeownership rate was approaching 70 percent in 2005, up from 64 percent in 1990. Great. A good cause shielded bad practices. The same complacency lulled ordinary Americans into paying ever-rising home prices. Something so embedded in the national psyche must be OK.

3   "House lust" is what Dan McGinn calls it in his book by the same title. McGinn documents—sympathetically, for he dotes on his own home—our housing excesses, starting with supersizing.[2] In Sweden, Britain and Italy, new homes average under 1,000 square feet. By 2005, the average newly built U.S. home measured 2,434 square feet, and there were many that were double, triple or quadruple that. After World War II, the first mass Levittown[3] suburbs offered 750-square-foot homes. (Full disclosure: McGinn is a *Newsweek* colleague.)

4   "We're not selling shelter," says the president of Toll Brothers, a builder of upscale homes. "We're selling extreme-ego, look-at-me types of homes." In 2000, Toll Brothers' most popular home was 3,200 square feet; by 2005, it had grown 50 percent, to 4,800 square feet. These "McMansions"[4] often feature marble floors, sweeping staircases, vaulted ceilings, family rooms, studies, home-entertainment centers and more bedrooms than people.

5   In a nation of abundant land—unlike Europe and Japan—our housing obsession is

understandable and desirable up to a point. People who own homes take better care of them. They stabilize neighborhoods. In a world where so much seems uncontrollable, a house seems a refuge of influence and individuality. In a 2004 survey, 74 percent of would-be home buyers preferred a new home to an existing house. One reason is that a new house often allows buyers to select the latest gadgets and shape the design. The same impulse has driven the remodeling boom, which totaled $180 billion in 2006.

6   "The most exciting thing was just watching the house go up piece by piece," said one buyer of a new, $380,000 home in Las Vegas. The fiftyish couple added a pool, hot tub and deck. They love their home.

7   Homes are a common currency of status. As McGinn notes, many jobs in an advanced economy are highly technical and specialized. "I could tell you more about (my job)," a woman informed him at a dinner party, "but you won't understand it, and it's not that interesting." By contrast, a home announces that, whatever the obscurities of your work, you've succeeded. There's a frantic competition to match or exceed friends, co-workers and (yes) parents.

8   Some house lust is fairly harmless. Several Web sites (Zillow.com and Realtor.com) provide estimated prices for homes. People can indulge their nosiness about their neighbors', friends', co-workers' or relatives' finances. They can also fantasize about their next real estate adventure by watching a cable channel (HGTV[5]) devoted to houses, home buying and renovation.

9   Other effects are less innocuous. Although house prices recently exploded, they have increased only slightly faster than inflation since the 1890s, concluded a study by Yale economist Robert Shiller. The recent sharp run-up may imply years of price declines or meager increases. "Buying a bigger house isn't an investment," warned *Wall Street Journal* columnist Jonathan Clements. It's "a lifestyle choice—and it comes with a brutally large price tag." Not only are mortgage payments higher; so are costs for utilities, furniture and repairs.

10   Worse, government subsidizes these supersize homes along with suburban sprawl and, just incidentally, global warming.[6] In 2008, the tax deduction for mortgage interest payments will cost the federal government $89 billion. The savings go heavily to the upper-middle class and the wealthy—the least needy people—and encourage ever-larger homes. Even with energy-saving appliances, those homes are likely to generate more greenhouse gases than their smaller

predecessors. As individuals and a society, we've over-invested in housing; we'd be better off if more of our savings went into productive investments elsewhere.

11　Sociologically, the "housing bubble" resembles the preceding "tech bubble". When people paid astronomical prices for profitless dotcom stocks, they doubtlessly reassured themselves that they were investing in the very essence of America—the pioneering spirit, the ability to harness new technologies.[7] Exorbitant home prices inspired a similar logic. How could anyone go wrong buying into the American dream? It was easy.

—Robert J. Samuelson

Notes

1. **subprime lending:** 次级抵押贷款(利率比银行最低贷款利率略高)

   In general, subprime lending (also known as B-paper, near-prime, or second chance lending) is lending at a higher rate than the prime rate. Prime rate is a term applied in many countries to a reference interest rate used by banks. The term originally indicated the rate of interest at which banks lent to favored customers, though this is no longer always the case. Some variable interest rates may be expressed as a percentage above or below prime rate.

2. McGinn documents—sympathetically, for he dotes on his own home—our housing excesses, starting with supersizing. 此句意为：麦克金评述说——令人同情的是，他本人也很爱自己的房子——我们对住宅的过分要求是从建造超大面积的住宅开始的。dote on：宠爱，溺爱。

3. **Levittown:** 莱维敦，美国著名的居住社区，堪称美国城市化住宅典范

   Levittown, Pennsylvania is a census-designated place (CDP) and suburban community located in Bucks County, Pennsylvania, within the Philadelphia metropolitan area. It was the second "Levittown" built by William J. Levitt, who is often credited as the creator of the modern American suburb. What set Levittown apart from other developments at the time was that it was built as a complete community. Levitt designed neighborhoods with traffic-calming curvilinear roads, in which there were no four-way intersections. Each neighborhood had within its boundaries a site for a public elementary school. Locations for churches and other public facilities were set aside on main thoroughfares. Other amenities included Olympic-sized public pools, parks, "greenbelts" baseball fields and playgrounds, and a shopping center located in Tullytown Borough that was considered large and modern at the time of its construction.

4. McMansion: (成批建造的)大型住宅(面积在 280～460 平方米)

   This word is to describe a particular type of housing that is constructed in an assembly line fashion reminiscent of food production at McDonald's fast food restaurants. The term is one of many McWords. A McMansion is generally considered a house between 3,000 ft² (280 m²) to 5,000 ft² (460 m²) in size in homogeneous communities that are often produced by a developer. Although they are generally large homes, they are mass produced and are not of the caliber of a mansion. Their cost places them in the purchasing range of the upper middle class segment of the population.

5. HGTV: 家居园艺电视网

   HGTV (Home & Garden Television) is a cable TV network in the U.S. that carries a variety of home and garden improvement, maintenance, renovation, craft and remodeling shows.

6. Worse, government subsidizes these supersize homes along with suburban sprawl and, just incidentally, global warming. 此句意为：更糟糕的是，政府不仅要补贴那些在郊区无计划扩展的超大型住宅，还要顺带为他们造成的全球变暖现象买单。sprawl：无计划发展(偶尔增长或向四周扩展，特别是由城市郊区房地产的发展而形成)

7. When people paid astronomical prices for profitless **dotcom stocks**, they doubtlessly reassured themselves that they were investing in the very essence of America—the pioneering spirit, the ability to harness new technologies. 此句意为：当人们以天文数字的价格买下毫无利润的网络公司的股票时，他们无疑在宽慰自己，他们在投资美国的精髓本质——开拓精神和掌控新技术的能力。

●**Reading Comprehension**

1. **Directions:** *Try to find out the reasons why Americans tend to buy big houses in the passage and then discuss with your partner which reason you think would be the most important one.*

2. **Directions:** *Fill in the column concerning American housing in the following table based on the information you get from the passage. Then compare with what you know about Chinese housing.*

Changing items in housing in the past decade or decades	the U.S.	China
price of house		
the homeownership rate		
the area of house		
people's attitude towards buying houses		

Part Three

Topic-related Activities

1. Solving the Problem

Step One

Directions: *Work within a group of 4 or 5. Look at the following pictures, and then try to find out what the problems are.*

Step Two

Directions: *Work with your group members, and brainstorm the possible reasons of these problems.*

Step Three

Directions: *Try to find out some possible solutions to the problems and evaluate carefully whether they will work or not.*

Step Four

Directions: *Choose one student from each group to present the solution to the problems in public.*

2. Believe It or Not

Step One

Directions: *Read the following list of Chinese social problems. Work in groups of 4 or 5 and discuss whether these problems are reflecting the reality or just being exaggerated. State your reasons.*

China is ushering in what could be its best period in the development of its economy and society. However, according to the latest issue of *Outlook Weekly* (a magazine issued in Columbus, USA), it listed some social problems which are hindering the development of China as follows:

1) Aggravating social contradictions due to loss of farmland;

2) Income gap further widened;

3) Long-term difficulty in employment;

4) Poverty-relief work still high on the agenda in the new century;

5) Sustainable development seriously hampered by resources, energy and environment;

6) Psychological changes in the fast economic growth period.

Step Two

Directions: *Conduct a survey among the group and select the top three Chinese social problems that you are most concerned. You may use the above problems as your reference or figure out new ones. Then come up with some ideas to help solve these three problems. Choose one student from each group to present the problems and solutions to the whole class.*

3. Case Study

Public Security Ministry spokesman Wu Heping on Friday said China would maintain strict controls on guns, while responding to the deadly rampage at a U.S. university on Monday.

"I would like to express my deep sympathy and condolences to the victims of the tragedy in the United States, which claimed the lives of many young students." Wu told *China Daily*.

Police destroy 30,000 replica guns confiscated from smugglers on Friday in Shanghai.

Wu said the tragedy also throws into focus gun ownership in China.

He said strict controls had helped China avoid a U.S.-style "gun culture", and the rampage had proved that it's necessary to maintain this policy.

U.S. media reported that more than 30,000 people die from gunshot wounds in the country annually and there are more guns in private hands than in any other country.

However in China, gun crime is rare, as private citizens are forbidden from owning and selling guns.

Wu said the ban aims to wipe out potential danger and protect the safety of every individual citizen. "If there's no access to the weapon, people cannot commit a gun crime," he said.

—Zhu Zhe

Questions

1. Compared with America, what different gun laws does China have?

2. Can you come up with any geographical, economical, historical or ethical factors that cause the totally different gun laws in these two different cultures?

Part Four

Topic-related Information

1. How Easy Is It to Buy a Gun in America?

America is one of the few countries which allow the law-abiding citizens to own and use their own guns. When their lives and properties or the lives and properties of their families, friends or just people around them are severely threatened, they can legally employ their guns to protect themselves or the weak. The second amendment of the U.S. Constitution asserts that "the right of the people to keep and bear arms shall not be infringed."

Gun Laws of America

Gun laws of America are extremely complicated. There are:

1) federal guns laws, state gun laws;

2) legislations of guns in local cities and towns;

3) bylaws of guns established by companies, stores and even individuals.

Though State gun laws vary widely, most Americans and greencard-holders can purchase firearms and carry concealed guns in given public places after a criminal background check. Anyone with a felony and certain misdemeanours such as domestic violence or mental health issues is rejected.

Where to Buy Guns?

People buy guns from such legal gun dealers as:

1) Gun Shop;

2) Shooting Range;

3) Gun Show;

4) Sports Stores;

5) through mail order.

However, guns can not be mailed to the buyers straightly.

Who Can Buy Guns?

Generally, the gun buyers must be:

1) Americans or greencard-holders;

2) without Class 1/2/3 Felony Charge;

3) not users of illegal medicine;

4) not mentally ill;

5) not soldiers kicked out from the army;

6) without domestic violence;

7) not a criminal at large;

8) over 18.

Anyone aged 18+ can buy long guns (rifles & shotguns) in all states. Some states allow handgun purchases for those aged 18-20. Anyone aged 21+ can buy long guns or handguns in all states. Wal-Marts in some states sell firearms.

2. New Interesting Social Phenomena Emerging in the Current World

1) Blogging (博客)

A blog (an abridgment of the term web log) is a website, usually maintained by an individual, with regular entries of commentary, descriptions of events, or other material such as graphics or video. A research showed that blogging is a social phenomenon with Asians primarily as a means to maintain and build their social connections and to express themselves. The report suggested that netizens in Asia are most interested in those blogs written by friends and family (74 percent) while blogs by work colleagues were the second most popular blog but were a distant second with only a quarter of respondents showing interest. The survey also shows that blogs are a relatively trusted source of information with half of respondents believing that blog content is as trustworthy as traditional media. Miniblog, as its name suggests, is a means letting people broadcast short messages to anyone in the world and is believed to be the quickest way to learn about news and current affairs.

2) Graffiti (街头涂鸦)

Graffiti has existed since ancient times, with examples going back to Ancient Greece and the Roman Empire. Graffiti can be anything from simple scratch marks to elaborate wall paintings. In modern times, spray paint and markers have become the most commonly used materials. In most countries, defacing property with graffiti without the property owner's consent is considered vandalism, which is punishable by law. Sometimes graffiti is employed to communicate social and political messages. To some, it is an art form worthy of display in galleries and exhibitions, to others it is merely vandalism. There are many different types and styles of graffiti and it is a rapidly evolving art form whose value is highly contested, being reviled by many authorities while also subject to protection, sometimes within the same jurisdiction.

3) Flash Mobs (快闪族)

Is it performance art or the ultimate surprise party? A social phenomenon known as the "flash mob", which began in New York and relies on e-mail, appears to be spreading worldwide.

Actually organizing a "flash mob" basically involves e-mailing a bunch of people with instructions to show up at a certain place for a few moments, then disappear. The flash mob members then voluntarily and simultaneously converge at the venue specified in the e-mail, then collect detailed instructions for the event. They usually have someone there to give secret signals. They partake in a silly and harmless activity and then disperse at a given time. To make sure the plan stays secret, participants aren't told exactly what the mob is supposed to do until seconds before it happens. They have to follow the timetable exactly.

Flash mobbing originated in the U.S. Its creator is reported to be someone called "Bill". He began the trend by e-mailing 50 people and asking them to gather at a shop in downtown Manhattan. Another flash mob saw hundreds of people perched on a stone ledge in Central Park making bird

noises. The "flash mob" craze spread to China as early as two years ago. The game rapidly swept across Xiamen, Hangzhou, Chengdu, Qingdao, Guangzhou, and, of course, Beijing. Mobbers usually gather quietly at the pre-determined place, like a church, square, or even a subway station.

"It's a spectacle for spectacle's sake—which is silly, but is also, as I've discovered somewhat to my surprise, genuinely transgressive, which is part of its appeal, I think," said the mysterious Bill in an e-mail exchange. "People feel like there's nothing but order everywhere, and so they love to be a part of just one thing that nobody was expecting."

Hyperlinks

[1] http://www.aacap.org/

[2] http://en.wikipedia.org/wiki

[3] http://english.people.com.cn/200501/24/eng20050124_171731.html

[4] http://www.digitalmediaasia.com/default.asp?ArticleID=20064

[5] http://www.abc.net.au/science/news/stories/s913314.htm

[6] http://english.cri.cn/3178/2006/12/21/167@176500.htm

[7] http://www.greatwalltour.com/greatwall_pages/miscellaneous/Housing.htm

[8] http://www.atimes.com/atimes/China_Business/IG06Cb02.html

References

[1] http://english.people.com.cn/200501/24/eng20050124_171731.html

[2] http://www.abc.net.au/science/news/stories/s913314.htm

[3] http://english.cri.cn/3178/2006/12/21/167@176500.htm

[4] http://www.ubasics.com/adam/personal/school/essay3.htm

[5] Richard Munday. Wouldn't You Feel Safer with a Gun? *The Times*[J], September 8th, 2007

[6] Robert J. Samuelson. Big Homes, Big Problems. *Newsweek*[J], Jan 2, 2008

[7] Zhu Zhe. *China Daily*, 2007-04-21

Unit 6

Social Etiquette

Part One

Lead-in

People fail to get along with each other because they fear each other, they fear each other because they don't know each other, they don't know each other because they have not communicated with each other.

—by Martin Luther King, Jr. (America)

人们不能彼此相处是因为他们害怕彼此，害怕彼此是因为不了解彼此，而不了解彼此是因为没有相互沟通。

——小马丁·路德·金(美国)

Etiquette is dependent on culture: what is excellent etiquette in one society may be shocking in another. Etiquette evolves within culture. Etiquette can vary widely between different cultures and nations. In China, for example, a person who takes the last item of food from a common plate or bowl without first offering it to others at the table may be seen as a glutton and insulting the generosity of the host, while in most European cultures a guest is expected to eat all of the food given to them, as a compliment to the quality of the cooking.

Part Two

Reading Passages

In-Class Reading

Warm-up questions:

1. What is an open cubicle workplace like? Describe it to your classmates.

2. Do you know any good manners on or outside the campus? Share them with your classmates.

Good Manners in Today's Workplace

1　Whether you work in the heat and heart of Silicon Valley or do business farther away from the high tech "fires," there is no work on earth that has not been permanently influenced by the way of life created by the information age and information tools. And, as we all have noticed by now, being able to do business at the speed of light has done enormous damage to conducting business in a human and **humane** fashion.

2　I would like to offer a few **ground rules** on insights into how to bring some consideration, grace and style back into your work life. Read on to rediscover good manners you may have **misplaced** and perhaps learn a few new tips you can incorporate into the way you work. And, as you read through the guides, grade yourself on how you generally conduct yourself at work right now, noting where you can improve.

3　Speaking. Use well-**modulated** tones when you speak in the office and over the phone. Raising your voice in haste, frustration, or anger is always inappropriate. It doesn't **foster** clear communication and leaves all parties concerned with an "emotional **residue**" that will interfere with getting work done.[1] And, when "speaking" in e-mail and online, all the same rules apply. Don't "flame" with insults and rudeness and don't "shout" by using **ALL CAPS**! Finally, do not swear, tell **off-color** jokes, or bring sexual topics or **overtones** into your work discussions. This is highly unprofessional and completely inappropriate at work.

4   Work **Attire**. Pages have been written on how to dress at work and while an entire column could be devoted to this topic, we offer a few simple guidelines here. Dress as those in your work group dress. Remember that being casual does not extend to poor **grooming**—always be clean and neat.[2] If your job requires you to interact with the public, you will probably be required to dress more formally. If this doesn't appeal to you, don't try to **buck** the system. Find another job. If you wish to climb the corporate ladder,[3] look at the people in positions you want and dress as they do. Avoid clothing extremes, revealing clothing, and evening or party wear in the workplace. And don't sacrifice comfort for trends or fashion. Use good taste or get help figuring out what is tasteful.

5   Personal Life at Work. Everyone makes friends at work and there is a fine line that is easy to cross when co-workers become friends. Remember to conduct your personal life outside the workplace and you won't go wrong. Use **moderation** in your exchanges with work friends so you don't spend too much time socializing. If it is necessary to discuss personal issues or conduct urgent personal business of any sort in your workplace, be brief and **discreet**, so you don't distract, disturb or offend those with whom you work. The best rule is to discuss personal issues in private and in moderation when at work, so you give your employer what he pays you for—your time, focus and work done well. Keep casual talk to a minimum. Don't bring family members, friends, and pets into the office for extended periods of time.

6   Interaction with Co-Workers. Don't interrupt your workmates. Schedule times to meet whenever possible to go over mutual work.[4] The occasional quick question is unavoidable, but don't let **spontaneity** rule you and ruin everyone else's schedule and concentration. Open **cubicles** already remove most of your co-workers' privacy, so respect their quiet. And observe the "shut door" of your co-workers who work in offices. Avoid **roaming** the floor and disturbing others at work when you are less busy. Take your breaks in a break area or cafeteria for the same reason. If you are interrupted or if a co-worker is making too much noise in an **adjacent** area, calmly and respectfully inform him that you need quiet. You can be polite and firm at the same time. And always treat your co-workers with consideration and respect in all exchanges.

7   Your Workspace. Maintain a high standard of neatness and professional **decorum** in your personal work area. Bringing personal items into that area is your decision, but be aware that what you display is a direct reflection of whom you are and how you wish to be perceived. If you line your cube walls with soda cans or toys, it may be amusing and show that "arty" or "witty" side of yourself, but it also presents you as

someone who wishes his sense of humor or playfulness to be the first and most important thing people observe about him. [5] Think about it first! And think twice about displaying controversial, religious, political or extremely personal items in your private work area. And, while it shouldn't have to be said, we must: Never take things from other people's workspace and return anything you borrow with haste! Use earphones if you wish to listen to music or the radio while you work. Don't use a speakerphone without shutting your office door and never use one in an open area. It is extremely rude to carry on your business to the **detriment** of everyone around you.

8   Sharing the Environment. Take care in shared areas. Don't leave your **clutter** in a conference room after a meeting. And share the "visual, sound and air space" politely at work, too. If you have nervous habits, break them. Don't twitch, **jiggle** your leg, tap pencils or other items on the table and so on. Never engage in personal grooming in your cube or in meetings. Comb hair, put on make-up, and engage in ALL personal grooming in the restroom or at home. Keep your casual and personal habits outside the workplace. Don't smoke, chew gum, play with your face, hands or other body parts, or absentmindedly snack, whistle or sing in a shared workplace. If you decide to eat snacks, breakfast, or lunch in your cubicle, be considerate of those around you; try to select foods that do not have strong or unpleasant aromas.

9   Group Politics. Don't be a **whiner**, complainer, or negativity "black hole." Do bring a positive attitude to meetings and discussions. You don't have to be rude or sarcastic to say "no." And, while saying "no" politely is a learned skill—it is the professional way to go. Further, don't gossip about or discuss other employees or their performance in any way in their absence. And if you have something you absolutely must say, say it to that person and in private. Avoid bringing a bad mood into your workplace. And never abuse others when you have a bad day. Learn how to be a "team player" and how to take action to make the changes you think are important. If you find this is impossible in your job and that you are distressed by your inability to affect change, maybe it's time to find a job where you can make changes. But don't destroy your current work environment with your unhappiness in the meantime.

10   In conclusion, putting together this list of "do's and don'ts" may be **daunting** at first, but every well-mannered, successful working adult should know and observe them. Take steps to become more than a mindless worker bee. Bring some style and grace into your work behavior today!

—Sue Fox

New Words and Expressions

adjacent	*a.*	close to; lying near 邻近的；靠近……的，毗连……的
attire	*n.*	clothing or array 服装，衣着
buck	*v.*	oppose directly and stubbornly; go against 竭力反对；反抗
clutter	*n.*	a confused or disordered state or collection; a jumble 混乱，无序；

一团

cubicle	*n.*	a small compartment, as for work or study 小书房，小房间(用于工作或学习)
daunting	*a.*	making someone feel afraid or worried about dealing with something 使人畏缩的
decorum	*n.*	appropriateness of behavior or conduct; propriety 正派得体，行为举止适宜
detriment	*n.*	damage, harm, or loss 损害，伤害，损失
discreet	*a.*	exercising, or showing prudence and wise self-restraint in speech and behavior 谨慎的，慎重的
foster	*v.*	promote the growth and development of; cultivate 促进，培养
groom	*v.*	care for the appearance of; make neat and trim 打扮；注意外表，使整洁
humane	*a.*	marked by an emphasis on humanistic values and concerns 高雅的，文雅的：将侧重点置于人文主义价值或所关心的事物上的
jiggle	*v.*	move or rock lightly up and down or to and fro in an unsteady, jerky manner 抖动
misplace	*v.*	put into a wrong place 把……放错地方
moderation	*n*	acting in a way that is reasonable and not extreme 适度
modulate	*v.*	change or vary the pitch, intensity, or tone of (one's voice or a musical instrument, for example) 调整音量，改变音量；改变或变换如噪音或音乐装置的音高、强度或音调
off-color	*a.*	exhibiting bad taste 伤风败俗的，展示不好的品味的
overtone	*n.*	an implication or a hint 暗示
residue	*n.*	the remainder of something after removal of parts or a part 残留物
roam	*v.*	wander over or through 来回走动或漫步于
spontaneity	*n.*	spontaneous behavior, impulse, or movement 行为冲动，自发动作
whiner	*n.*	哀诉者
all caps	*n.*	all in capital letters 全部大写
ground rule(s)	*n.*	a basic rule of procedure or behavior 基本规则

Proper Name

Silicon Valley   硅谷(位于美国加利福尼亚州西部，以其高科技设计和生产工业闻名)

Notes

1. It doesn't foster clear communication and leaves all parties concerned with an 'emotional residue' that will interfere with getting work done. 此句意为：那并不能促进明白无误的交流，只会让所有人都受到那种不良情绪的困扰，使得工作不能顺利完成。

2. Remember that being casual does not extend to poor grooming—always be clean and neat. 此句意为：记住，穿着随意不能到邋遢的地步，务必一贯保持干净、整洁。

3. If you wish to climb the corporate ladder…: 如果你想进入公司的高层……

4. Schedule times to meet whenever possible to go over mutual work. 此句意为：尽一切可能安排时间聚在一起共同研讨工作。times: suitable moments 适当时机。

5. If you line your cube walls with soda cans or toys, it may be amusing and show that "arty" or "witty" side of yourself, but it also presents you as someone who wishes his sense of humor or playfulness to be the first and most important thing people observe about him. 此句意为：如果你的工作间的壁柜上堆满了苏打水瓶或玩具，这可能会表现出你的艺术气质或诙谐的一面，但也表明你希望别人第一时间看到你是一个具有幽默感和童心未泯的人，这对你来说至关重要。

● **Reading Comprehension**

1. Directions: *Discuss the following questions with your classmates.*

1) Where is Silicon Valley? What is it famous for?

2) What does the author think is the consequence of people's way of doing business in the information age?

3) If you want to display your personal items in your private work area, what do you have to be cautious about?

4) Since people in today's workplace work in open cubicles, what does the author mean by saying "observe the 'shut door' of your co-workers" (Para. 6)?

5) What does a "mindless worker bee" mean in the last paragraph?

2. Directions: *Read the following statements carefully, and decide whether they are true (T) or false (F) according to the text.*

_____ 1) The author thinks that the way of life created by the information age and information tools has done enormous damage to conducting business in a human and humane fashion in Silicon Valley.

_____ 2) You are advised to always wear business suits in the workplace if you want to get a promotion in the corporation.

_____ 3) It can be inferred in the passage that when communicating in e-mail and online, using all letters in capital is considered inappropriate.

_____ 4) According to the passage, when communicating with your co-workers, you should keep friendly and intimate relations with them.

_____ 5) Open cubicles in today's workplace have deprived office workers of most of their privacy.

After-Class Reading

Passage One

Warm-up questions:

1. Have you ever been to a pub? What is it like? If you have not, what is it like in your mind?

2. Do you think pubs are good places where you can easily make friends?

The Basics of British Pub Etiquette

1   "Pub" is short for "Public House". The publican opens part of his or her "house" to the public —a bit like giving a party in your own home every day! [1] The home-like qualities of the British pub are perhaps why tourists often find our pubs more cozy and welcoming than bars and cafes in other parts of the world.

2   In other parts of the world, cafes and bars often display the words "café" or "bar" in a prominent position on the facade or signage. You will rarely see the word "pub" anywhere on a British pub. However, there is one important external feature which can tell you that it is a pub: the pub-sign. The pub-sign is mounted about 15 to 25 feet from the ground, either sticking out at right-angles to the building or swinging in a wooden frame at the top of a pole outside the building. The sign usually measures about 3 by 4 feet, and displays both the name of the pub and a pictorial representation of the name.

3   By law, pubs are not allowed to open until 11 a.m. (noon on Sundays). They cannot serve drinks after 11 p.m. (10.30 on Sundays)—although you are allowed 20 minutes to finish any drinks already purchased. In Scotland pubs generally open until midnight. Do not even try to get served outside these legal "licensing hours". It is also illegal for pubs to serve alcoholic drinks to anyone under the age of 18, and you will be breaking the law if you try to buy an alcoholic drink for anyone who is under 18.

4   Here are some unofficial, unspoken rules of pub etiquette which are complex but important.

5   First, there is no waiter service in British pubs. You have to go up to the bar to buy your drinks, and carry them back to your table.

6　　Once they are aware of the no-waiter-service rule[2] in British pubs, most tourists recognize it as an advantage, rather than an inconvenience. Having to go up to the bar for your drinks ensures plenty of opportunities for social contact between customers.

7　　In bars and cafes in other parts of the world, waiter service can isolate people at separate tables, which makes it more difficult to initiate contact with others. Perhaps many cultures are more naturally outgoing and sociable than the British, and do not require any assistance in striking up a conversation with those seated near them.

8　　The British, however, are a somewhat reserved and inhibited people, and we need all the help we can get! It is much easier to drift casually into a spontaneous chat while waiting at the bar than deliberately to break into the conversation at another table. Like every other aspect of pub etiquette, the no-waiter-service system is designed to promote sociability.

9　　This is very good news for tourists who wish to make contact with the natives. The bar counter[3] in a pub is possibly the only site in the British Isles in which friendly conversation with strangers is considered entirely appropriate and normal behaviour.

10　　Second, it is customary for one or two people, not the whole group, to go up to the bar to buy drinks.

11　　Bar staff are generally very tolerant people, but large packs of tourists crowding the bar counter can try their patience. It is best if only one or at the most two members of the group approach the bar to purchase drinks for the group. Other members of the group should either stand back from the bar or go and sit down at a table.

12　　Third, to get served, you must attract the attention of the bar staff without making any noise or resorting to the vulgarity of too-obvious gesticulation. In the pub, we gather haphazardly along the bar counter, and the bar staff are aware of each person's position in the "invisible" queue. There are strict rules of etiquette involved in attracting the attention of bar staff.

13　　Don't ever try to "jump" the invisible queue. The people who reached the bar before you will be served before you.

14　　Do start by trying to identify the best position at the bar counter. When the bar is busy, find positions[4] which may be favourable for making eye-contact with bar staff.

15　　Don't call out to the bar staff,[5] tap coins on the counter, snap your fingers, wave like a drowning swimmer, bang your hand on the counter, shout "service" or "barman" or wave money about. In fact, it is best to avoid all speech or obvious gesticulation.

17　　Do let the bar staff know you are waiting to be served by holding money or your empty glass in your hand. You may tilt the empty glass, perhaps even turn it slowly in a circular motion (some say that this indicates the passing of time).

18　　Don't scowl, frown or glare at the bar staff, or make your impatience obvious by heavy sighing and angry muttering. The bar staff are doing their best to serve everyone in turn, and rudeness will not help your cause.

19   Do adopt an expectant, hopeful, even slightly anxious facial expression. If you look too contented and complacent, the bar staff may assume you are already being served.

20   Don't ring the bell. Some pubs have a large bell attached to the wall at one end of the bar. This is used by the publican or bar staff to signal "last orders" and "time".

21   Do stay alert and keep your eye on the bar staff at all times. This will increase your chances of making eye-contact.

22   When you achieve your goal of making eye contact with the barman, a quick lift of the eyebrows and upwards jerk of the chin, accompanied by a hopeful smile, will let him know that you are waiting. In a busy bar, do not expect a verbal response.

23   Fourth, if you wish to pay for your drinks individually, then order individually; if you order as a group, the bar staff will total the cost and expect a single payment.

24   Fifth, in most British pubs, you pay for your drinks in cash,[6] immediately when you order them. You should also expect to pay for each drink or round of drinks when you order it.

25   Sixth, when ordering beer[7], tell the bar staff whether you want bitter, lager or another sort of beer, and whether you want a pint,[8] a half, or one of the wide variety of imported and domestic beers sold by the bottle. You just say "A half of lager, please" or "A half of bitter, please". This is very often shortened to "Half a lager, please" and so on. The "please" is important.

26   Seventh, it is not customary to tip the publican or bar staff in British pubs.[9] Instead, the common practice is to buy them a drink. Just say "and one for yourself", or "and will you have one

yourself?" at the end of your order.

27　Eighth, when ordering food, drinks must almost always be purchased at the bar. The best strategy is to go up to the bar first, order your drinks and ask the bar staff what the procedure is for ordering food. And do not expect the staff who bring your food to take orders for drinks as well.

28　Pubs are not just about food and drink: they give you the opportunities for friendly chats with the bar staff and other natives. They are about sociability, and every trip to the bar to buy drinks is another chance to make contact.

Notes

1. "The publican opens part of his or her 'house' to the public—a bit like giving a party in your own home every day." 此句大意为：酒馆老板把他或她的房子的一部分向公众开放——有点像每天在自己家里举行聚会。

2. **the no-waiter-service rule:** For this rule, there are regional variations. You may find waiter service in some pubs in Northern Ireland, but not all. Even there, waiter service is not common in city-centre pubs, and some pubs only use waiters at very busy times. Where waiter service is available, it is a supplement to bar service, not a replacement.

3. the bar counter: In Britain, the term "bar" can mean either the actual counter at which drinks are served, or any room in the pub which contains one of these counters. You may come across pubs with rooms marked "Public Bar" and "Lounge Bar" or "Saloon Bar". The Public Bar usually has more modest and functional furnishings, and houses pub-games such as pool and darts, while the Lounge or Saloon Bar is more luxurious, comfortable and conducive to quiet conversation. Traditionally, both prices and social classes were lower in the Public Bar, but these distinctions no longer apply. 吧台

4. positions: Here are two favorable positions. One is immediately opposite the till, as bar staff must return there after each sale. Skilled bar staff, however, are aware of the "till-position-manoeuvre" and may have perfected gaze-avoidance techniques to prevent customers who adopt this strategy from jumping the queue. A more potentially effective strategy is to position yourself next to a person currently being served, as bar staff will find it hard to avoid eye-contact with you when they hand over drinks and take money from your immediate neighbour.

5. Don't call out to the bar staff. There are exceptions: If you hear people calling out "Get a move on!" or "I've been stood here since last Thursday!" or "Any chance of a drink sometime this week?" to the bar staff, do not imitate them. The only people permitted to make such remarks are established regulars, and the remarks are made in the context of the special etiquette governing relations between bar staff and regulars.

6. "…you pay for your drinks in cash." In terms of financial transactions, the ordinary British local is not a 20th-century business. Although you will find some exceptions, the majority of local pubs do not take credit cards for drinks, and you will have to ask if you want a receipt. Credit

cards are becoming more widely accepted when ordering meals, but ask before relying on them.

7. beer: There are hundreds of different varieties of beer available, each with its own distinctive taste and characteristics. Pubs often have a range of around 20 different beers behind the bar, many of them on draught (on tap), some in bottles and a few in cans. They range from dark stouts, through mild ales and bitter to lager—a light, gold-coloured beer. (You would normally get lager if you just asked for a beer in most other countries, including Europe, the United States and Australia.) In Scotland, bitter is described as "heavy" or "70/-" (Seventy Shilling Ale). If you are interested, there is a lot more to find out about the endless different varieties of traditional British beers. Some publicans and bar staff are very knowledgeable, and will be happy—when they are not too busy serving the stuff—to explain it all to you. Some natives are also extremely well-informed on this subject, and will probably tell you much more than you could ever wish to know about the merits of different beers.

8. a pint: 0.568 litres (i.e. quite a big drink). "A half" means a half-pint.

9. "...it is not customary to tip the publican or bar staff in British pubs." To understand this particular element of pub etiquette, you need to understand both the British attitude towards money, and the social structure of the pub. The British tend to be rather squeamish and embarrassed about money. Any sign of excessive interest in money is considered vulgar, and obvious displays of wealth are viewed with contempt rather than admiration. The publican and bar staff may be providing you with a service in exchange for money, but it is not appropriate to emphasize this aspect of the relationship. The social structure of the pub is egalitarian: those serving behind the bar are in no way inferior to the customers—indeed, the publican often commands great respect. To give them a tip would be a reminder of their "service" role, whereas to offer a drink is to treat them as equals.

● **Reading Comprehension**

1. Directions: *Try to find out mainly how many rules in a British pub are introduced, what they are and then comment on some of them.*

2. Directions: *Read the following statements carefully, and fill the blanks according to the text.*

1) A British pub gives you the feeling of _____.

2) _____ can tell you what a pub is.

3) The lawful open time of British pubs is _____.

4) _____ is recognized as an advantage rather than an inconvenience because it allows more opportunities for social contacts between customers.

5) It is customary for _____ to go up to the bar to buy drinks.

6) In order to get served, you can attract the attention of the bar staff by_____.

7) If you order drinks as a group, the bar staff will _____.

8) Pubs give you the opportunities for _____.

Passage Two

Warm-up questions:

1. Have you ever been invited to a western meal? If yes, how do you like it? If not, what do you suppose it should be like?

2. Do you know the table manners in a western meal? List some of them.

Dining Etiquette for the Fast-food Generation

1   Everyone needs an etiquette book on his or her shelf, one of those five-pound encyclopedias of everything related to manners. I think it should be a mandatory gift to every graduate, right along with the PDA[1] and new briefcase. I received one when I finished high school and I still have it on my bookshelf. It's a little dog-eared, but the advice within isn't showing its age (unlike its owner).[2]

2   Why is this book so important? You'll be glad you have it when you're faced with an invitation to a formal event. It will teach you first how to properly respond to the invitation and then, how to eat that multi-course meal[3] with dozens of utensils, plates and glasses. It can help you plan a wedding, teach you how to write a letter, even how to get along with your co-workers.

3   But in this fast-food era, many people have forgotten—or were never taught—the fundamentals of dining etiquette. Which way should I pass? Which fork is mine? What do I do with my napkin? What follows are the answers to the basic questions many people have about dining.

4   The first thing to do after being seated at a table is to immediately place your napkin in your lap. Unfold it into either a large triangle or rectangle. Never use your napkin as a tissue, but have one close by if you think you'll need to wipe your nose during the meal. Ladies should blot their lipstick with a tissue before eating so that they don't soil the cloth napkin and glassware. Don't flip over your coffee cup or other glassware you won't be using. If a beverage is served during the meal that you don't want, simply hold your hand over the cup and say, "No, thank you."

5   If you have to leave the table during the meal, say a soft "excuse me" to the people on either side of you, leave your napkin on your chair (not the table) and push the chair under the table as you leave.

6   As you look at your place setting, remember that solids are on the left and liquids are on the right. In other words, your bread plate is on the left side above your forks and your drinking glasses are on the right side above the knife and spoons. Use silverware from the outside in. The first fork you will need will probably be your salad fork, the one farthest on the left. The larger fork directly to its right is your dinner fork. On the far right side of your place setting will most likely be a soup spoon, and on its left, a teaspoon followed by the knife. If you see utensils placed horizontally across the top of your place setting, save those for dessert. Remember—once a utensil has been used for eating, it never again touches the tablecloth, only the china!

7   Your "real estate" at a table consists of, not only your place setting, [4] but also the other items directly in front of you. It is your responsibility to take notice of those things and initiate their use. Roll baskets, butter, cream, salad dressings, sugar, salt and pepper—if they're within your reach, pick them up and start them around. Pass to the right and refrain from helping yourself first. Those items should make a complete pass around the table before you get your turn. If you just can't stand not having first choice of the rolls, turn to your neighbor on your right and say, "Would you mind if I help myself first?" They'll always say yes.

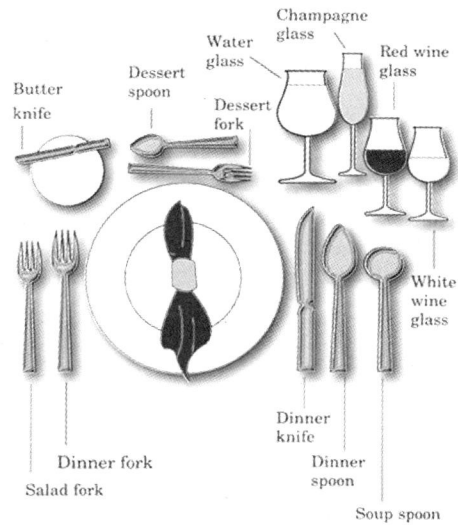

Whenever you pass something with a handle, such as dressings, pass it with the handle facing the other person so that they can grasp it easily. And always pass the salt and pepper as a set, even if only one was requested.

8   It's important that you place the butter first on the bread plate before buttering your bread. Break up your bread or rolls into one- or two-bite morsels for buttering and eating. Whatever you take up to your mouth to eat should be eaten in one or two consecutive bites. Your tablemates don't want to see the part that didn't quite fit in your mouth placed back on your bread plate!

9   To eat soup properly, draw the spoon away from you and quietly sip the soup from the side of the spoon. Tilt the bowl away from you to get to the last drops. When you're finished, place the spoon on the plate beneath the soup bowl. If there is no plate, rest the spoon in the bowl. Follow these same guidelines for any dessert served in a bowl.

10   Salads should be prepared so that they consist of bite-size pieces. But if the salad contains leaves that are too big to eat, use your salad fork to cut them into smaller pieces. And if that doesn't work, use your dinner knife. But only use the knife when all other methods have failed. Why? Because you'll also need that knife for the main course, and after you've used it for the salad, there's no place to put it so that it doesn't also disappear with the salad plate.

11   When eating the main course, pace your speed of eating to that of your tablemates so that you don't make them feel uncomfortable. In the United States, we eat "American Style". Here's how to do it. Cut your food with the fork in your left hand and the knife in your right hand. Cut only one piece at a time. Then lay your knife down along the top edge of the plate and transfer the fork to your right hand. Bring the food up to your mouth with the tines on the fork facing upward. Don't stab your food or hold the silverware with your fists. And be careful not to gesture or point with your silverware, whether or not it has food on it.

12   If you must remove something from your mouth as you eat, take it out the way it went in. In other words, if it entered your mouth on a fork, remove it with your fork. If it was finger food, use your fingers to remove it. Hold your napkin in front of your mouth to mask the removal, then place the item on the side of your plate. Don't try to hide it under the plate, because as soon as the plates are cleared it will be left behind on the tablecloth! Don't hide any paper trash you've accumulated during the meal under your plate either. Just place it on the edge of your bread plate.

13   At the conclusion of the meal, imagine your dinner plate as a clock and place your utensils in the 4:20 position. It's considered rude to push your plates away, stack them up or hand them to the server. Place your loosely-folded napkin on the table just as you stand to leave, not before.

14   Maneuvering through a meal doesn't have to be scary. Like all elements of etiquette, it boils down to common sense combined with kindness[5]. Knowing the guidelines for dining etiquette gives you confidence so that you can relax and enjoy the meal and company. And in this fast-food age, it can also make you unforgettable!

Notes

1. PDA: A PDA (Personal Digital Assistant) is a computer that fits in your hand. These small computers are sometimes called palmtops and are a great way to store telephone numbers, email addresses, access the internet, make calculations, keep a digital calendar and play games. 掌上电脑

2. "It's a little dog-eared, but the advice within isn't showing its age (unlike its owner)." 此句大意是：书已经旧得边角卷起了，但是里面的建议却一点没显出它的年纪(不像书的主人)。作者以幽默的方式表明自己年岁已大，而年轻时学的礼仪却不会过时。

3. **multi-course meal:** Most western-world meals include several courses in a standard sequence, with each course interacting harmoniously with those that introduce and follow it. The meal usually begins with an appetizer, a small serving that usually does not include red meat. This may be followed by a variety of dishes, including a possible fish course, each with some kind of vegetable. Following these is the "main course" or central part of the meal. This is the most important course and is usually a larger portion than all others. Next comes the salad course. The meal will often culminate with a dessert, either hot or cold, sometimes followed with a final serving of hot or cold fruit and accompanied by a suitable dessert wine.

4. place setting: the arrangement of eating utensils and dishwares for a single diner 为某一人准备的(进餐前放在进餐者面前的)餐位餐具

5. "Like all elements of etiquette, it boils down to common sense combined with kindness." 此句大意为：正如礼仪的所有要素一样，(就餐时的策略)归结起来就是常识加上善意。

●Reading Comprehension

1. Directions: *Choose the best answer for each of the following questions.*

1) Where should you put your napkin once you are seated?

   A. On the table.

   B. In your lap.

   C. In your hand.

   D. Wherever you like.

2) Which of the following is NOT true about your utensils in your place setting?

   A. The first fork you will need will probably be your salad fork, the one farthest on the left.

   B. Solids are on the left and liquids are on the right.

   C. On the far right side of your place setting will most likely be a dinner spoon.

   D. Utensils placed horizontally across the top of your place setting are those for dessert.

3) Which of the following is regarded as appropriate behavior when eating soup?

   A. Sip the soup from the tip of your spoon.

   B. Do not tilt the bowl away from you to get to the last drops.

   C. When you're finished, place the spoon on the tablecloth.

   D. Eat quietly without making any unpleasant noises.

4) At the conclusion of the meal, what should you do with your utensils?

   A. Push them away.

   B. Stack them up.

   C. Put them in the 4:20 position in the plate.

   D. Hand them to the server.

2. Directions: *Read the following statements carefully, and decide whether they are true (T) or false (F) according to the text.*

_____ 1) Ladies should wipe off their lipstick before eating to avoid soiling the glassware.

_____ 2) If items like butter, cream, salad dressings, sugar, salt and pepper are within your reach, it's your responsibility to pass them around, to the left first.

_____ 3) Before buttering your bread, you should place the butter first on the bread plate.

_____ 4) Americans will cut the food with the fork in the left hand and then transfer the fork to the right hand to bring food to the mouth.

_____ 5) When you stand to leave at the end of the meal, don't forget to leave your loosely-folded napkin on the chair.

Part Three

Topic-related Activities

1. Test Your Social Etiquette

Business and social etiquette can be tricky, and making the right moves can make a big difference. Take this quiz and see how you fare in the following business situations.

1. You're at a table in a restaurant for a business dinner. Midway through the meal, you're called to the telephone. What do you do with your napkin?

   A. Take it with you.

   B. Fold and place it to the left of your plate.

   C. Loosely fold it and place it on the right side.

   D. Leave it on your chair.

2. When you greet a visitor in your office, what will you do?

   A. Say nothing and let her/him sit where s/he wishes.

   B. Tell her/him where to sit.

   C. Say "Just sit anywhere."

   D. Say nothing and let her/him stand there.

3. You are invited to a reception and the invitation states "7:00 to 9:00 PM". You should _____.

   A. arrive at 7:00 PM

   B. arrive anytime between 7:00 and 9:00 PM

   C. arrive between 7:00 and 7:30 PM

   D. go early and leave early

4. You have forgotten a lunch with a business associate. You feel terrible and know he's furious. What will you do?

   A. Write a letter of apology.

B. Send flowers.

C. Keep quiet and hope he forgets about it.

D. Call and set up another appointment.

5. Your boss, Ms. Alpha, enters the room when you're meeting with an important client, Mr. Beta. You rise and say "Ms. Alpha, I'd like you to meet Mr. Beta, our client from San Diego." Is this introduction correct?

6. You're entering a cab with an important client. You position yourself so the client is seated close to the curb (人行道). Is this correct?

7. You're hosting a dinner at a restaurant. You've pre-ordered for everyone and indicated where they should sit. Are you correct?

8. Is it proper for women to apply lipstick at the table after a meal?

9. At a formal dinner party, how do you properly serve and remove the dishes and glasses?

10. What is the best way to utilize a home-office (SOHO) telephone system?

2. Case Study

Why does a minute's silence become so harsh?

My friend Richard is a Canadian teacher and he taught oral English at a Chinese university. He liked his work and enjoyed his life in China. Lately, however, he found that one of his classes is awfully quiet and seemed unwilling to respond to whatever he asked. He felt uncomfortable with the quietness and could not figure out the reason. He tried everything: reorganizing teaching plans, constantly changing topics to interest them, telling jokes to lighten up the atmosphere, etc. But nothing worked. One week in his class, when he asked a question, as usual, no one responded. He then asked again, and he got nothing but silence. Then he asked the students whether they understood the question, still, no response. The whole class remained silent for another minute until he got frustrated and walked out of the classroom.

In this case, the foreign teacher could not stand it and left the class. Why does the one-minute silence become so harsh?

Part Four

Topic-related Information

1. Introduction to the Driving Etiquette in Some Foreign Countries

Germany

On German motorways, there is no general speed limit for cars. For lorries and any other vehicles exceeding a weight of 3.5 tons, there is. This creates a problem in that it "forces" every driver to leave the right lane for the use of trucks only—disregarding the simple fact that the law requires you to drive on the right lane when you're not overtaking. The left lane, on the other hand, is strictly reserved for two kinds of people: Drivers of Mercedes, BMWs (preferably dark coloured). When you're driving a really fast car which happens to be another brand you can just about get away with using this lane if it's dark blue. If it's white, forget it. Nice, balanced, well-meaning drivers who want to introduce a speed limit (of about 100-120 km/h) or simply detest speeding usually indicate right when they see somebody approaching fast in the rear view mirror—and switch the indicator off when the other car is nearly on their trunk (without changing lanes, naturally). Of course, this is done purely as an educational measure. Incidentally, they never dare "educating" when the approaching car is a dark Mercedes or BMW.

The real trouble starts when there are only two lanes, which usually leads to frenetic honking, repeated headlight- flashing and indicating on the left lane, while the right lane lies deserted apart from the odd lonely lorry every now and then.

When you try to overtake somebody on the right lane, be careful not to exceed their speed by more than 5 mph. When in a traffic jam, always change to the lane which goes fastest. Every inch counts, and it's not your fault that everybody tries to do the same. When there's no movement on any lane, use the hard shoulder, that's what it's there for (apart from undertaking).

France

"French driving etiquette" is something of an oxymoron. On the surface, the French have some

good ideas. For instance, you can go through a red light if the way is clear, which stops a lot of frustration from sitting at an empty junction for no reason. However, most French drivers tend to amend this law in their heads to "you can go through red lights whenever you like, including when pedestrians are crossing the road having been beckoned by a little green man".

Also, on the autoroutes the speed limits are sensibly set at two different speeds for wet and dry conditions. Top speed is 130 km/h (about 85 mph). Again, drivers refuse to accept that it is ever raining, even when it is, and stick to the maximum limit at all times. Drivers rarely (read: never) indicate as they swap lanes, and aggressively cut back in when they have overtaken.

Thank-yous, via flashing headlights or waving, are rare. Save them for visually alerting other drivers how annoyed you are with them.

Ireland

It would appear that overtaking is a manoeuvre to be attempted at every opportunity: on a bend, on a hill, when the car you're overtaking is overtaking another car, into oncoming traffic, and along narrow one-way streets. It would also appear that it is compulsory to drive as fast as possible whilst attempting these, or any other manoeuvres. Unfortunately, many of the roads are not only narrow but badly surfaced, and full of drivers that never took a test. This was due to a massive waiting list in the late 1970s causing the government to issue a full licence to anyone that asked for one.

It seems the only really important thing to remember when driving around Ireland is the subtle form of greeting that is also common in rural areas of the UK (particularly in the Midlands). When one comes across a farmer traveling in the other direction on foot they will, out of politeness, raise their index finger by way of greeting. The driver should respond by raising the index finger of their right hand whilst keeping the entire hand on the steering wheel.

It is common for regular drivers who know many people in certain local areas to save time, and drive with their index finger permanently pressed to the windscreen in a continuous greeting mode.

2. Urban etiquette—New York City

At the Bar

If a lady is holding a cigarette and you are a man, it's your job to light it without disturbing her or her conversation. For this, smoker or not, you should carry a lighter, otherwise you will have to scramble for a pack of matches and, as soon as you try to light one, a wind will suddenly appear. Feel free to silently curse The Fates.

The goes-around and comes-around principle must be assumed for a night of drinks to go smoothly. This means you offer to buy a round when it's your turn and not wait to be reminded. Any members of the party not "buying their share" should be explicitly told when it's their turn, to save them any long-standing resentment their friends may carry afterwards.

Bartenders should always be tipped a dollar on every drink unless the bartender is cruel, slow or bad. If the dollar is too fixed for you, think to yourself. If I was the type to tip my friends, would he or she qualify as a friend? If so, how good a friend? Though buy-backs are recently illegal in New York, good tipping will encourage a free drink to you. If you are entertaining out-of-town guests who do not normally tip at home, do not let them get away with any feeble excuses.

At the Restaurant

It's always better to be over-dressed at a restaurant than under-dressed. For men: shorts are not acceptable, except at lunch, on vacation, in your hotel room, a million miles away from anyone you know. For women: women can generally wear whatever they wish at the table and not look like fools doing it: they can even wear hats. The jury's still out on culottes, though.

If the restaurant offers coat check, you may refuse it and hang your coat on the back of your chair. However, if you've been shopping all day and have a dozen bags, these must be checked as it's impolite to stuff them under your table and make your fellow diners jealous. If the restaurant gently insists that you check your coat, do so. Coat-check people should be tipped a dollar, regardless of whether or not they rummage around in your bags and rifle through your pockets.

A cell phone may not be used in a restaurant. Ever. If you must take a call (and that phone better has been on vibrate mode), excuse yourself and walk outside—not to the bar, not to the hall, not to the bathroom: outside. If you must place a call, you're wrong: that call isn't necessary. But if you continue in this delusion, go outside and start dialing once the door is closed. We don't care if your baby's crying, your mother's dying, or your husband set his pants on fire; we're trying to enjoy our meal, and we'd like to do so in quiet.

Women order first. If the waiter motions to the man to order before a lady, it is the man's responsibility to look down humbly. It is the lady's responsibility to order first, no matter what, unless she's formed an agreement with her partners to order last because she hasn't made up her mind. Also, if the lady disagrees with this rule, she may order whenever she wants; we are only trying to be courteous.

Asking for the check with the flourish of a hand is OK; asking for the check by barking, waving, or commandeering stray waitresses is not.

Never be talked into ordering a wine that is too expensive. Never fear asking how much the specials cost. Always take home the leftovers, whether in bag, bottle, or purse.

At the Party

If you've been invited to a party, you are likely expected to bring something: a bottle of wine, a dessert, flowers (exceptions: business parties, launch parties, book parties, or parties thrown by the obscenely wealthy who probably wouldn't want anything you can afford). Even if the host insists you should not bring something, they're lying, and they will think better of you than the other guests when you arrive with a bottle of wine, a box of chocolates, and a dozen roses.

A smart guest will consult the host on what type of wine to bring; a smarter guest will bring two bottles.

If you are a guest of someone invited, you are also expected to bring something to the party, of similar—but more expensive—nature, in order to compensate for your lack of invitation. It would also be wise to compliment the host's apartment, even if it's a dump.

If you've been invited to a dinner party—large or small—you should assume that the host expects to be hosted in return. You should submit your invitation within three weeks of the host's party, but no sooner than ten days after said party; you don't want to seem eager or unappreciative, but a conscientious good friend.

On the Street

Be mindful that others on the street are trying to get someplace—fast; and also be aware that they should assume that you're trying to get someplace—fast. This is why people on the streets of New York walk so quickly. It's the "quickly" part that aids the "fast" part. So step quickly, sirs and madams. And, please, please, no serpentining down the sidewalk.

It's impolite to broach strangers on the street and tell them how awful they look. It's also impolite to start fights with homeless people. However, it is unbelievably rude to do both at the same time, while impersonating a homeless person. This has been witnessed.

At night, if you're a man and you're walking along a street on which a woman is walking, and there is no one else around, do not walk behind her. Switch to the other side of the street and make a subtle noise—jingle change, half-whistle (but not wolf-whistle), scuff your shoes—so as to alert the female that a slightly eccentric but completely non-threatening male is within a hundred yards. By no means may you speak to her, unless this is a case of genuine true love, at which point you should speak to her. Say something witty, simple and urbane-think timeless, like "Sorry, do you have the time?"—that will allow for further conversation. However, if it's difficult to discern whether or not this is a true-love scenario, it isn't.

Hyperlinks

[1] http://www.bellaonline.com/subjects/6328.asp

[2] http://chineseculture.about.com/od/etiquette/Chinese_Etiquette.htm

[3] http://www.cyborlink.com/

References

[1] http://www.jbbjcc.cn

[2] http://www.cnwto.com.cn/2007-05-17

[3] http://www.sirc.org/publink/pub.html

[4] http://www.bremercommunications.com/Dining_Etiquette.htm

[5] http://www.ukstudentlife.com/Britain/Food/Pubs.htm

[6] http://www.nytimes.com/slideshow/2008/04/13/travel/0413-PUBS_index.html

[7] http://www.pbase.com/lindarocks/image/31486333

[8] http://www.pbase.com/lindarocks/image/31486333

[9] http://www.tysy.net/dag/bylw/2006/wenke/wyx/6.doc

Unit 7

Social Welfare

Part One

Lead-in

The road to hell is paved with good intentions.

—Samuel Johnson (Britain)

通往地狱的路上铺满善意。

——塞缪尔·约翰逊（英国）

we need child care to be affordable

Social welfare is a system that offers aids to needy persons, such as persons with low incomes, parents with dependent children, unwed mothers, the unemployed, etc. Undoubtedly, it is well-intended. However, it is not rare that good intentions result in disastrous consequences. Then, did you ever expect that welfare would cause crimes or other social problems? What is needed to be done to reform social welfare system in China?

Part Two

Reading Passages

In-Class Reading

Warm-up questions:

1. Are unwed mothers entitled to the welfare benefits from the government? Why or why not?

2. What do you think is the most important influence of a family on young children?

Welfare and Crimes

1   My name is Michael Tanner and I am the director of health and welfare studies at the Cato Institute[1]. I appreciate the opportunity to appear before the committee on an issue of extreme importance to the American people. There is no doubt that **juvenile** crime is a serious and continuing problem in this country. There are many factors contributing to the rise in juvenile violence and crime, from the **glorification** of violence in the media to the failure of the "war on drugs." But, today, I would like to focus on a factor that has received far less attention—the relationship between the welfare state and crime.

2   Last year, the Maryland NAACP released a report concluding that "the ready access to a lifetime of welfare and free social service programs is a major **contributory** factor to the crime problems we face today." Their conclusion appears to be confirmed by academic research. For example, research by Dr June O'Neill's and Anne Hill for the U.S. Department of Health and Human Services showed that a 50 percent increase in the monthly value of combined AFDC[2] and food stamp[3] benefits led to a 117 percent increase in the crime rate among young black men.

3   Welfare contributes to crime in several ways. First, children from single-parent families are more likely to become involved in criminal activity. According to one study, children raised in single-parent families are one-third more likely to exhibit anti-social behavior. Moreover, O'Neill found that, holding other **variables constant**, black children from single-parent households are twice as likely to commit crimes as black children from a family where the father is present. Nearly 70 percent of juveniles in state reform institutions come from fatherless homes, as do 43 percent of prison inmates.[4] Research indicates a direct **correlation** between crime rates and the number of single-parent families in a neighborhood.

4   As Barbara Dafoe Whitehead noted in her seminal article for *The Atlantic Monthly*: The relationship between single-parent families and crime is so strong that controlling for family **configuration** erases the relationship between race and crime and between low income and crime. This conclusion shows up time and again in the literature. The nation's mayors, as well as police officers, social workers, **probation** officers, and court officials, consistently point to family

break-up as the most important source of rising rates of crime.

5   At the same time, the evidence of a link between the availability of welfare and out-of-wedlock births is overwhelming. There have been 13 major studies of the relationship between the availability of welfare benefits and out-of-wedlock birth. Of these, 11 found a statistically significant correlation. Among the best of these studies is the work done by June O'Neill for the U.S. Department of Health and Human Services. Holding constant a wide range of variables[5], including income, education, and urban vs. suburban setting, the study found that a 50 percent increase in the value of AFDC and food stamp payments led to a 43 percent increase in the number of out-of-wedlock births. Likewise, research by Shelley Lundberg and Robert Plotnick of the University of Washington showed that an increase in welfare benefits of $200 per month per family increased the rate of out-of-wedlock births among teenagers by 150 percent.

6   The same results can be seen from welfare systems in other countries. For example, a recent study of the impact of Canada's social-welfare system on family structure concluded that "providing additional benefits to single parents encourages births of children to unwed women."

7   Of course women do not get pregnant just to get welfare benefits. It is also true that a wide array of other social factors has contributed to the growth in out-of-wedlock births. But, by removing the economic consequences of an out-of-wedlock birth, welfare has removed a major incentive to avoid such pregnancies.[6] A teenager looking around at her friends and neighbors is liable to see several who have given birth out of wedlock. When she sees that they have suffered few visible immediate consequences (the very real consequences of such behavior are often not immediately apparent), she is less inclined to modify her own behavior to prevent pregnancy.

8   Proof of this can be found in a study by Professor Ellen Freeman of the University of Pennsylvania, who surveyed black, never-pregnant females age 17 or younger. Only 40 percent of those surveyed said that they thought becoming pregnant in the next year "would make their situation worse." Likewise, a study by Professor Laurie Schwab Zabin for the Journal of Research on **Adolescence** found that: "in a sample of inner-city black teens presenting for pregnancy tests, we reported that more than 31 percent of those who elected to carry their pregnancy to term[7] told us, before their pregnancy was diagnosed, that they believed a baby would present a problem..." In other words, 69 percent either did not believe having a baby out-of-wedlock would present a problem or were unsure.

9   Until teenage girls, particularly those living in relative poverty, can be made to see real consequences from pregnancy, it will be impossible to gain control over the problem of out-of-wedlock births. By disguising those consequences, welfare makes it easier for these girls to make the decisions that will lead to unwed motherhood.

10   Current welfare policies seem to be designed with an **appalling** lack of concern for their

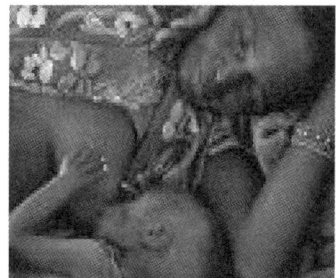

impact on out-of-wedlock births. Indeed, Medicaid[8] programs in 11 states actually provide **infertility** treatments to single women on welfare.

11   I should also point out that, once the child is born, welfare also appears to discourage the mother from marrying in the future. Research by Robert Hutchins of Cornell University shows that a 10 percent increase in AFDC benefits leads to an 8 percent decrease in the marriage rate of single mothers.

12   As welfare contributes to the rise in **out-of-wedlock** births and single-parent families, it **concomitantly** contributes to the associated increase in criminal activity.

13   Secondly, welfare leads to increased crime by contributing to the **marginalization** of young black men in society. There are certainly many factors contributing to the increasing **alienation** and marginalization of young black men, including racism, poverty, and the failure of our educational system. However, welfare contributes as well. The welfare culture tells the man he is not a necessary part of the family. They are in effect **cuckolded** by the state.[9] Their role of father and breadwinner is **supplanted** by the welfare check.

14   The role of marriage and family as a civilizing influence[10] on young men has long been discussed. Whether or not strict **causation** can be proven, it is certainly true that **unwed** fathers are more likely to use drugs and become involved in criminal behavior.[11] Indeed, single men are five times more likely to commit violent crimes than married men.

15   Finally, in areas where there is a high concentration of welfare, there may be an almost total lack of male role models. This can lead to crime in two ways. First, as the Maryland NAACP puts it, "A child whose parents draw a welfare check without going to work does not understand that in this society at least one parent is expected to rise five days of each week to go to some type of job."

16   Second, boys growing up in mother-only families naturally seek male influences. Unfortunately, in many inner-city neighborhoods, those male role models may not exist. As George Gilder, author of *Wealth and Poverty*, has noted, the typical inner-city today is "almost a **matriarchy**. The women receive all the income, dominate the social-worker classes, and most of the schools." Thus, the boy in search of male guidance and companionship may end up in the company of gangs or other undesirable influences.

17   Given all of the above, I believe it is clear that our current social welfare system is a significant cause of juvenile crime and violence in America today. Exactly how welfare should be reformed is undoubtedly beyond the scope of this **hearing**. The Cato Institute's position, however, is well known. Our research indicates that the current federal welfare system cannot be reformed. Accordingly, we have suggested that federal funding of welfare should be ended and responsibility for charity should be shifted first to the states and eventually to the private sectors.

18   In conclusion, let me simply say that, whatever Congress eventually decides to do in the way of welfare reform, I hope that you will recognize the disastrous consequences of our current welfare system. The status quo[12] is plainly and simply unacceptable. The relationship between our

failed social welfare system and juvenile violence and crime is one more urgent reason for reform.

New Words and Expressions

adolescence	*n.*	the period of physical and psychological development from the onset of puberty to maturity 青春期，从青春发育期到成熟期的一段生理与心理的发展阶段
alienation	*n.*	the act of making sb. feel that they do not belong in a particular group 离间
appalling	*a.*	shocking 令人震惊的
causation	*n.*	the process of one event causing or producing another event 诱因，起因
cuckold	*v.*	make a man a person whose wife has sex with another man 使某人妻子不贞
concomitantly	*ad.*	happening at the same time as sth. else, especially because one thing is related to or causes the other 同时发生地，伴随地
configuration	*n.*	an arrangement of the parts of sth. or a group of things; the form or shape that this arrangement produces 结构，构造，格局
constant	*a.*	unchanging in nature, value, or extent; invariable 永恒的；在性质、价值、范围上持久不变的
contributory	*a.*	helping to bring about a result 有助于促成某一结果的
correlation	*n.*	a causal, complementary, parallel, or reciprocal relationship, especially a structural, functional, or qualitative correspondence between two comparable entities 相互关联；一种互为因果的、互相补充的、平行或互惠的关系，尤指结构上、功能上、数量上两个可比方面之间的相应关系
glorification	*n.*	the act of giving glory, honor, or high praise to 颂扬
hearing	*n.*	an official meeting at which the facts about a crime, complaint, etc. are presented to the person or group of people who will have to decide what action to take 审讯，听审；听证会
infertility	*n.*	the persistent inability to conceive a child 不孕，不育
juvenile	*a.*	of, relating to, characteristic of, intended for, or appropriate for children or young people 青少年的
marginalization	*n.*	the act of making sb. feel as if they are not important and can not influence decisions or events or to put sb. in a position in which they have no power 被忽视；被排斥
matriarchy	*n.*	a social system that gives power and authority to women rather than men 母权制，母系社会

out-of-wedlock   *a.*   of parents not legally married to each other 私生的，父母不是合法地结合在一起的

probation   *n.*   a process or period in which a person's fitness, as for membership in a working or social group, is tested 检验期，检验某人是否适于做某事或加入某工作或社会团体的过程或时期

supplant   *v.*   to take the place of 取代，替代

unwed   *a.*   not married 未婚的

variable   *n.*   a situation, number or quantity that can vary or be varied 可变情况；变量

Proper Names

Maryland   马里兰州(美国中部偏东的一个州，1788 年成为最早的十三个殖民地之一)

NAACP   National Association for the Advancement of Colored People (美国)全国有色人种协进会

the U.S. Department of Health and Human Services   美国健康和人类服务部

The Atlantic Monthly   《大西洋月刊》

Notes

1. the Cato Institute: 卡图研究所

   The Cato Institute was founded in 1977 by Edward H. Crane. It is a non-profit public policy research foundation headquartered in Washington, D.C. The Cato Institute seeks to broaden the parameters of public policy debate to allow consideration of the traditional American principles of limited government, individual liberty, free markets and peace.

2. **AFDC: Aid to Families with Dependent Children** (对需要抚养孩子的家庭的资助) was the name of a federal assistance program in effect from 1935 to 1997, which was administered by the United States Department of Health and Human Services. This program provided financial assistance to children whose families had low or no income.

3. **food stamp:** a stamp or coupon, issued by the government to persons with low incomes, that can be redeemed for food at stores. 食物券(由政府发放给低收入者的票或券，可以在商店中换取食物)

4. Nearly 70 percent of juveniles in state reform institutions come from fatherless homes, as do 43 percent of prison inmates. 此句大意为：在国家罪犯改造机构中，70%的年轻人来自没有父亲的家庭，而因犯罪进监狱的年轻人中有 43%同样来自没有父亲的单亲家庭。

5. Holding constant a wide range of variables… 这是一个现在分词短语，在整个句子中作状语。这个短语中，a wide range of variables 是动词 hold 的宾语，而 constant 是 a wide range of variables 的宾语补足语，这一补足语被提前了。该短语的意思是：在维持许多可变量不变的情况下

6. But, by removing the economic consequences of an out-of-wedlock birth, welfare has removed a major incentive to avoid such pregnancies. 此句大意为：可是福利制度解决了抚养非婚生子女经济上的后顾之忧，这样一来人们就更加不用顾及未婚生子了。

7. carry their pregnancy to term: 怀孕直到孩子满月生下来

8. **Medicaid**: a program in the United States, jointly funded by the states and the federal government, that reimburses hospitals and physicians for providing care to qualifying people who cannot finance their own medical expenses 医疗补助计划——美国的一项由国家和联邦政府联合拨款方案，替负担不起自己医疗费用的人向医院和医生支付费用

9. They are in effect cuckolded by the state. 此句的字面意思说他们实际上让政府给戴了绿帽子。作者在这里想要表明：实际上是政府的福利制度使他们失去了作为丈夫、作为家庭经济支柱这样的角色。

10. a civilizing influence: 使人变得文明的影响力

11. Whether or not strict causation can be proven, it is certainly true that unwed fathers are more likely to use drugs and become involved in criminal behavior. 此句大意为：不管严格的因果关系能否被证实，有一点是千真万确的，那就是未婚爸爸更容易吸毒和参与犯罪活动。

12. status quo: 现状

● **Reading Comprehension**

1. Directions: *Discuss the following questions with your classmates.*

　1) According to the article, what factors can lead to the increase in juvenile violence and crimes?

　2) What is the relationship between crimes and single-parent families?

　3) What undesirable consequences do the welfare benefits bring to out-of-wedlock births?

　4) How come that the welfare can lead to the growth in out-of-wedlock births?

　5) How does welfare cause alienation and marginalization?

　6) Can marriage and family help young men keep away from drugs and crimes?

　7) What problems will boys growing in mother-only families have?

　8) What's wrong with the current social welfare system in America?

2. Directions: *Read the whole article again and summarize the undesirable consequences of welfare benefits.*

The current welfare system in America leads to more crimes by contributing to:

　1) _____;

　2) _____;

　3) _____;

　4) _____.

● **Discussion**

1. Discuss with your classmates about the living situation of unwed mothers in China. What's the

attitude of our society towards unwed mothers? Do you think China should also make a welfare system to aid unwed mothers? If so, what should the welfare system be like?

2. What's the importance of male models to the growth of children? Could you show some examples?

After-Class Reading

Passage One

Warm-up questions:

1. What do you know about the birth rate of Western countries?

2. Can you compare the birth rate of China with that of Western countries?

Should Governments Subsidize Child Care and Work Leaves?

1　Germany and the United States, among many other countries, have been criticized for not having the extensive system of benefits to parents who have children found throughout Scandinavia and some other countries[1]. For example, the Swedish government not only heavily subsidizes day care activities for young children with working mothers, but also allows up to eighteen months of paid leave to care for a newborn child. These benefits are open to both mothers and fathers, but mothers take practically all leaves. Benefits almost fully compensate for the loss in earnings during the first 12 months of leave, while they offset more than half of earnings during the next 6 months of leave. Also companies have to take their employees back at comparable jobs when they decide to return to work from a child leave.

2　The many advocates of a Swedish-type childcare system believe it permits mothers of young children to work while guaranteeing that their children have adequate childcare at government-run facilities. At the same time, it allows mothers to care for their young children without losing their jobs. In addition, these subsidies tend to encourage families to have more children since they reduce the cost of having and raising children.

3　Despite these claims, I believe it would be a mistake for the U.S., Germany, or other countries to emulate the Swedish approach. For starters, middle class and rich families can pay for their own childcare services for young children, such as preschool programs, whether or not the mothers are working. In fact, the majority of such families in the United States do send their young children to day care programs. It is much more efficient to have better off families buy childcare services in a private competitive market than to spend tax revenue on preschool government-run programs for the children of these families. The Swedish childcare system was insightfully criticized along these lines in a controversial but I believe correct analysis[2] by my late[3] colleague Sherwin Rosen (see "Public Employment, Taxes and the Welfare State in Sweden", NBER Working Papers 5003, 1995).

4　It could make sense to subsidize the preschool activities of children of poor families since these children may well receive inadequate care without such subsidies. The U.S. takes this approach by only subsidizing preschool care of low-income families. These subsidies appropriately take the form of a voucher system[4] rather than government-run pre-school programs. Poor families are in essence given vouchers each month that they can spend on any approved private day care program for young children. The market is highly competitive and I believe works well, although there are few careful evaluations of this system. Still, I believe it provides an example of how a voucher system might work for older children in school.

5　The case is also weak for following Sweden[5] by providing all women who work with generous and lengthy government-financed paid leaves. The U.S. does not have this system, yet many working women leave their jobs at least temporarily, or work part time, in order to care for their children. The vast majority of parents are very concerned about the well-being of their children, and give that a lot of weight when deciding whether to care for them rather than using preschool programs and other outside help.

6　Government–financed payments to working mothers who take a leave of absence to care for their young children subsidizes women who work compared to women who decide to stay home fulltime to care for children and engage in other activities[6]. It is still controversial whether there is a significant benefit to children from having mothers who stay home to care for them instead of having mothers who work, and care for their children (perhaps more intensely) only before and after work and on weekends. On the whole, I believe that work decisions are best left to parents without government subsidies or other government involvement.

7　Generous government childcare and work benefits for families with young children are advocated sometimes because they promote larger families. European and some Asian countries are particularly receptive to this argument since their birth rates are so low that their populations would begin to decline soon unless births increased a lot, or they accepted large numbers of immigrants[7]. Yet while the Swedish total fertility rate is quite a bit above that of Germany, Italy, and some other European nations, it is still too low to prevent its population from declining in the near future, despite the world's most generous system of work and child care benefits for families with young children.

8　This may be because the Swedish-type system promotes larger families in an indirect and inefficient manner. The most direct and best way to encourage births, if that is the goal[8], is to provide monthly allowances to families that have an additional child. Subsidizing births directly encourages larger families without mainly targeting women who work, or women who value childcare services a lot. Moreover, since the vast majority of families even in Europe have at least one child without government subsidies, an efficient family allowance program should concentrate

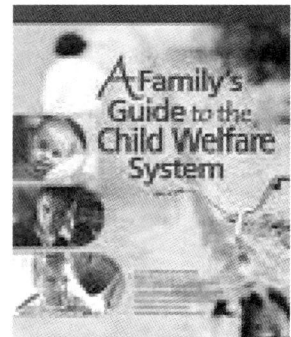

subsidies on the marginal fertility decision; that is, on second, third, or higher order births that may not happen without subsidies.

9   France has an extensive and complicated system of direct allowances mainly to families that have more than one child. The best study of the effects of this program (see Laroque, Guy & Salanié, Bernard, 2005, "Does Fertility Respond to Financial Incentives?" CEPR Discussion Papers, 5007) shows that it has had a significant effect in raising French birth rate to among the highest in Western Europe, although other factors are also important. However, the system is expensive, and the French total fertility rate is still considerably below its replacement level.

10   The U.S. does not apparently need any stimulation to family size since its total fertility rate is the highest of any developed country, and it is even above that of many much poorer countries, like China or South Korea. The case for general subsidies to childcare and for work leaves to employees with young children is also weak. So I believe that present American policy in these areas is much better than the Swedish approach, and does not need drastic changes.

—Gary Becker and Richard Posner

Proper Name

Scandinavia   斯堪的纳维亚(半岛) (瑞典、挪威、丹麦、冰岛的泛称)

Notes

1. Germany and the United States, among many other countries, have been criticized for not having the extensive system of benefits to parents who have children found throughout Scandinavia and some other countries. 此句大意为：和其他许多国家一样，德国和美国一直因为没有像斯堪的纳维亚半岛以及其他一些国家一样给予有孩子的父母广泛的福利体制而受到批评。

2. in a controversial but I believe correct analysis: 在这个短语中，controversial 和 correct 都是 analysis 的修饰语，but I believe 是插入语。

3. late: 已故的

4. **voucher system:** 票券制度

   It was 50 years ago when the economist Milton Friedman proposed a voucher system to improve American education. Some American children get a private education paid for with public money. School choice programs let parents move their child out of a failing public school. The parents can choose a private school and pay for it with a government payment "voucher". Today about 36,000 students are served by vouchers.

5. The case is also weak for following Sweden… 该句中的 following 是动词 follow 的分词形式，意为"跟随，遵循"。

6. Government–financed payments to working mothers who take a leave of absence to care for their young children subsidizes women who work compared to women who decide to stay home fulltime to care for children and engage in other activities. 此句大意为：政府只对那些暂时请假

照顾孩子的有工作的母亲发薪水,而不会资助那些留在家里全职照顾孩子、料理家事的母亲。

7. European and some Asian countries are particularly receptive to this argument since their birthrates are so low that their populations would begin to decline soon unless births increased a lot, or they accepted large numbers of immigrants. 该句大意为:欧洲和一些亚洲国家特别能接受这一论点,因为其出生率太低了。除非出生率能快速增长,或者接纳大量的移民,否则这些国家的人口数量会急速下降。

8. if that is the goal 是插入语,不作句子的任何成分,意为"如果这是目标的话"。

● **Reading Comprehension**

1. **Directions:** *Read the article carefully; try to answer the following questions.*

    1) What is the Swedish-type childcare system?

    2) Why does the author believe it would be a mistake for the U.S., Germany or other countries to emulate the Swedish approach?

    3) How does the U.S. subsidize child care?

    4) What is the most direct and best way to encourage births?

    5) How will you describe French allowance system?

2. **Directions:** *Read the following statements carefully, and decide whether they are true (T) or false (F) according to the text.*

    _____ 1) The Swedish government not only heavily subsidizes day care activities, but also allows eighteen months of paid leave.

    _____ 2) More families will have more children in Sweden since the cost of having and raising children is reduced.

    _____ 3) The U.S. government subsidizes preschool care of all families.

    _____ 4) The U.S. does not provide women who work with government financed paid leave, because all children are sent to private day care center.

    _____ 5) It is still not certain whether there is a significant benefit for children whose mothers stay home to care for them.

    _____ 6) Since the Swedish total fertility rate is quite a bit above that of other European nations, its population will not decline.

    _____ 7) Swedish-type system does not promote larger families in a direct and efficient way.

    _____ 8) Swedish-type childcare system is not suitable for America.

Passage Two

Warm-up questions:

1. Do you know any Chinese welfare program(s)?

2. What kind of welfare program are you concerned about most?

The Dynamics of Chinese Welfare Reforms

1   Responding to the changing socio-economic contexts of the reform period, the CCP embarked on extensive welfare reforms which came in the form of a series of social insurance programs covering a range of contingencies, e.g. old age, unemployment, illness, work injury and maternity leave. All these programs are now under the overall responsibility of the recently established Chinese Ministry of Labor and Social Security (MOLSS), although in practice they may be administered at or below the provincial level. So far the schemes that have received most attention are old-age insurance and unemployment insurance; while health care, work injury and maternity insurance schemes are on the agenda as well. We shall first look through these highly profiled social insurance schemes, then examine the newly emerging patterns of Chinese social welfare using welfare-state concepts and topics arising from a Western framework before we go on to compare them with those in East Asian capitalist societies.

Old-age Insurance[1]

2   As we have noted earlier, under the labor insurance system established in the 1950s, urban work units provided retirement pensions to their workers, and each work unit was responsible for funding its own pension expenditures. Owing to the reform period emphasis on enterprise efficiency, the government has argued the need to relieve the pension burden on enterprises. Initiated in 1984, the Old-age Insurance System Reform was designed to divide the burden of pension costs among employees and various kinds of enterprises. The Reform obligated urban workers for the first time to contribute directly to pension funds run by local governments. It also aimed to pool pensions among enterprises of different kinds in state-run pension funds, so that pension costs could be distributed more evenly among old enterprises that have many retirees and new enterprises that have fewer. Employees' pensions were to be paid from the fund, rather than by the enterprise itself.

3   In 1991, the State Council proposed a three-tier retirement insurance system for employees in urban enterprises, with the *basic* retirement program managed by the state, *supplementary* retirement programs funded by enterprises, and *individual savings* retirement programs chosen by each employee. The three-tier arrangement has been hailed by the Chinese government as a means to diversify pension finance, enhance the pooling of risk[2], and encourage individual enthusiasm. Estimates suggest that currently employers contribute around 20 percent of the wage bill for pension insurance and employees contribute 4 percent. State contributions are made via tax breaks on employee pension contributions and via financial support to enterprises unable to fulfill their

pension fund obligations.

4   The 1991 proposal also called for changing unified financing programs from the city and county to the provincial level. It included enterprises with different forms of ownership—state, collective, private, individual and foreign-funded enterprises[3]—to provide pension coverage for all urban employees. It continued to exclude, however, those classified as rural enterprises, such as the TVEs[4]. In 1997, the government adopted a Decision on Establishing a Uniform Basic Old-age Insurance System for Enterprise Employees. According to a white paper[5] released by the Information Office of the State Council, employees participating in the old-age insurance program had increased from 86.71 million in late 1997 to 108.02 million by the end of 2001. The number of those enjoying basic old-age pension has also increased from 25.33 million to 33.81 million.

Unemployment Pension[6]

5   Because of the full employment policy of the Mao era, no unemployment insurance existed prior to the mid-1980s. In 1986, unemployment insurance was introduced, initially to state-owned enterprises. The scheme aimed primarily to facilitate enterprise reform and promote labor mobility by providing a safety net for workers made redundant. Official estimates suggested that by the end of 1998, the number of persons participating in the scheme reached 79.3 million, and the number of those who were granted unemployment benefits was almost 1.6 million. In 1999, the State Council announced Unemployment Insurance Regulation. Under the new scheme, enterprises pay 1 percent of their total wage bill to an unemployment insurance fund, and employees contribute 2 percent of their wage. The new scheme also extends unemployment coverage to collective enterprises, and in some areas to private and foreign-funded enterprises. So far, the new unemployment insurance scheme has been introduced in 24 provinces and provincial level cities. According to official estimates, 98.0 million workers across the country were participating in the scheme by the end of 1999, and the unemployment insurance fund accumulated 11.0 billion *yuan* or 1.3 billion U.S. dollars. However, still many fall through this safety net, especially the rural migrants[7] and those who are not registered as unemployed such as the laid-off workers.

Medical Insurance[8]

6   Prior to the reform period, urban workers and their dependents received comprehensive health-care coverage from their work unit. The enterprise reform as well as the changes in urban demographics led the government to reform the urban medical insurance system. Trial reforms have focused on pooling enterprise contributions and creating individual employee accounts. In the city of Zhenjiang, for example, enterprises pay the equivalent of 10 percent of an employee's gross

wage to a fund, of which 50 percent goes into an individual account in the worker's name. Employees contribute 1 percent of their total annual pay to their individual accounts. Employees' medical expenses are first paid from the individual accounts and then by the individuals themselves. However, after self-paid expenses exceed 5 percent of annual income, they are paid from the social fund.

7   Similar to old-age insurance and unemployment insurance, newer and wealthier enterprises are often reluctant to participate. Despite this, the State Council issued the Decision on Establishing the Basic Medical Insurance System for Urban Employees, which aimed to set up a basic medical insurance system throughout China by 1999. Estimates suggested that by the end of 2001, 97 percent of prefectures and cities had started such reforms programs, and 76.3 million employees had participated in basic medical insurance programs.

Work Injury Insurance[9]

8   Work insurance was stipulated in the 1951 Labor Insurance Regulations. Like other forms of insurance, it exerted huge financial pressure on public enterprises. Since the late 1980s, reforms have been introduced with the aim of pooling contributions and setting up individual accounts. According to official estimates, by the end of 2001, the national average rate of industrial insurance premium had been about 1 percent, and over 43.45 million employees were covered by the industrial injury insurance scheme.

Maternity Insurance[10]

9   According to the 1951 Labor Insurance Regulations, women in public enterprises were entitled to 56 days paid maternity leave, and hospital treatments were paid by their employers as well. In 1988, new regulations extended the paid maternity leave to 90 days. In 1995, the former Chinese Ministry of Labor issued Provisional Measures for Enterprise Maternity Insurance. Under these rules, all urban enterprises are required to contribute to maternity insurance fund, while individuals do not make contributions. According to official estimates, by the end of 2001, the national average maternity insurance expense rate had been 0.7 percent, with 34.55 million employees covered by the scheme.

Social Relief[11]

10   As we have noted earlier, the social welfare in pre-reform China was supplemented by a system of social relief targeting at those who fall outside the workplace-based social insurance system. The primary recipients were disabled and elderly people and orphaned children. Since the economic reforms, unemployment and inflation have created greater income inequalities. In response, the government is broadening the scope of social relief provision. In the urban areas, the government is trying out a minimum living standard security system. Introduced in Shanghai in

1993, the minimum living standard scheme has been expanding rapidly to cities and towns throughout the country. It is reported that in 2001, there were 11.7 million urban residents nationwide drawing the minimum allowance, whereas in the first half of 2003, the figure increased to 21.8 million. The average drawing per person per month was 55 *yuan* or 6.6 U.S. dollars, though it varied enormously from region to region.

11   An old-age insurance system similar to that in the cities is being set up in the rural area. But rural relief payments are much lower than urban payments and have risen much more slowly than urban relief spending as well.

Proper Names

CCP (=Chinese Communist Party) (缩写)中国共产党

Chinese Ministry of Labor and Social Security (MOLSS) 中国劳动和社会保障部

State Council 国务院

Decision on Establishing a Uniform Basic Old-age Insurance System for Enterprise Employees 关于统一建立企事业单位职工基础养老保险体制的决定

Information Office of the State Council 国务院新闻办公室(国新办)

Zhenjiang 镇江市(位于中国江苏省)

Chinese Ministry of Labor 中国劳动部(中国劳动和社会保障部的前身)

Notes

1. **old-age insurance:** 养老保险

2. the pooling of risk: 风险共担

3. **state, collective, private, individual and foreign-funded enterprises:** 国有、集体、私人、个体以及外资企业

4. **TVE:** town or village enterprise (缩写)乡镇企业

5. **white paper:** 白皮书(政府部门关于某一问题的官方报告)

6. **unemployment pension:** 失业救济金

7. **rural migrant:** 农民工

8. **medical insurance:** 医疗保险

9. **work injury insurance:** 工伤抚恤金

10. **maternity insurance:** 生育保险

11. **social relief:** 社会救济

●Reading Comprehension

1. Directions: *Study the following table and fill in the missing information based on Paragraphs 2-5.*

Year	Social Insurance Program	Content	Aim	Disadvantage
1950s	Labor insurance system	Urban work units provided retirement pensions to their workers.		1)
1984	Old-age Insurance System Reform	Urban workers should contribute to pension funds run by local governments.	2)	
1991	3)	Managed by the state, supplementary retirement programs funded by enterprises, and individual savings retirement programs chosen by each employee.	Diversify pension finance, enhance the pooling of risk, and encourage individual enthusiasm.	4)
5)	No unemployment insurance existed			
1986	Unemployment insurance	Introduced initially to state-owned enterprises.	6)	
1999	7)	Enterprises pay 1% of their total wage bill to an unemployment insurance fund, and employees contribute 2% of their wage.		8)

2. Directions: *Read the following statements carefully, and decide whether they are true (T) or false (F) according to the text.*

_____ 1) The CCP launched extensive welfare reforms, but excluded health care, work injury and maternity insurance.

_____ 2) The number of people who benefited from the Decision on Establishing the Old-age Insurance System in late 1997 to the end of 2001 had increased considerably.

_____ 3) Under the Provisional Measures for Enterprise Maternity Insurance, all urban enterprises as well as individuals are required to contribute to maternity insurance fund.

_____ 4) Trial reforms of medical insurance have focused on social fund, enterprise contributions and individual employees' gross wage.

_____ 5) Because of economic reforms, unemployment and inflation, the scope of social relief recipients is broadened.

Part Three

Topic-related Activities

1. Which Is the Best One?

Step One

Directions: *Before class, work in groups of 4 or 5 to find out the child care system in a country you are interested in. You can surf the net or consult some encyclopedia from the library.*

Step Two

Directions: *Choose one student from each group to present the country's system. Please explain the system as clearly as possible.*

Step Three

Directions: *After all the group finish their presentations, students in the whole class can choose their favorite child care system by writing the country's name on the paper. Finally the one that gets the most votes will be the best one.*

2. The More Information the Better!

Step One

Directions: *"Railroad Retirement System", "Food Stamp Program", "Earned Income Tax Credit" are programs among the complicated social security system of U.S. Do you know any details of these programs? Do you know any other welfare programs? Go to the internet or the library to find as much information about as many programs as you can.*

Step Two

Directions: *Discuss with your group members about your findings and compare all the programs in your group to find out the most beneficial or meaningful program. Then, one of your group members presents this program to the whole class.*

3. Case Study

Chinanews, Zhengzhou, Mar. 29—Zhang Yingmei, a 24-year-old student from Anyang Normal College of Henan Province recently called for designing November 1 as International Single Parent Day, and appealed to people to take care of children raised by single parents. Zhang herself is from a single-parent family.

According to Henan Business News, Zhang was a fashionable lady, wearing red boots and a yellow jacket. She told our reporter that she had launched activities aiming to commemorate single parents in the past two years.

"I had a happy family in the past, but my life became miserable after my parents got divorced," she said. Zhang revealed that she was born in Baimasi County in Luoyang, Henan Province. She was forced to live with her grandparents in the countryside because her parents quarreled every day. In Zhang's memory, her father had come to see her only two or three times, which made her often think he was her "uncle." After her father remarried, she never met him again. Nobody mentioned him ever since.

Because she was from a single-parent family, Zhang was often laughed at by her classmates, and was insulted by a man from the same county.

Zhang also finds that children from single-parent families are stubborn and lonely, and she believes that, if a special commemorative day is devoted to them and their families, things may turn better.

Questions

1. Will you support Zhang Yingmei? Why or why not?
2. What do you think our society and government should do to aid the single-parent children and their families?

Part Four

Topic-related Information

1. Baby Bonus and Childcare in Different Countries

Canada

A baby bonus was introduced in Canada following the Second World War. A family allowance scheme known as the "baby bonus" made regular monthly payments of $5 to $8 to all parents of children under 16. In 1988, the Quebec government introduced the Allowance for Newborn Children that paid up to $8,000 to a family after the birth of a child.

Maternity benefits for working mothers and parents remain the responsibility of the federal government. Canada's Employment Insurance (EI) gives paid maternity leave for 15 weeks, and only a birth mother is eligible to receive these benefits. Even surrogate mothers, or those whose babies do not survive, may apply. Parental benefits are paid for 35 weeks, and partners and adoptive parents may receive these benefits as well. If parents share benefits, the total between them may not exceed 50 weeks. In addition, there is a 2-week waiting period on the shared claim, so the total time away from work is 52 weeks.

Singapore

The Child Development Co-Savings Scheme (more commonly known as the Baby Bonus) was first introduced in

Singapore in April 2001, with enhancements made in August 2004 and August 2008. The objective of this scheme is to improve on the country's fertility rate by providing cash incentives, with the hope of reducing the financial burden of raising children and thereby encouraging them to have more children. The cash payouts are S$4,000 each for the first and second child, and S$6,000 each for the third and fourth child. Under the scheme, the Singapore government also contributes a dollar for a dollar matching the amount of savings that parents contribute to their child's savings in the Children Development Account (CDA) (savings in this account may be used for educational or medical-related expenses for the child up to the age of 6), which is capped at S$6,000 each for the first and second child, and S$12,000 each for the third and fourth child, and S$18,000 each for the fifth and subsequent child.

Spain

Spain has launched a financial incentive scheme to encourage families to have more children, becoming the latest in a list of countries employing such a tactic to boost population numbers. The family of every child born in Spain will get 2,500 euros to help raise the country's low birth rate and support the fast-growing economy.

Baby-related schemes offer paid maternity leave for six weeks before and 10 weeks after childbirth, at a maximum of 80 percent of earnings, for the first and second child. For a third child, it is eight weeks before and 18 weeks after childbirth. French fathers also get time off. Paternity leave extends to 14 days of paid leave and to 21 days in the case of multiple births.

Germany

The "Elterngeld" or "parent money" program in Germany allows an adult who stops work after a child is born to continue to claim two-thirds of their net wage, up to a maximum €2,000 per month. Low earners can claim 100 percent compensation for lost wages. One parent can claim for up to 12 months; if both parents take a turn, they can claim the benefit for a total of 14 months—a program designed to encourage more fathers to help.

The United Kingdom

Britain introduced a so-called "baby bonds" scheme in 2004, giving a €500-voucher to every newborn to start a trust fund.

The government of the United Kingdom has taken some significantly proactive steps when it comes to the maternity rights of mothers. As of 2007, a mum has the ability to take 39 weeks of work with pay

following the birth of a baby. At the conclusion of this time period a mum has the right to go back to work at the same or comparable position. Moreover, if a mother so desires, she can take additional time of 13 more weeks off for maternity leave without jeopardizing her job. However, this additional time will be without pay. If a mum is self-employed, she may qualify for maternity leave which is paid directly to her by the government.

The United States

The United States is one of four countries in the world (of 168 countries surveyed) that do not have national policies for maternity leave. The other three are Lesotho (莱索托), Swaziland (斯威士兰), and Papua New Guinea (巴布亚新几内亚). Currently, the only law that is national is the Family and Medical Leave Act. This law allows for up to 12 weeks in any 12 month period for the birth or adoption of a child, the care of a family member with a serious medical condition, or to treat a medical condition of the employee.

China

The maternity leave of female staff and workers shall be ninety (90) days, including fifteen (15) days of antenatal leave. An extra maternity leave of fifteen (15) days shall be granted in case of dystocia (难产). Female staff and workers who have borne more than one child in a single birth shall be granted an extra maternity leave of fifteen (15) days for each additional baby borne.

Female staff and workers who have a miscarriage (流产) shall be granted a certain period of maternity leave by the units employing them according to a certificate from a medical department.

2. Do You Know?

In the USA, there are about 10.4 million single-mother families.

In the United Kingdom, the number is around 1.9 million.

Japan has about 1.1 million single moms.

In Canada, there are 550,000 single-mother families.

And in Australia, there are 500, 000 single-mother families.

One out of every two children in the U.S. will live in a single-parent family at some time before they reach the age 18.

Since 2001 31% of babies born in Australia were born to unmarried mothers.

In the UK, 86% of single parents are white and 9% are single fathers.

According to the Chinese Ministry of Civil Affairs, nearly 1.2 million Chinese couples were divorced in 2002, an average 3,225 couples a day.

3. Europe, East and West, Wrestles with Falling Birthrates

Birthrates have reached a historic and prolonged low in European countries, from Italy and Germany to Poland and the Czech Republic, straining pension plans and depleting the work force across the Continent. The number of elderly already exceeds the number of young people in many countries, and the European Union's executive arm, alarmed by the trend, estimates that the bloc will have a shortfall of 20 million workers by 2030 if the low birthrates persist. Immigration from non-European countries, already highly contentious across the EU, would not be sufficient to fill the gap even if Europe's relatively homogenous countries were willing to embrace millions of foreign newcomers.

1) Factors Contributing to the Decline of Fertility across Europe

a. Greater educational and professional opportunities for women have provided an alternative to motherhood and encouraged some to delay having children, at times until it is too late.

b. The average age for having a first child has risen sharply in the last 20 years, from the early 20s to around 30s in many countries. With that delay, grandmothers, the traditional caregivers in much of southern Europe, may be too old to help out, especially for a second child.

c. The widespread availability and use of contraceptives turned childbearing into a conscious choice rather than an act of nature. The legalization of abortion in many countries has had a similar effect.

d. The marketplace, meanwhile, has provided many new costs and temptations: mortgages to buy apartments, vacations, malls with Benetton.

e. Like many countries in Europe, the Czech Republic provides for long maternity leaves, generally three years, so that mothers can take care of young children. But low payments—even though recently doubled to about €230 a month—do not go far and are unrelated to previous income, and the long hiatus makes it harder for women to re-enter the work force.

2) Results

Birthrates are the lowest in the world—and the lowest sustained rates in history: 1.2 per woman in the Czech Republic, Slovenia, Latvia and Poland, far below the rate of 2.1 needed to maintain population. West European countries are also suffering: Greece, Italy and Spain have had rates of 1.3 and under for a decade. But Eastern Europe is faced with a desperate double whammy: plummeting birthrates combined with emigration to Western Europe for work, made easier by membership in the EU.

In 1990, no European country had a fertility rate less than 1.3; by 2002, there were 1.5, with six more below 1.4. No European country is maintaining its population through births, and only France—with a rate of 1.8—has the potential to do so, according to a recent report from the Organization for Economic Cooperation and Development.

3) Some Approaches

In an attempt to turn the tide, the Czech Parliament voted unanimously this year to double the payment given to women on maternity leave to encourage new births. To maintain the country's work force, the Czech Labor Ministry several years ago set up a program to encourage emigration from Bulgaria, Croatia, Kazakhstan and Ukraine, although so far with limited results.

France has long encouraged larger families through incentives, from direct per-child payments to allocations for clothing and school supplies, and it recently offered women €750, or $960, a month for a year if they had a third child. Austrian women have been offered €450 a month for three years for a first birth.

Hyperlinks

[1] http://www.centrelink.gov.au/internet/internet.nsf/payments/maternity.htm

[2] http://www.babybonus.gov.sg/bbss/html/index.html

[3] http://en.wikipedia.org/wiki/Parental_leave

[4] http://www.world-psi.org/TemplateEn.cfm?Section=Maternity_protection&CONTENTFILEID=
5394&TEMPLATE=/ContentManagement/ContentDisplay.cfm

References

[1] http://www.becker-posner-blog.com/archives/2005/10/should_governme.html

[2] http://www.crazyenglish.org/xinwen/zuixinbaodao/20070914/12714.html

[3] http://www.siis.org.cn

[4] Social Welfare. The Columbia Encyclopedia, 6th ed. Columbia University Press, 2007

[5] https://www.babybonus.gov.sg/bbss/html/index.html

[6] http://en.wikipedia.org/wiki/Baby_Bonus

[7] http://www.babybonus.com.au/

[8] http://www.iwpr.org/pdf/parentalleaveA131.pdf

[9] http://en.wikipedia.org/wiki/Parental_leave

[10] http://www.cato.org/testimony/ct-wc67.html

Unit 8

Work

Part One

Lead-in

Every man's work, whether it be literature, or music or pictures or architecture or anything else, is always a portrait of himself.

——Samuel Butler (American educator)

每个人的工作，不管是文学、音乐、美术、建筑
还是其他工作，都是自己的一幅画像。

——塞缪尔·巴特勒（美国教育家）

People's attitude towards work has been changing as time goes by. Some people live to work. They devote themselves to their work. The aim for which they work is to realize the value of life. On the contrary, other people work to live. They regard work as a way of making a living. Good life is an assurance of smooth work. Only when we realize this can we live happily and work well.

Part Two
Reading Passages

In-Class Reading

Warm-up questions:

1. What factors are taken into consideration when you choose a job?

2. Do you think that there are any differences in work attitude between you and your parents?

What Gen Y Really Wants

1   With 85 million baby boomers[1] and 50 million Gen Xers[2], there is already a **yawning** generation gap among American workers—particularly in their ideas of work-life balance. For baby boomers, it's the **juggling act** between job and family. For Gen X, it means moving in and out of the workforce to accommodate kids and outside interests. Now along come the 76 million members of Generation Y.[3] For these new 20-something workers, the line between work and home doesn't really exist. They just want to spend their time in meaningful and useful ways, no matter where they are.

2   The first challenge for the companies that want to hire the best young workers is getting them in the door. They are in high demand—the baby boomers are retiring, and many Gen X workers are **opting out of** long hours—and they have high expectations for personal growth, even in entry-level jobs. More than half of Generation Y's new graduates move back to their parents' homes after collecting their degrees, and that **cushion** of support gives them the time to pick the job they really want. Taking time off to travel used to be a résumé red flag;[4] today it's a learning experience. And **entrepreneurship** now functions as a safety net for this generation. They grew up on the Internet, and they know how to launch a **viable** online business. Facebook,[5] for example, began in a college dorm room.

3   With all these options, Generation Y is forcing companies to think more creatively about work-life balance. The employers who do are winning in the war for young talent. The consulting firm Deloitte[6] was alarmed by the high **turnover** of its youngest employees, so it asked one of its consultants, Stan Smith, to find out more about what attracts them to and keeps them at a job. His research reveals that job hopping is not an end in itself but something young workers do when they see no other choice.

4   "People would rather stay at one company and grow, but they don't think they can do that," he

says. "Two-thirds of the people who left Deloitte left to do something they could have done with us, but we made it difficult for them to transition." So Smith, who is now in charge of **recruit**ing and retaining Generation Y as national director of next-generation **initiatives**, created programs at Deloitte that focus on helping people figure out their next career move. Smith is betting that in many cases, the best place for a restless young person is simply another spot in Deloitte. This saves the company the $150,000 cost of losing an employee—not to mention the stress for employees of changing jobs.

5   Old assumptions about what employees value in the workplace don't always apply with Gen Y. Friendship is such a strong motivator for them that Gen Y workers will choose a job just to be with their friends. Boston-based Gentle Giant Moving once hired an entire athletic team. "It looked like a great work environment because of the people," says rower Niles Kuronen, 26. "It was huge to be able to work with friends." It feels normal for Gen Y employees to check in by BlackBerry all weekend as long as they have flexibility during the week. Sun Microsystem's telecommuting program, for example, has kicked into high gear in response to Generation Y's demands. Today more than half of Sun's employees work remotely.

6   Generation Y's search for meaning makes support for volunteering among the benefits it values most. More than half of workers in their 20s prefer employment at companies that provide volunteer opportunities, according to a recent Deloitte survey. The software company Salesforce.com[7] gives 1% of profits to its foundation, which pays for employees to volunteer 1% of their work time. Salesforce.com staff will do 50,000 hours of community service this year. "This program has dramatically increased our ability to recruit and retain high-quality employees," says CEO Marc Benioff. It's what attracted Eliot Moore, 26. "When I heard about the Salesforce.com Foundation, it was plus after plus for me[8]," he says. "It's a way to take the skills I learned in the corporate **arena** and give back to the community without leaving the company."

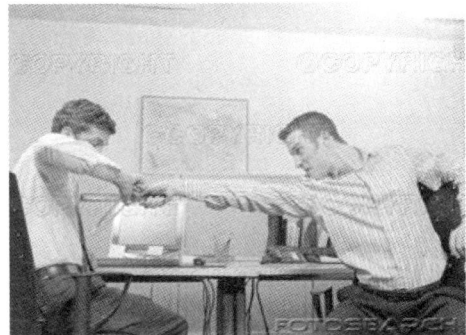

7   Understanding Generation Y is important not just for employers. Older workers—that is, anyone over 30—need to know how to adapt to the values and demands of their newest colleagues. Before too long, they'll be the bosses.

—Penelope Trunk

New Words and Expressions

arena	*n.*	a place where important political or other events unfold 竞争场所，活动场所
cushion	*n.*	something acting as a cushion, especially to absorb a shock or impact 垫状物，缓冲器，减震垫
entrepreneurship	*n.*	the quality of being an entrepreneur 企业家身份，企业家精神
initiative	*n.*	a new development; a fresh approach to something; a new way of dealing with a problem 首创精神，进取心
opt	*v.*	make a choice, decide 选择，决定
recruit	*v.*	supply with new men, as an army; fill up or make up by enlistment 雇用，聘用
turnover	*n.*	the rate at which people enter and leave employment, etc. 就业变动人数
viable	*a.*	feasible, esp. economically 切实可行的，可实施的
yawn	*v.*	be wide open (深坑，裂口等)张开；裂开
juggling act		the situation that you try your best to deal with 尽力对付的局面
opt out of		choose not to participate in 决定不参加

Proper Names

Deloitte	德勤(美国公司名)
BlackBerry	黑莓手机网

Notes

1. **Baby boomers:** 婴儿潮

Baby boomer is a term used to describe a person who was born during the Post-World War II baby boom between 1946 and the early 1960s. Following World War II, several English-speaking countries—the United States, Canada, Australia, and New Zealand—experienced an unusual spike in birth rates, a phenomenon commonly referred to as the "baby boom". The terms "baby boomer" and "baby boom", along with other expressions, are also used in countries with demographics that did not mirror the sustained growth in American families over the same interval.

2. **Generation Xers:** X 代人

Generation X is a term used to describe generations in many countries around the world born from 1965 to around 1980. The term has been used in demography, the social sciences, and marketing, though it is most often used in popular culture. In the U.S. Gen X was originally referred to as the "baby bust" generation because of the small number of births following the baby boom.

3. **Generation Yers:** Y 代人

Generation Y refers to the cohort of individuals born, roughly, between 1980 and 1994. "Generation Y" alludes to a succession from Generation X, a term popularized by the Canadian fiction writer Douglas Coupland in his 1991 book *Generation X: Tales for an Accelerated Culture*. Generation Y are primarily the children of Baby boomers, though some are the children of older members of Generation X.

4. **a résumé red flag:** something that should be avoided in the résumé　履历表上的禁忌

5. **Facebook:** Facebook is a social networking website launched on February 4, 2004. The free-access website is privately owned and operated by Facebook, Inc. Users can join networks organized by city, workplace, school, and region to connect and interact with other people. People can also add friends and send them messages, and update their personal profile to notify friends about themselves. The website's name refers to the paper facebooks depicting members of a campus community that some American colleges and preparatory schools give to incoming students, faculty, and staff as a way to get to know other people on campus. (一个社交网站)

6. Deloitte: Deloitte Touche Tohmatsu is a privacy conscious global organization. It has been more than 150 years since William Welch Deloitte opened his own accountancy office across the street from Bankruptcy Court on Basinghall Street in London. Deloitte member firms offer clients a broad range of audit, tax, consulting and financial advisory services. Its client service teams, under the leadership of a Lead Client Service Partner, help create powerful business solutions for organizations operating anywhere in the world. This integrated approach combines insight and innovation from multiple disciplines with business knowledge and industry expertise to help its clients exceed their expectations. 世界四大会计师事务所之一的德勤会计师事务所(Deloitte & Touche)是德勤全球(Deloitte Touche Tohmatsu)在美国的分支机构，后者在 126 个国家内共有 5.9 万名员工。公司的咨询部门德勤咨询(Deloitte Consulting)在全美有 2900 名员工，是业内最大的公司之一。其特长在于国际商务。德勤咨询无疑完善了母公司的业务范围。公司所强调的是维持与客户之间的长期业务关系，其 75%以上的业务都来自于老客户。

7. Salesforce.com: Salesforce.com is a Multi-Tenant Business Network. Salesforce.com customers will be able to securely connect and share information between individual salesforce.com deployments with the click of a button. Just as Facebook is revolutionizing how individuals connect, Salesforce to Salesforce is revolutionizing how companies connect and share business information.

8. When I heard about the Salesforce.com Foundation, it was plus after plus for me. 此句意为：当我听说 Salesforce.com 基金会的事，那对我来说是再好不过了。

●Reading Comprehension

1. Directions: *Discuss the following questions with your classmates.*

1) What are the differences among baby boomers, Gen Xers and Gen Yers as far as work-life balance is concerned?

2) What does Gen Y really want according to the text?

3) What forces companies to think more creatively about work-life balance of Gen Y?

4) What does the example of the consulting firm Deloitte tell us?

5) In choosing a job, what is valued most by Gen Y?

6) In the current work market many changes occur such as people's assumption about what employees value. What other changes are mentioned in the text?

2. Directions: *Read the following statements carefully, and decide whether they are true (T) or false (F) according to the text.*

_____ 1) The first challenge for the companies that want to hire the best young workers is to provide the highest salary for them.

_____ 2) Gen Y has high expectations for personal growth only in those executive positions.

_____ 3) Gen Yers get in touch with the Internet even when they are very small, so they know how to start a profitable online business.

_____ 4) The programs created by Stan Smith at Deloitte benefit not only the company but also the employees.

_____ 5) The Salesforce.com Foundation attracts a lot of high quality employees because they can get some money every year as a reward for good performance in their work.

_____ 6) It matters a lot to understand Gen Y's attitude towards work not only for the employers but also for those potential bosses.

●Discussion

Finding work-life balance in today's frenetically paced world is no simple task. Whether the problem is too much focused on work or too little, when your work life and your personal life feel out of balance, stress, along with its harmful effects, is the result. Discuss with your classmates about how to keep the balance in the current society.

After-Class Reading

Passage One

Warm-up questions:

1. Look at the picture on page 171, and give a vivid description.

2. Which notion is dominating our lives now, "work to live" or "live to work"?

Work until You Drop How the Long-hour Culture Is Killing Us

With the longest working week in Europe, experts say Britain's health and productivity will decline unless something is done about it.

1   In Japan they call it *karoshi* and in China it is *guolaosi*. As yet there is no word in English for working yourself to death, but as more and more people put in longer hours and suffer more stress there may soon be.

2   This week, an American survey concluded that long working hours increased an individual's chances of illness and injury. It noted that for those doing 12 hours a day, there was a 37% increase in risk compared to those working fewer hours.

3   Ronald Reagan was wrong, it seems, when he said: "Hard work never killed anyone." Death from overwork is not a new phenomenon in Britain but it is largely unremarked upon.

4   In 2003, Sid Watkins, a paediatrician who was exhausted after working up to 100 hours a week, died after injecting himself with anaesthetic in an attempt to cope with his workload. The coroner at Dr Watkins' inquest described the hours he had to work as "crazy".

5   In 1994, the parents of Alan Massie, a junior doctor who collapsed and died after working an 86-hour week at a Cheshire hospital, claimed that their 27-year-old son was worked to death. He had worked seven days and three nights, including two unbroken periods of 27 hours and one of 24 hours.

6   In the same year, British Airways pilot David Robertson, 52, died while flying. Work stress and long working hours were implicated.

7   The American study, published in *Occupational and Environmental Medicine*, points out that overtime and extended work schedules are associated with an increased risk of hypertension, cardiovascular disease, fatigue, stress, depression, musculoskeletal disorders, chronic infections, diabetes and other general health complaints[1]. In Japan, most karoshi victims succumb to brain aneurisms, strokes and heart attack[2].

8   Professor Cary Cooper, a stress expert at Lancaster University[3] Management School, says the

risk is not just confined to those who work more than 60 hours but hits those that put in more than 45. "If you work consistently long hours, over 45 a week every week, it will damage your health, physically and psychologically. In the UK we have the second-longest working hours in the developed world, just behind the States and we now have longer hours than Japan," he says.

9   Professor Cooper advocates "working smarter", not longer, and introducing flexibility into the workplace. He acknowledges that the Department of Trade and Industry[4] is trying to encourage business to adopt such practices, but it is a slow process.

10   Derek Simpson, the general secretary of Amicus[5], the manufacturing, technical and skilled persons' union, agrees with Prof Cooper. "UK employees work the longest hours in Europe, yet all the evidence shows that long working hours are bad for our health, equality, our families and for society. People's jobs are by far the biggest single cause of stress, and stress-related illness is the silent killer in our workplaces, impacting on workers' physical and mental health. As well as being bad for individuals, our long-hours culture is also bad for business because lower working hours relate directly to higher productivity. It is no coincidence that the UK has the least-regulated economy in Europe and is the least productive in the industrialized world. Yet while other European governments are aiming to reduce weekly working hours below the working-time directive limit of 48 hours, our government is still desperately trying to keep the opt-out[6]."

11   In a survey, Amicus found that almost one in five workers was put off sex because of long hours. The union found a third of people said they didn't have enough time to spend with partners or children. Community work, socializing, personal fitness and hobbies all lost out to excessive working hours[7]. Earlier this month, the law firm Peninsula published a survey of 1,800 employers. It found that four out of five of them worked more than 60 hours a week and revealed that seven out of 10 got only four hours' sleep a night.

12   In her recent book *Willing Slaves: How the Overwork Culture Is Ruling Our Lives*[8], the *Guardian* writer Madeleine Bunting points out that Britain's full-time workers put in the longest hours in Europe at 43.6 a week compared with the EU average of 40.3. The number of people working over 48 hours has more than doubled since 1998, from 10% to 26%. And one in six of all workers is doing more than 60 hours.

13   Roger Vincent, a spokesman for the Royal Society for the Prevention of Accidents, says that overwork inevitably leads to lapses in concentration and therefore accidents. "Between a third and a quarter of all road accidents are in some way work-related. That means that somewhere between 800 and 1,000 deaths each year on Britain's roads are to do with somebody driving or being on the road as a result of their jobs."

14   In 1987, the Japanese Ministry of Labor acknowledged that it had a problem with death from overwork and began to publish statistics on karoshi. In 2001, the numbers reached a record level with 143 workers dying. Now, death-by-overwork lawsuits are common, with the victims' families demanding compensation payments. In 2002-2003, 160 out of 819 claimants received

compensation.

15　The health and safety magazine *Hazards* has continually warned that karoshi does exist in the UK. It said: "In July 2003 the government proposed abolishing the mandatory retirement[9] of 65 years." The old notion that "we work to live, not live to work" could soon be superseded by "we work until we drop."

Nose to the Grindstone in Europe's Sweatshop[10]

16　The UK's long-hours culture means that on average many of us are now working a 43.6-hour week. Our counterparts in the rest of Europe do 40.3 hours. The last seven years have seen a significant rise in the number of employees working in excess of 48 hours a week, rising from 10% in the late 90s to 26% now. Women in the workforce have also experienced changes to their work pattern. Since 1992 there has been a leap of 52% in the number of women expected to do 48 hours a week. The number of people working a long week has also jumped. Estimates from 2000—2002 suggest that those clocking up 60 hours a week have increased by a third, which equates to one sixth of the UK labor force.

17　We may be working more hours but many of us waste the opportunity to take time off. Recent surveys estimate that only 44% of workers use up their full entitlement to annual leave. Reasons cited for not taking paid holiday often include a heavy workload or fear of upsetting the boss. The right to take a full hour for lunch seems at odds with[11] our modern workplaces, with 65% of UK workers not using the full 60 minutes. The average time for a break is now 27 minutes, and more of us remain at our workstation.

Proper Names

Alan Massie	艾伦·马西
Cary Cooper	卡里·库珀
David Robertson	大卫·罗伯森
Derek Simpson	德里克·辛普森
Madeleine Bunting	马德琳·班廷
Roger Vincent	侯杰·凡松
Ronald Reagan	罗纳德·里根(美国前总统)
Sid Watkins	西德·沃金斯

Notes

1. The American study, published in *Occupational and Environmental Medicine*, points out that overtime and extended work schedules are associated with an increased risk of hypertension, cardiovascular disease, fatigue, stress, depression, musculoskeletal disorders, chronic infections, diabetes and other general health complaints. 此句意为：在《职业病与环境医学》中，美国

的一项研究指出，加班和延长工作时间表往往会带来更多的疾病风险，如高血压症、心血管疾病、过度劳累、压力、抑郁、肌骨骼混乱、慢性疾病、糖尿病以及其他健康问题。

2. ...succumb to brain aneurisms, strokes and heart attack. 此句大意为：因为脑瘤、中风和心脏病突发而死。succumb to sth. 表示"因患……而死"，"被压垮"或"劳累而死"。

3. Lancaster University Management School: 兰卡斯特大学创建于 1964 年，是英国十所最佳的研究型大学之一。兰卡斯特大学管理学院是兰卡斯特大学最大的学院，由六个系组成，其研究和教学水平在英国大学商学院中排在首位。英国高教拨款委员会最近评出两所六星级的商学院，一所是伦敦商学院，而另一所就是兰卡斯特大学商学院。所谓六星级的商学院是指此商学院是国际商业管理研究中心。

4. Department of Trade and Industry: 英国贸易与工业部

5. Amicus: 英国制造业技术工人联合会

6. opt-out: 拒绝参加(做出决定)

7. ...lost out to excessive working hours. 此句意为：被过度的工作时间所取代。lost out to 在句中意为"被……取代"。

8. *Willing Slaves: How the Overwork Culture Is Ruling Our Lives*:《心甘情愿的奴隶：加班文化如何统治我们的生活》

9. **mandatory retirement:** 指令性的退休年龄

10. Nose to the Grindstone in Europe's Sweatshop: 在欧洲榨取工人血汗的工厂里拼命地工作

11. at odds with: 与……不一致

● **Reading Comprehension**

1. **Directions:** *Find out the author's attitude towards the long-hours culture from the text, and discuss with your classmates whether his attitude is well-grounded.*

2. **Directions:** *Discuss the following questions with your classmates.*

　　1) Why did the author say that Reagan was wrong when he said "hard work never killed anyone"? What do you think Reagan meant by saying "hard work never killed anyone"?

　　2) What is the cause of David Robertson's death?

　　3) When a person overworks, what risks is he running?

　　4) Why does long-hours culture do harm to individuals and businesses as well?

　　5) Why couldn't a third of people find enough time to stay with their families?

　　6) What does the author mean by saying "we work till we drop"?

　　7) Why would the notion "we work to live, not live to work" soon be replaced by "we work until we drop"?

　　8) Why do many workers give up the opportunities of annual leave?

Passage Two

Warm-up questions:

1. What do you know about the situation of Chinese farmers?

2. Where is the largest cotton-growing region in China? Do you know how much share it occupies in the cotton market in 2007?

A Tale of Cotton Pickers

Cotton production in Xinjiang has boosted migrant farmers' income and self-confidence

1   When autumn settles in the rolling cotton fields in Xinjiang Uygur Autonomous Region[1] and the fluffy snowy flowers burst out of their shells, the cotton harvest season arrives. For farmers like Wu Caixia, a resident of Linze County in northwestern Gansu Province, it is time to embark on their journey to the cotton fields in Xinjiang.

2   Wu and her husband make a living by growing two thirds of a hectare of corn in their hometown, which yields an annual income of about $1,450. Her husband also works as a construction worker here and there, bringing in another $400. Last autumn, the couple spent two months in Xinjiang picking cotton, making $700, which boosted their family savings and self-confidence. With this money, the couple bought a refrigerator, a DVD player, an electric fan; the remaining was set aside for social security for their parents and tuition fees for their child.

White Gold

3   Located in the northwest corner of China, Xinjiang Uygur Autonomous Region is blessed with a cotton-friendly climate. Xinjiang is the largest cotton-growing region in China, producing about 40 percent of the country's cotton in 2007. Statistics from the China Cotton Association (CCA)[2] show that the national gross output of cotton reached 6.73 million tons during the 2006/07

cotton season and is estimated to be 7.5 million tons in 2007/08. Cotton production and related industries have become a backbone of Xinjiang's economy, generating one sixth of the local gross domestic product (GDP).

4   "And when the cotton balls get rotten, you can't pick very much cotton," an English nursery rhyme says. Cotton growers in Xinjiang understand it too well. If cotton is not picked in time, it is wasted in the field.

5   Labor is abundant in China, but not in Xinjiang during the cotton harvest season. With an area four times the size of California, Xinjiang accounts for one sixth of the total landmass of China and a little over 1 percent of the total population. While rich coastal cities frown upon the influx of rural migrant workers, cotton growers there have to compete fiercely for scarce labor resources.[3] During the cotton harvest season, Yang Huowa, a cotton grower in Xinjiang frequents the local railway station to recruit farmers.[4] "From dawn to dusk, I crane my neck for migrant labors, yelling at the top of my voice to attract their attention. As soon as I see one, I lobby him to work on my farm. In addition to a regular wage, I offer them perks such as delicious free meals." On one unlucky day, he only managed to recruit four farmers. Yang planted about 15 hectares of cotton. Due to labor shortages, in one year, his cotton was still swaying in the field when snow blanketed the ground in winter.

6   In 2007, Xinjiang attracted about 1 million farmers from other inland provinces of China, half of whom were from the neighboring Gansu Province. These migrant farmers picked most of the cotton produced in Xinjiang, earning a total of 2 billion yuan ($0.27 billion) in two months or so. The majority of migrant farmers are women. To ladies such as Wu Caixia, cotton-picking is no more onerous than other fieldwork. They have time to spare in autumn anyway. Cotton-picking not only brings them off-budget revenue[5] but also provides a rare chance to see the world outside their hometown.

Cotton Picker Economics

7   We can hardly talk about cotton pickers without mentioning the textile and apparel industry. The textile industry is a labor-intensive industry that offers employment opportunities to a large number of low-skill workers. Many countries used to impose quota and tariffs[6] on textile imports to protect their own industry. The Multifiber Agreement (MFA)[7], signed in 1974, restricts international competition in the industry with bilateral quotas. Under the MFA, the total textile exports from an exporting country cannot exceed a certain share of total imports in the country of destination. In 1995, the MFA was replaced by the World Trade Organization (WTO) Agreement on Textiles and Clothing (ATC)[8], which set procedures for the phasing out of MFA quotas by 2005. Since the expiration of MFA in 2005, clothing products are no longer subject to quotas under a special regime outside normal WTO/GATT (The General Agreement on Tariffs and Trade)[9] rules. China entered the WTO in 2001, which granted China increased access to international market.

Many foreign apparel companies such as Nike, JC Penney, and Adidas have outsourced production to Chinese companies[10].

8   Now, China has a very large textile industry that captures a large share of the global market. The industry gobbles up millions of tons of cotton each year. The migrant farmers working in Xinjiang's vast cotton fields are part of the global supply chain of textile and apparel. Demand for these farmers and the wages offered to them are associated in some sense with how much clothing shoppers buy in stylish stores lining the streets of cities such as Beijing, Shanghai, New York and Paris, and how much cotton is produced on the plantations outside of Xinjiang. The number of migrant farmers picking cotton in Xinjiang each year has increased from about 10,000 a decade ago to 1 million now.

9   The globalization of the textile industry is illustrated by Pietra Rivoli, a business professor with Georgetown University. In her book *The Travels of a T-Shirt in the Global Economy*, Professor Rivoli traced the fascinating journey of a t-shirt around the globe and the politics involving each leg of the shirt's journey. Professor Rivoli learned that the t-shirt she bought for six dollars was woven with cotton planted on a farm around Lubbock, Texas. Further investigation led her to a factory in Shanghai, China, where the cotton from Texas was spun and woven into cloth. The cloth was cut and sewn into a t-shirt, and then was shipped back to the United States, where it was bought by Professor Rivoli.

10   "We are moving away from an economic system in which national markets are distinct entities, isolated from each other by trade barriers and barriers of distance, time and culture and toward a system in which national markets are merging into one huge global marketplace," she said.

11   In 2005, Thomas Friedman, a foreign affairs columnist for *The New York Times* identified 10 factors that have leveled the global playground, including the rise of information technology and new business models such as outsourcing and offshoring.

12   Although China is the world's largest cotton producer now, domestic supply still falls significantly behind ballooning demand fueled by the growing textile industry.[11] The world cotton price is lower than the domestic price due to the higher production efficiency of foreign farmers and subsidies from their governments. According to the U.S. Cotton Council[12], from 2004 on, about half of cotton consumed in China was from imports, and about one-half of China's imported cotton was from the United States, with the rest from West Africa, the former Soviet Union and Australia.

13   Traditionally, cotton in China was primarily produced by Chinese farmers along the Yellow River. The fields were patchy and production costs were high. In 2004, the government began to subsidize grain crop farmers in 13 major grain-producing provinces in east and central China[13] (farmers in western provinces are not covered because they are not located in the major grain belt), according to a U.S. Department of Agriculture study authored by Fred Gale, Bryan Lohmar and Francis Tuan. This was the first time that the Chinese Government had offered direct subsidies to

farmers.

14　After the turn of this century, China's agriculture accounted for only 15 percent of GDP and 5 percent of tax revenue. China's WTO accession renders farmers vulnerable to global competition. The government decided to end the century-old agricultural tax and introduced direct subsidies. The amount of subsidies varies across regions and across crop types. The subsidy enticed many cotton growers in China's heartland to shift to grain production. Foreign cotton took up half of the cotton market in China. In 2004, Xinjiang had a bumper harvest of cotton, yet cotton growers suffered from declining cotton prices and a shortage of migrant cotton-picking farmers. Their woes were exacerbated by dwindling demand from cotton mills.[14] High cotton prices the previous year forced some mills to close down and others to reduce capacity.

15　Recent booms in the textile and cotton market gave birth to the spectacular phenomenon of migrant cotton pickers. Year after year, like migrant birds taking wing in the autumn wind, cotton-picking farmers embark on their journey to the vast cotton fields in Xinjiang, harvesting a better life.

16　The market has a cool head and a cold heart when picking losers and winners. Recently, Xinjiang cotton growers acquired another helper, the cotton-picking machine. Each machine can pick as much cotton as 600 farmers, at a cost of 0.4 yuan ($0.05) per kg of cotton, 60 percent lower than the labor cost of human cotton pickers. How this will affect the landscape of the cotton fields of Xinjiang is a question for tomorrow.

Proper Names

Bryan Lohmar　　　布赖恩·洛马尔(美国经济学家)

Francis Tuan　　　段志煌(美国经济学家)

Fred Gale　　　弗雷德·盖尔(美国经济学家)

Pietra Rivoli　　　皮翠拉·瑞沃莉(美国经济学家)

Thomas Friedman　　　托马斯·弗里德曼(美国经济学家、专栏作家)

Notes

1. **Xinjiang Uygur Autonomous Region:** 新疆维吾尔自治区

   Autonomous region of northwest China. The capital is Urumqi. Industries include oil, chemicals, iron, textiles, coal, copper, and tourism. Cereals, cotton, and fruit are grown, and there is animal husbandry.

2. China Cotton Association (CCA): 中国棉花协会

   China Cotton Association is a non-profit organization in the area of cotton with the status of national mass organization legal person, which is voluntarily established by cotton farmers, cotton farmers' cooperative organizations, enterprises engaged in cotton production, purchase, processing and operation, cotton textile enterprises, cotton research institutes and other organs, and which accepts the supervision and management of the Ministry of Civil Affairs and the professional guidance of the All-China Federation of Supply and Marketing Cooperatives.

3. While rich coastal cities frown upon the influx of rural migrant workers, cotton growers there have to compete fiercely for scarce labor resources. 此句大意是：当富有的沿海城市为民工大量涌入担忧的时候，那里的棉农还得为稀缺的劳动力资源展开激烈的竞争。

4. Yang Huowa, a cotton grower in Xinjiang frequents the local railway station to recruit farmers. 此句大意是：新疆棉农杨火娃频繁地到当地火车站去招募民工。

5. off-budget revenue: 预算外收入

6. **quota and tariffs:** Tariff (关税) is a tax imposed on an imported good. Quota (配额) is a legal limit on the quantity of a good that may be imported. 两者都属于贸易壁垒，都是不利于出口国、出口商的。中国加入 WTO，大的趋势就是降低关税，扩大配额，尽可能地实现贸易自由化。

7. The Multifiber Agreement (MFA): 《多种纤维协定》

8. the World Trade Organization (WTO) Agreement on Textiles and Clothing (ATC): WTO《纺织品和服装协定》

9. **GATT (The General Agreement on Tariffs and Trade):** 关贸总协定

The General Agreement on Tariffs and Trade (GATT) was first signed in 1947. The agreement was designed to provide an international forum that encouraged free trade between member states by regulating and reducing tariffs on traded goods and by providing a common mechanism for resolving trade disputes. GATT membership now includes more than 110 countries.

10. outsourced production to Chinese companies: 把产品外包给中国公司生产

11. Although China is the world's largest cotton producer now, domestic supply still falls significantly behind ballooning demand fueled by the growing textile industry. 此句大意是：尽管中国现在是世界上最大的棉花生产国，但国内棉花供应量仍然远远跟不上日益增长的纺织工业所带来的对棉花的飞涨需求。

12. the U.S. Cotton Council: 美国棉花署

13. **13 major grain-producing provinces in east and central China:** 中国东部和中部的 13 大粮食主产省(河北、河南、黑龙江、吉林、辽宁、湖北、湖南、江苏、江西、内蒙古、山东、四川、安徽)

14. Their woes were exacerbated by dwindling demand from cotton mills. 此句大意是：随着棉花厂对棉花需求的萎缩，他们的担忧日益加剧。

● **Reading Comprehension**

1. Directions: *Choose the best answer for each of the following questions.*

1) How much did Wu and her husband earn in that year when they spent 2 months in Xinjiang picking cotton?

    A. $1,450.   B. $1,850.   C. $2,150.   D. $2,550.

2) From 2004 on, about half of cotton consumed in China was from imports, and about one-half of China's imported cotton was from _____.

  A. the United States   B. Australia

  C. the former Soviet Union   D. West Africa

3) According to Thomas Friedman, which of the following is NOT one of the factors that have leveled the global playground?

  A. The rise of information technology.

  B. The fall of the Berlin Wall.

  C. The influx of rural migrant workers.

  D. New business models such as outsourcing and offshoring.

4) According to the article, which of the following is NOT true?

  A. Xinjiang accounts for one sixth of the total landmass of China.

  B. Xinjiang is three times bigger than California.

  C. After the turn of this century, China's agriculture accounted for only 15 percent of GDP and 5 percent of tax revenue.

  D. Xinjiang accounts for less than 1 percent of the total population of China.

5) The passage is mainly about _____.

  A. cotton harvest in China   B. cotton economics in the whole world

  C. Chinese agriculture policies   D. the situation of cotton pickers in China

2. Directions: *Read the following statements carefully, and decide whether they are true (T) or false (F) according to the text.*

_____ 1) Cotton production and related industries have become a backbone of Xinjiang's economy, generating 40% of the local gross domestic product (GDP).

_____ 2) In 2007, Xinjiang attracted about 0.5 million farmers from the neighboring Gansu Province.

_____ 3) China is a major exporting country of cotton in the world.

_____ 4) To ladies such as Wu Caixia, cotton-picking is harder than other fieldwork.

_____ 5) The textile industry is a labor-intensive and low-skilled industry.

_____ 6) Located in the northwest corner of China, the climate of Xinjiang Uygur Autonomous Region is very good for growing cotton.

_____ 7) The number of migrant farmers picking cotton in Xinjiang each year is 100 times that of 10 years ago.

_____ 8) Since China is the world's largest cotton producer now, domestic supply can meet ballooning demand fueled by the growing textile industry.

Part Three

Topic-related Activities

1. For or Against

It's a fact of life in the 21st century workplace: the boss may well be monitoring your use of computer by using two types of spying software (network-based programs that monitor all traffic passing through a system and programs that sit directly on an employee's desktop). Fierce debate arises as to whether this practice should be furthered or eliminated.

Step One

Directions: *The whole class is divided into several groups of 4 or 5. Each group should decide on which side you take. Discuss in groups and try to list all the persuasive points to illustrate your points.*

Step Two

Directions: *One representative from each side is going to have a debate. Time limit is 2 minutes. After the debate, the winner stays and challenges the followers. The last student is the winner of the whole competition. Choose one student from each group as a judge and evaluate the performance of each group based on the criteria provided by the teacher.*

Suggested criteria: 1) Pronunciation and intonation (2 points)

2) Language (fluency and correctness) (3 points)

3) Content (3points)

4) Humor (1 point)

5) Manner (1 point)

Total points: (10 points)

2. Work Ethics: Old Generations vs. Post-80s Generation

Now, there is a distinct contrast of work ethics between old generations and post-80s generation. The old generations are complaining about the post 80s' laziness, irresponsibility, indulging in recreation, while the post-80s show contempt on the old generations' long-hour culture with low productivity. You may get some hints from the sentences stated below.

"Many in my generation despise work. They are lazy, addicted to entertainment and recreation… They are utterly unwilling to put in the planning, effort, dedication and self-sacrifice that are vital to meaningful accomplishment…"

—Julia Nelson

Discussion: *As a member of the post-90s, what is your opinion of the statement above? Discuss in groups.*

3. Case Study

Directions: *Read the following two statements. Can you figure out the work ethics of westerners and Japanese? In what way is the Chinese work ethic much alike?*

Akio Morita, chairman of Sony has once said that western society looks ten minutes ahead while the Japanese look ten years ahead. It's quite difficult for Japanese to shift from one job to another within a company. While in U.S an individual is not bound to the company and has the flexibility to move in order to further one's personal goals. Movement is often looked upon as an asset to the individual's résumé but not disloyalty.

Japanese tend to answer the boss' questions in terms of what they think will please the inquirers rather than answer with a disagreeable truth. No confrontation occurs. While Americans feel free to speak openly to his co-workers and supervisors without fear of recourse.

4. Writing

Directions: *Write a composition of no less than 150 words based on the following picture.*

Part Four

Topic-related Information

1. Teleconference

A teleconference is a telephone meeting among two or more participants involving technology more sophisticated than a simple two-way phone connection. At its simplest, a teleconference can be an audio conference with one or both ends of the conference sharing a speaker phone. With considerably more equipment and special arrangements, a teleconference can be a conference, called a videoconference, in which the participants can see still or motion video images of each other. Because of the high bandwidth of video and the opportunity for larger and multiple display screens, a videoconference requires special telecommunication arrangements and a special room at each end. As equipment and high-bandwidth cabling become more commonplace, it's possible that videoconferences can be held from your own computer or even in a mobile setting. One of the special projects of Internet is to explore the possibility of having teleconferences in which all participants actually appear to be in the same room together. Today's audio teleconferences are sometimes arranged over dial-up phone lines using bridging services that provide the necessary equipment for the call.

2. Asian Work Ethics vs. American Ethics

Basic ethical values in Asian business systems are influenced by three philosophical and religious traditions: the Shinto Ethic, the Confucian Ethic, and the Buddhist Ethic and also the Parent-Child Ethic. Shinto was the primitive religion of Japan before Confucius and Buddha. The chief deity of Shinto is Amaterasu, the Sun Goddess from whom the Imperial Family of Japan traces its origin. Lesser clans, in turn, claim descent from the lesser Shinto deities. Shinto has only one command, the necessity of being loyal to one's ancestors. This precept binds all Japanese in a bond of unity to a degree unknown in rest of the world. Shintoism stresses that harmony is necessary to keep man and things right with the cosmos. Each individual is obligated to do whatever is expected of him whatever the cost so as to bring honor to his family. Those in superior positions are obligated to take care of those who serve. Selflessness, kindness, helpfulness, loyalty, will bring trust, honor, confidence, and respect from others. Confucius insisted on respect for superior persons and things.

Western culture is based on Christian philosophy which preaches the equality of men and emphasizes man's freedom as a rational being. Man has a free will and can choose to act in accordance with this principle. Consciousness, choice, and freedom are the key principles. The fundamental work philosophy in the U.S. is capitalism. Webster's dictionary defines capitalism as an economic system characterized by private or corporate ownership of capital goods, by investments that are determined by private decision rather than by state control, and by prices, production, and the distribution of goods that are determined mainly by competition in a free market.

These basic philosophical differences have resulted in very different corporate ethics for western and Asian cultures. Because of their ties to their past, the Asians place more emphasis on the long-term success of their country and the long-term growth of their company and connected partners who are seen as family. In Western society the company is only a means to an end, namely the way to support one's individual or family lifestyle. In the U.S. an individual is not bound to the company and has the flexibility to move in order to further one's personal goals. In conclusion, these two cultures often find it difficult to understand and accept each other's differing corporate goals and management styles and misunderstandings are frequent.

3. SOHO

SOHO is the abbreviation of "Small Office, Home office", which refers to those people who work at home by means of computers, fax machines, Internet and other advanced technology. Compared with traditional ways, SOHO is a totally different way to make a living and has formed a strong challenge to traditional ways since it can bring people many benefits. Working at home, people will not suffer from the painful experience of squeezing into the crowded bus every morning with sleepy eyes. The time spent on the commute between home and office can be saved, and people will have more time to stay with their families, sharing their feelings and discussing their problems. Furthermore, without bearing the dull and depressive environment in the office, people can choose the fittest place to do the job. In short, SOHO can reduce people' troubles, save their time and improve their working efficiency, but the most important one is that they can enjoy the life while making a living. Through this way, people can do better in balancing their work and life. SOHO will be more and more popular in this digital era.

4. 18 Rules of International Business Ethics

Rule 1: If you strive to understand the values of different cultures, you will find common points.

Rule 2: If you analyze the facts, you will realize that honesty and reliability benefit you.

Rule 3: If you analyze case studies from different perspectives, you will discover the benefits of fair play.

Rule 4: Respecting your colleagues is the smartest investment you can make.

Rule 5: To increase productivity, provide safe and healthy working conditions.

Rule 6: To inspire trust, make your performance transparent.

Rule 7: Your loyal dissent can lead your institution in the right direction.

Rule 8: Downsizing your labor force is only beneficial when you respect each stakeholder.

Rule 9: To establish your brand name, act as a fair competitor.

Rule 10: Reduce the gap between the rich and poor by developing a new social security system.

Rule 11: If you act against discrimination, you will increase your productivity and profitability.

Rule 12: If you protect intellectual property, all stakeholders will receive their due share.

Rule 13: Ongoing changes in information technology require new forms of loyalty.

Rule 14: Your public relations strategy will only secure your reputation if it witnesses your drive for quality and excellence.

Rule 15: Your economic achievements will only stand on firm ground if you diminish corruption.

Rule 16: Long-term success urgently calls you to constantly care for the environment.

Rule 17: To become a refined player, sharpen your discernment and cultivate good manners.

Rule 18: Care for your business by caring for society.

5. Flextime System

Flextime (or flexitime, flexi-time, originally derived from the German word Gleitzeit which literally means "sliding time") is a variable work schedule, in contrast to traditional work arrangements requiring employees to work a standard 9 a.m. to 5 p.m. day. Under flextime, there is typically a core period (of approximately 50% of total working time/working day) of the day when employees are expected to be at work (for example, between 11 a.m. and 3 p.m.), while the rest of the working day is "flextime", in which employees can choose when they work, subject to achieving total daily, weekly or monthly hours in the region of what the employer expects, and subject to the necessary work being done.

A flextime policy allows staff to determine when they will work, while a flexplace policy allows staff to determine where they will work.

Hyperlinks

[1] Resources for Baby boomer, Generation X, Generation Y

http://en.wikipedia.org/wiki

http://www.youtube.com/watch?v=kF05oDvHPq8

http://cio.it168.com/i/2007-06-05/200707031114953.shtml

http://www.southcn.com/opinion/cartoon/200606230749_608834.gif

http://news.xinhuanet.com/comments/2006-08/31/xinsrc_4920903011600531207804.jpg

[2] Resources for proverbs related to work

http://www.hxen.com/englishstudy/yanyumingyan/2007-03-22/2535.html

http://www.great-quotes.com/quotes/category/work.htm

References

[1] http://www.time.com/time/magazine/article/0,9171,1640395,00.html

[2] http://www.guardian.co.uk/uk/2005/aug/20/britishidentity.health

[3] http://www.bjreview.com.cn/print/txt/2007-12/27/content_93775.htm

[4] http://www.oppapers.com/essays/Japanese-Work-Ethics-Vs-American-Ethics/96027

[5] http://www.scu.edu/ethics/publications/ethicalperspectives/business-china.html

[6] http://www.4ewriting.com/read.asp?id=641

[7] http://www.scu.edu/ethics/publications/ethicalperspectives/business-china.html

[8] Penelope Trunk. What Gen Y Really Wants. Time [J], July 5, 2007

Unit 9

Food

Part One

Lead-in

Tell me what you eat and I will tell you who you are.

—Brillat-Savarin (France)

告诉我你吃什么，我就能知道你是什么样的人。

——布里亚-萨瓦兰(法国)

Food is not just what we eat. Most traditions have a recognizable cuisine, a specific set of cooking traditions, preferences and practices, which creates distinctive catering culture. By looking at food, the ages we are living in, the culture of different regions and the history of human beings can be better understood.

Part Two
Reading Passages

In-Class Reading

Warm-up questions:

1. What role does food play in your life and in your family?

2. Do you think that food is just what we eat? Why or why not?

The Food Chains That Link Us All

1   C.L.R James, the great Trinidadian essayist, once wrote of his favorite sport, "What do they know of cricket, who only cricket know?" The same question should be asked of food. To write about food only as food misses the point, or many points, about the great universal human experience between birth and death. Food is not just what we eat. It charts the **ebbs and flows** of economies, reflects the changing patterns of trade and **geopolitical** alliances, and defines our values, status and health—for better and worse. The famous **dictum** of the early 19th century French **gastronome** Jean Anthelme Brillat-Savarin, "Tell me what you eat and I will tell you who you are," should be expanded. Tell me what you eat and I will tell you who you are, where you live, where you stand on political issues, who your neighbors are, how your economy functions, your country's history and foreign relations, and the state of the environment. By looking at food, the age we live in is better understood.

2   Once, food was defined by a very small geographic zone, prescribed by the products and traditions in that area. Where there were wars, food was modified. Arabs conquered Europe; cane sugar went with them. Immigration left a mark, too. The Chinese entered Japan and the soybean entered the Japanese diet. Jews fleeing Portugal brought chocolate to southwestern France. African slaves brought frying and **okra** to the Caribbean and the American South. It seemed every time a royal marriage was arranged in France, the **cuisine** gained a few ingredients and dishes. Modern historians question the influence of Catherine de' Medici[1] when she arrived in Paris in 1533 at the age of 14, with an extensive Italian cooking staff. The event probably did not revolutionize French cooking as is sometimes suggested, but it did bring the artichoke north. And when Louis XVI[2] married Marie Antoinette[3] from Lorraine[4], sauerkraut[5] became fashionable in Paris and remained popular far longer than she did.

3   Never has food been more of a global commodity than it is today. Witness the rise of the **franchised** superchef, the **ubiquity** of **fusion fare**, and the ease with which exotic ingredients cross borders and oceans. But not all of this is a modern phenomenon. Purely local cuisines have always been rare. Take the **spice** trade. While fortunes were being made in Asian, African and American commerce, European food **was laced with** excessive quantities of **nutmeg**, **mace**, ginger,

black pepper and **cinnamon**. In the Caribbean, where history is an endless succession of migrations and conquests, there is almost nothing **indigenous** in the "local" food. Even China, **possessed of** great cuisines, is full of imports in its traditional food, such as the hot peppers the Portuguese transported from the Americas.

4   All of the processes by which cooks were introduced to new products and new ideas began to speed up in the 19th century as transportation became faster—an acceleration so **relentless** that over the past 50 years the changes have seemed **bewildering**.[6] Today trade is swift and global, and therefore food no longer reflects its place or time. No longer do you know where you are or what month it is by the food that is available.[7] Every day organic vegetables from California, freshly caught turbots packed in dry ice from France, fresh Portuguese sardines, New Zealand oysters and smelly durian from Asia land in the airports of the world. More than ever in our history, we are now offered endless choices in food. But we may be embracing this excitement **at the cost of** the **erosion** of our own cultures.

5   Globalization has not led to equality either. Food remains **classist**. The poor still eat mostly **carbohydrates** and fats, while the rich get the protein—something that can even be seen in the difference between airline meals in first class and economy. I once had to attend a **black-tie** food event in New York City while on a **low-carb** diet. From **caviar** to fish, all of the **deluxe** fare suited my **regime**.

6   The great restaurants, with their low-carb dishes that take a paragraph to explain on a menu, prepare food that is too complicated for most people to prepare at home. It is also too expensive. Most of the great cities of the world, once **refuge**s for the poor, are increasingly **enclaves** for the wealthy where cooks and even farmers can experiment without considering cost. New York City has established a much loved system of neighborhood "farmers' markets[8]." No longer do you know where you are or what month it is by the food that is available. Originally a movement to take control back from corporate industrial agriculture, these markets, **serviced** by local farmers **trucking in** their goods, are a most fascinating **collusion** of **small-scale** farming and wealthy consumers. There is almost no limit to the price such farmers can ask for their produce. Farmers traditionally like to grow crops as large as possible because the ratio of weight to effort is better. People like baby vegetables because they are cute—tiny carrots, peanut-like **squash** and bean-sized brussels sprouts[9]. If the customer pays enough, the farmer will pick the vegetable when it's tiny. Precious small radish-sized potatoes from white to purple, and very **waxy** to very **floury**, sell in New York City for a price per size comparable to Manhattan **real estate**. The wealthy, of course, reject industrial farming, which was always intended to mass produce for the poor. To see just how much resistance to industrial agriculture there is among the rich, travel to rural areas where wealthy **urbanites** have their vacation homes and watch them pay fees for the privilege of stooping in the field to harvest a crop.

7   But the three-star restaurants are not the ones charting the course of food. History has shown

that food almost always impacts culture from the poor up, not from the rich down. The creativity of great French chefs **belies** the fact that there is less and less cooking going on in the average French home, almost none of it in any way resembling the food of restaurants; that it is becoming increasingly difficult to find good bread in France because few want to be a baker, a hard and low-paying job; that more **rarefied** crafts like chocolate making are difficult to continue because adolescents now go to school instead of **apprenticing**; and that industrial farming continues to **squeeze out** small, quality producers.

8   And yet, industrial food is out of fashion. Today there is a global market for organic fruits and vegetables, **free-range** birds, oysters from microbeds. Technology is in. **Genetically** modified food offers many opportunities, not the least[10] of which is crops that are so insect **repellent** they need no **pesticides**. But—to the **fury** of some farmers—some of the same people who reject pesticides and call for organic food are now calling for a ban on genetically modified food. The argument, though a bit **murky**, is powerful. While there is no **solid** proof of the evils of such food, why trust hi-tech food from the same corporations that brought us industrial food?

9   Climate change is also changing our food, particularly through its impact on that great supplier, the ocean. Water is becoming not only warmer but less salty. The oceans, however, have been **assaulted** with not only climate change, but with pollution and **destructive** industrial fishing. Many predictions about seafood stocks are **dire**. Will most of them be seriously **depleted** by the year 2048, as one marine biologist recently predicted? Has the number of large fish in the ocean decreased by 90% over the past 50 years, as another scientist reported? Are 31% of the 274 commercially important fish stocks in America overfished, as a 2002 U.S. government report **asserted**? Are 60% of the fish species studied by the U.N. Food and Agriculture Organization (FAO) either fully exploited or depleted, as an FAO report claims? What is clear is that popular fish such as Atlantic salmon, cod and tuna are vanishing. We are now eating varieties that 40 years ago were considered "trash fish." On the coast of Cornwall, in England, monkfish is the largest catch in ports that used to be known for sardines, herring and cod. But what happens if the monkfish start to vanish too? The only certainty is that the survival of the ocean's fish can no longer be assumed—something that **portends** not just a crisis for biology, but one of the most dramatic shifts in food consumption ever seen.

10   History carries tremendous burdens—the age of empire, the Industrial Revolution—that influence our lives and what we eat today. To understand the food of today, the past must be remembered. For the same reason, if future historians want to look back at what life was like in the early 21st century—the technological and information revolutions, the **blessings** and dangers of globalization, the challenges to the survival of a healthy planet—they would do well to look at our food. Changes in food have always been a function of changes in society. We are—and will always be—what we eat.

—Mark Kurlansky[11]

New Words and Expressions

apprentice	v.	work for an employer for a fixed period of time in order to learn a particular skill or job 当学徒
assault	v.	attack something in a violent way 攻击，袭击
assert	v.	state firmly that something is true 断言，声称
belie	v.	give someone a false idea about something 掩饰
bewildering	a.	confusing, especially because there are too many choices or things happening at the same time 令人困惑的，使人混乱的
black-tie	a.	of parties or other social occasions at which people wear special formal clothes, such astuxedos for men 要求宾客穿半正式礼服的
blessing	n.	something that you have or something that happens which is good because it improves your life, helps you in some way, or makes you happy 祝福
carbohydrate	n.	foods such as rice, bread, and potatoes that contain carbohydrates 含碳水化合物的食物
caviar	n.	the preserved eggs of various large fish, eaten as a special very expensive food 鱼子酱
cinnamon	n.	a sweet-smelling brown substance used for giving a special taste to cakes and other sweet foods 肉桂，桂皮
classist	a.	having bias based on social or economic class 有阶级偏见的
collusion	n.	a secret agreement that two or more people make in order to do something dishonest 共谋，勾结
cuisine	n.	a particular style of cooking 厨房烹调法，烹饪
deluxe	a.	of better quality and more expensive than other things of the same type 华丽的，奢侈的
deplete	v.	reduce the amount of something that is present or available 耗尽，使衰竭
destructive	a.	causing damage to people or things 破坏(性)的
dictum	n.	a formal statement of opinion by someone who is respected or has authority 格言
dire	a.	extremely serious or terrible 可怕的；灾难的
ebb	n.	a period of decline 衰减时期
enclave	n.	a distinctly bounded area enclosed within a larger unit 一个被较大单位围住的明显划出界线的区域
erosion	n.	the process by which something is gradually reduced or destroyed 腐蚀，侵蚀

exotic	*a.*	unusual and interesting, (as if) from a foreign country 异国情调的，外来的，奇异的
fare	*n.*	(written) food, especially food served in a restaurant or eaten on a special occasion 食物
floury	*a.*	soft and powdery 粉状的
franchise	*v.*	grant a franchise to 赋予特权
free-range	*a.*	relating to a type of farming which allows animals such as chickens and pigs to move around and eat naturally, rather than being kept in a restricted space 在农场自由放养的
fury	*n.*	extreme, often uncontrolled anger 狂怒，狂暴
fusion	*n.*	a combination of separate qualities or ideas 融合
gastronome	*n.*	a connoisseur of good food and drink; a gourmet 美食者，爱吃的人
genetically	*ad.*	relating to genes or genetics 基因方面地
geopolitical	*a.*	relating to the way that a country's position, population, etc. affect its political development and its relationship with other countries 地理政治学的
indigenous	*a.*	originating and growing or living in an area or environment 本土的
low-carb	*a.*	having low carbohydrate 低碳水化合物的
mace	*n.*	a spice made from the dried shell of a nutmeg 豆蔻香料
murky	*a.*	complicated and difficult to understand 含糊的
nutmeg	*n.*	a brown powder made from the seed of a tropical tree, which is used as a spice 肉豆蔻
okra	*n.*	秋葵荚
pesticide	*n.*	a chemical substance used to kill insects and small animals that destroy crops 杀虫剂
portend	v.	be a sign that something is going to happen, especially something bad 预示
rarefied	*a.*	only available to or understood by a small group of people 秘传的
real estate	*n.*	property in the form of land or houses 房地产
refuge	*n.*	a place that provides shelter, or protection from danger 避难所
regime	*n.*	a special plan of food, exercise, etc. that is intended to improve your health 养生法
relentless	*a.*	steady and persistent 无情的
repellent	*a.*	resistant or impervious to a substance 排斥的
service	*v.*	provide people with something they need or want 提供服务
small-scale	*a.*	involving only a small number of things or a small area 小规模的
solid	*a.*	sound; reliable 坚固的；可靠的

spice	*n.*	a type of powder or seed, taken from plants, that you put into food you are cooking to give it a special taste 香料，调味品
squash	*n.*	one of a group of large vegetables with solid flesh and hard skins, such as pumpkins 南瓜属植物
ubiquity	*n.*	existence or apparent existence everywhere at the same time 普遍存在
urbanite	*n.*	people who live and work in towns and cities 都市人
waxy	*a.*	smooth and lustrous 柔软的，蜡的
at the cost of		at the price of 以……为代价
be laced with		have some of a quality 带有……的特点
be possessed of		have a particular quality, ability, etc. 占有，拥有
ebb and flow		prosperity and decline 盛衰
squeeze out		do something so that someone or something is no longer included or able to continue 榨出，挤出
truck in		take something somewhere by truck 用卡车运输

Proper Food Names

artichoke	朝鲜蓟
durian	(马来群岛产的)榴莲果
herring	青鱼
monkfish	安康鱼
okra	黄秋葵，秋葵荚
oyster	牡蛎
radish	萝卜
salmon	鲑鱼
sardine	沙丁鱼
tuna	金枪鱼
turbot	大比目鱼

Notes

1. Catherine de' Medici: 凯瑟琳·美第奇

   Catherine de' Medici (April 13, 1519—January 5, 1589) was born in Florence, Italy. In 1533, at the age of fourteen, she married Henry, second son of King Francis I of France and Queen Claude and became queen consort of King Henry II of France from 1547 to 1559.

2. Louis XVI: 路易十四

   Louis XVI (23 August 1754—21 January 1793), born Louis-Auguste, ruled as King of France and Navarre from 1774 until 1791, and then as King of the French from 1791 to 1792.

Suspended and arrested during the 10th of August 1792 Insurrection, he was tried by the National Convention, found guilty of treason, and executed on 21 January 1793.

3. Marie Antoinette: 玛丽·安托瓦内特

Maria Antonia (November 2, 1755—October 16, 1793) was born in Austria and later became Queen of France and Navarre. At fourteen, she was married to Louis-Auguste, Dauphin of France, the future Louis XVI. She was the mother of Louis XVII, who died in the Temple Tower at the age of ten during the French Revolution. Marie Antoinette is perhaps best remembered for her legendary excesses and for her death: she was executed by guillotine at the height of the French Revolution in 1793 for the crime of treason.

4. Lorraine: a district located in the northeast of France 洛林 (法国东北部一地区)

5. sauerkraut: a German food made from cabbage that has been left in salt so that it tastes sour 德国泡菜的一种

6. All of the processes… bewildering. 这个长句的大意是：在 19 世纪，随着运输的发展，厨师们接触新产品和新思想的过程也开始加快。这个加速过程非常迅速，在过去的 50 年中，变化快得让人不知所措。

7. No longer do you know where you are or what month it is by the food that is available. 这是一个倒装句。此句大意是：你再也不能根据上市的食物来判断地点和月份了。

8. **farmers' markets:** 农贸市场

Farmers' markets, sometimes called green markets, are markets, usually held out-of-doors, in public spaces, where farmers can sell produce to the public. Farmers' market produce is renowned for being locally-grown and very fresh. Farmers' markets often feature produce grown naturally or organically, meats that are raised humanely on pasture, handmade farmstead cheeses, eggs and poultry from free-range fowl, as well as heirloom produce and heritage breeds of meat and fowl.

9. brussels sprouts: a small round green vegetable that looks like a very small cabbage 芽甘蓝

10. not the least of 用于陈述重要理由或举出重要例子，常译为"其中重要的一个"。如: There were several reasons for dismissing him from his post, not the least of which was his neglect of duty. 撤消他的职务的理由有几条，其中重要的一条是他玩忽职守。

11. Mark Kurlansky: 马克·克兰斯基

Mark Kurlansky is the author of *Cod: A Biography of the Fish That Changed the World* and *Salt: A World History*. His latest book is *Nonviolence: 25 Lessons from the History of a Dangerous Idea.*

●Reading Comprehension

1. Directions: *Discuss the following questions with your classmates.*

1) What examples are given to elaborate how the development of transportation sped up the changes of food in the 19th century?

2) Why does the author think that "food remains classist"?

3) Why do the rich resist the industrial farming, according to the author?

4) What facts are covered by the seemingly thriving picture of French cooking?

5) What is the most important opportunity provided by the GM food?

6) How do you understand the famous dictum "Tell me what you eat and I will tell you who you are" after reading this article?

2. Directions: *As is indicated in Paragraph 2, food was once defined by a small geographic zone. Several aspects are mentioned to illustrate the causes of food changes from one place to another. Fill in the form based on the information provided in Paragraph 2. The first one has been done for you.*

Causes	Who	Food Involved	From	To
war	Arabs	cane sugar	Arabia	Europe

● **Discussion**

1. Which place do you prefer to shop for food, grocery stores, supermarkets or farmers' markets? Why?

2. What is GM food? What advantages does it have? Are you a fan of this kind of food? Why or why not?

After-Class Reading

Passage One

Warm-up questions:

1. Which do you like better, Chinese food or Western food? Why?

2. Do you know something about British eating habits? Tell each other something about it if possible.

British Food

British Cuisine

1   Yes, we do have a wide and varied cuisine in Britain today. No more do we suffer under the

image of grey boiled meat! After years of disparagement by various countries (especially the French) Britain now has an enviable culinary reputation.[1] In fact some of the great chefs now come from Britain. I kid you not!

2   Traditional British cuisine is substantial, yet simple and wholesome. We have long believed in four meals a day. Our fare has been influenced by the traditions and tastes from different parts of the British Empire: teas from Ceylon[2] and chutney[3], kedgeree[4], and mulligatawny[5] soup from India.

A Brief History

3   British cuisine has always been multicultural, a potpourri[6] of eclectic styles. In ancient times, it is influenced by the Romans, and in medieval times[7], the French. When the Frankish Normans[8] invaded, they brought with them the spices of the east: cinnamon, saffron, mace, pepper, and ginger. Sugar came to England at that time, and was considered a spice—rare and expensive. Before the arrival of cane sugars, honey and fruit juices were the only sweeteners[9]. The few Medieval cookery books that remain record dishes that use every spice in the larder, and chefs across Europe saw their task to be the almost alchemical transformation of raw ingredients into something entirely new (for centuries the English aristocracy ate French food) which they felt distinguished them from the peasants.

4   Despite being part of Europe today, we've kept up our links with the countries of the former British Empire, now united under the Commonwealth.[10] One of the benefits of having an empire is that we did learn quite a bit from the colonies. From East Asia (China) we adopted tea (and exported the habit to India), and from India we adopted curry-style spicing, we even developed a line of spicy sauces including ketchup, mint sauce, Worcestershire sauce and deviled sauce to indulge these tastes.[11] Today it would be fair to say that curry has become a national dish.

5   Unfortunately a great deal of damage was done to British cuisine during the two world wars. Britain is an island and supplies of many goods became short. The war effort used up goods and services and so less were left over for private people to consume. Ships importing food stuffs had to travel in convoys[12] and so they could make fewer journeys. During the Second World War food rationing[13] began in January 1940 and was lifted only gradually after the war.

6   The British tradition of stews, pies and breads, according to the taste buds of the rest of the world, went into terminal decline.[14] What was best in England was only that which showed the influence of France, and so English food let itself become a gastronomic joke[15] and the French art of Nouvell Cuisine[16] was adopted.

Today

7   In the late 1980's, British cuisine started to look for a new direction. Disenchanted with the overblown (and under-nourished) Nouvelle Cuisine, chefs began to look a little closer to home for inspiration. Calling on a rich (and largely ignored) tradition, and utilizing many diverse and

interesting ingredients, the basis was formed for what is now known as modern British food. Game has enjoyed a resurgence in popularity although it always had a central role in the British diet, which reflects both the abundant richness of the forests and streams and an old aristocratic prejudice against butchered meats.[17]

8   In London especially, one can not only experiment with the best of British, but the best of the world as there are many distinct ethnic cuisines to sample, Chinese, Indian, Italian and Greek restaurants are amongst the most popular.

9   Although some traditional dishes such as roast beef and Yorkshire pudding, Cornish pasties, steak and kidney pie, bread and butter pudding, treacle tart, spotted dick or fish and chips[18], remain popular, there has been a significant shift in eating habits in Britain. Rice and pasta have accounted for the decrease in potato consumption and the consumption of meat has also fallen.[19] Vegetable and salad oils have largely replaced the use of butter.

10   Roast beef is still the national culinary pride. It is called a "joint," and is served at midday on Sunday with roasted potatoes, Yorkshire pudding, two vegetables, a good strong horseradish, gravy, and mustard.

11   Today there is more emphasis on fine, fresh ingredients in the better restaurants and markets in the UK offer food items from all over the world. Salmon, Dover sole, exotic fruit, Norwegian prawns and New Zealand lamb are choice items[20]. Wild fowl and game are other specialties on offer[21].

12   In fact fish is still important to the English diet. We are after all in an island surrounded by some of the richest fishing areas of the world. Many species swim in the cold offshore waters: sole, plaice, cod (the most popular choice for fish and chips), halibut, mullet and John Dory. Oily fishes also abound as do crustaceans like lobster and oysters. Eel, also common, is cooked into a wonderful pie with lemon, parsley, and shallots, all topped with puff pastry.

The Sunday Roast

13   Every Sunday thousands of British families sit down together to eat a veritable feast of roasted meat served with roast potatoes, vegetables and other accompaniments. It is a tradition with a long pedigree. In medieval times the village serfs served the squire for six days a week. Sundays however were a day of rest, and after the morning church service, serfs would assemble in a field and practice their battle techniques. They were rewarded with mugs of ale and a feast of oxen roasted on a spit[22].

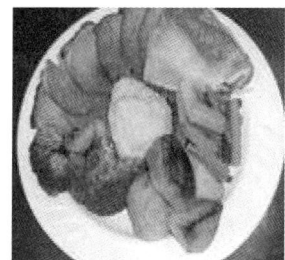

Fish and Chips

14   Fish and chips is the traditional take-away food of England. Long before McDonald's we had

the fish and chip shop. Fresh cod is the most common fish for our traditional fish and chips; other types of fish used include haddock, huss, and plaice.

15   The fresh fish is dipped in flour and then dipped in batter and deep-fried. It is then served with chips (fresh not frozen) and usually you will be asked if you want salt and vinegar added. Sometimes people will order curry sauce, mushy peas[23] or pickled eggs[24].

16   Traditionally fish and chips were served up wrapped in old newspaper. Nowadays (thanks to hygiene laws) they are wrapped in greaseproof paper[25] and sometimes paper that has been specially printed to look like newspaper. You often get a small wooden or plastic fork to eat them with too, although it is quite ok to use your fingers.

British Cheese

17   Cheese is made from the curdled milk[26] of various animals: most commonly cows but often goats, sheep and even reindeer, and buffalo. Rennet is often used to induce milk to coagulate, although some cheeses are curdled with acids like vinegar or lemon juice or with extracts of vegetable rennet.

18   Britain started producing cheese thousands of years ago. However, it was in Roman times that the cheese-making process was originally honed and the techniques developed. In the Middle Ages, the gauntlet was passed to the monasteries that flourished following the Norman invasion.[27] It is to these innovative monks that we are indebted for so many of the now classic types of cheese that are produced in Britain.

19   The tradition of making cheese nearly died out during WWII, when due to rationing only one type of cheese could be manufactured—the unappealingly named "National Cheese". The discovery and revival of old recipes and the development of new types of cheese has seen the British cheese industry flourish in recent years and diversify in a way not seen since the 17th century.

The Future

20   The food industry in Britain is now undergoing major changes. From a resurgence of interest in organic food to the other extreme—genetically modified (GM) food[28]. GM food has so incensed the general public that there have been mass demonstrations against it all over the country.

Proper Food Names

saffron	藏红花
ginger	生姜
sole	鳎鱼

exotic fruit	奇异果
plaice	蝶鱼
cod	鳕鱼
halibut	比目鱼
mullet	鲻鱼
dory	海舫
crustaceans	甲壳类
lobster	龙虾
oyster	牡蛎
eel	鳗鱼
parsley	欧芹
shallot	葱
haddock	熏鳕鱼
huss	鲨鱼肉
rennet	凝乳酶

Notes

1. After years of disparagement by various countries (especially the French) Britain now has an enviable culinary reputation. 此句大意为：很多年来，烹饪方面，英国一直受到许多国家(尤其是法国)的轻蔑，但是现在英国在这方面获得了令人羡慕的声誉。

2. Ceylon: 锡兰

3. chutney: 酸辣酱

4. kedgeree: 印度鸡蛋葱豆饭

5. mulligatawny: 咖喱肉汤

6. potpourri: 肉菜杂烩

7. medieval times: 中世纪

8. Frankish Normans: 法兰克诺曼底人

9. sweetener: 甜味佐料

10. Despite being part of Europe today, we've kept up our links with the countries of the former British Empire, now united under the Commonwealth. 此句大意为：英国虽然是欧洲的一部分，但它仍然与前大英帝国的其他国家保持着联系，作为英联邦帝国的成员,我们仍然紧密团结。

11. From East Asia (China) we adopted tea (and exported the habit to India), and from India we adopted curry-style spicing, we even developed a line of spicy sauces including ketchup, mint sauce, Worcestershire sauce and deviled sauce to indulge these tastes. 此句大意为：从东亚，尤其是中国，我们学会了喝茶，(然后又把这个习惯带到了印度)。在印度，我们学会了使用具有咖喱风味的调料，我们甚至研制出了一系列的新辣酱，有番茄酱、薄荷酱、伍斯

特郡酱与芥末酱，使人们的味蕾得到了无尽的享受。

12. travel in convoys: 集结而行

13. food rationing: 食物配给

14. The British tradition of stews, pies and breads, according to the taste buds of the rest of the world, went into terminal decline. 此句意为：炖菜、馅饼、面包这些英国传统菜肴，彻底被其他国家人们的味蕾拒绝了。

15. gastronomic joke: 烹饪笑话 (指在烹饪方面被其他国家的人看不起)

16. **Nouvelle Cuisine:** 新派法国菜派系

The food industry in Britain is now undergoing major changes. From a resurgence of interest in organic food to the other extreme—genetically modified (GM) food, GM food has so incensed the general public that there have been mass demonstrations against it all over the country.

17. Game has enjoyed a resurgence in popularity although it always had a central role in the British diet, which reflects both the abundant richness of the forests and streams and an old aristocratic prejudice against butchered meats. 此句大意为：虽然猎物在英国饮食中一直占有非常重要的地位，现在再度兴极一时，这不仅反映了英国森林资源和溪水资源的丰富，也反映了老派贵族们对于屠宰肉的歧视之意。

18. roast beef and Yorkshire pudding, Cornish pasties, steak and kidney pie, bread and butter pudding, treacle tart, spotted dick or fish and chips: 烤牛肉、约克布丁、康尔郡菜肉烘饼、牛排、腰子派、面包黄油布丁、蜜糖馅饼、炸鱼加土豆条

19. Rice and pasta have accounted for the decrease in potato consumption and the consumption of meat has also fallen. 此句大意为：由于米、面食用量的增加，土豆食用量减少，肉的食用量也减少了。

20. choice item: 上等的食物

21. on offer: 出售中

22. mugs of ales and a feast of oxen roasted on a spit: 几杯淡啤和烤肉签上的牛肉大餐

23. mushy peas: 豌豆泥

24. pickled eggs: 腌蛋

25. greaseproof paper: 防油纸

26. the curdled milk: 凝乳

27. In the Middle Ages, the gauntlet was passed to the monasteries that flourished following the Norman invasion. 此句大意为：在中世纪，修道院曾兴极一时，随着诺曼底人的侵入，改良奶酪的重任于是交给了他们。

28. genetically modified food: 基因改良食品

● **Reading Comprehension**

1. Directions: *Fill in the table according to the passage about the British Cuisine.*

The history:

➢   British cuisine has always been __1__, a potpourri of __2__ styles, but it was damaged greatly during __3__ in January 1940.

1)   British cuisine has been influenced by __4__ and __5__.

2)   From __6__. we adopted tea, from __7__ we adopted curry-style spicing.

Today:

➢   In the late 1980s, British started to look a little closer to __8__ for inspiration.

1)   __9__ enjoys resurgence in popularity.

2)   __10__ is the nation culinary pride.

3)   Today, there is more emphasis on fine, fresh __11__ in the better restaurant.

4)   __12__ is still important to English diet.

The future:

➢   The food industry in Britain is undergoing major __13__.

__14__ has incensed the general public and aroused mass demonstrations.

---

2. Directions: *Read the following statements carefully, and decide whether they are true (T) or false (F) according to the text.*

_____ 1) French had showed contempt to British cuisine for many years before British got enviable culinary reputation.

_____ 2) British cuisine has adopted styles of different countries, and thus becomes multicultural.

_____ 3) Due to goods shortage, food rationing began during the First World War.

_____ 4) Many traditional dishes remain popular, so the eating habits have been almost the same in Britain.

_____ 5) It was very difficult for people to get to buy fish and chips before it became part of McDonald's menu.

_____ 6) Many types of classic types of cheese were created by the monasteries in the Middle Ages.

Passage Two

Warm-up questions:

1. What is your favorite Chinese food?

2. What is the most impressive characteristic of Chinese food in your mind?

Chinese Food Cultural Profile

Nutrition and Food

"Fashion is in Europe, living is in America, but eating is in China."

1   The phrase is a testament to the popularity of Chinese food around the world. Food is an important part of daily life for Chinese people. Chinese not only enjoy eating but believe eating good food can bring harmony and closeness to the family and relationships.

Bok choy

2   Shopping daily for fresh food is essential for all Chinese cooking. Unlike the fast food society of the U.S., the Chinese select live seafood, fresh meats and seasonal fruits and vegetables from the local market to ensure freshness. This means swimming fish, snappy crabs, and squawking chickens[1]. Even prepared foods such as dim sum or BBQ duck for to go orders must gleam, glisten, and steam[2] as if just taken out of the oven.

3   Chinese people in general are not as concerned about nutrition as Western culture. They are more concerned with the food's texture, flavor, color, and aroma[3]. These are the crucial points for good Chinese cooking. Chinese daily meals consist of four food groups: grains, vegetables, fruit, and meat. A typical Chinese's meal usually consists of rice, soup and three to four side dishes. Dishes are made of seasonal vegetables, fresh seafood or bite-size portion of meat or poultry. In Chinese food, meat portions are usually small, and often used for the purpose of flavoring the dish or soup. Vegetables, fruits, and meats are usually fresh. Some exceptions include preserved vegetables such as snow cabbage or mustard greens, preserved eggs, also known as "thousand year old eggs" or salted and dried fish. Other exceptions include snack items such as beef jerky,

cuttlefish jerky, sweet and sour preserved plums, or dehydrated[4] mango slices. Canned or frozen foods are seldom eaten. After dinner, families usually eat seasonal fruit as dessert. Chinese desserts such as red bean soup, sweet white lotus's seed soup, or steam papaya soup are served every so often as a special treat on a hot summer's night.

"Yi xing bu xing"

4   Chinese hardly waste any section of the animal and have found ways to cook nearly every part. Chinese culture believes that "yi xing bu xing", which means by using any shape or part of the animal the same part of the human body can be replenished and strengthened[5]. For example, shark fin soup and bird nest soup (bird's saliva) is served to replenish strength and increase appetite, crocodile meat strengthens the bronchia[6], dehydrated tiger testicle increases stamina for men[7], while monkey brains add wisdom. These foods are considered to be delicacies and tonics[8]. Shark fin soup or bird nest soup is often served at special occasions such as at a Chinese banquet dinner. Other items are rarely prepared.

Regional Cuisine

5   There are many different cuisines in China. Each province has its own special style of cooking. There is Beijing cuisine, Hunan or Hubei cuisine, Shanghai cuisine, Sichuan cuisine, Cantonese cuisine, Hakka cuisine[9], etc. The most well known cuisines are Sichuan and Cantonese. The Sichuan cuisine has the spiciest dishes. They use a lot of chili paste, red pepper, and hot oil in their food. The most famous Sichuan dishes are hot chili eggplant, twice-cooked pork, Sichuan beef, Ma Po Tofu, and Kung Pau Chicken. These dishes are all very spicy and delicious.

6   The Cantonese cuisine is the most well known cuisine in the Chinese community. In fact, in China, they say, "Eating is in Canton." Cantonese people are known to be quite particular and have high expectations about their food. All the vegetables, poultry, and ingredients have to be fresh. The timing on the cooking is very crucial. Dishes must not be overcooked, and the texture of the food has to be just right with the freshness and tenderness still remaining. For this reason, Cantonese food is very popular. Soup is also essential in Cantonese cuisine. It consists of different ingredients and herbs and is boiled to a rich and tasty soup before it is served. There are many kinds of soup and each soup has its own function or purpose. Cantonese women believe that "to win a man's heart, she must first learn how to cook a good pot of soup."

Yin Yang Foods

7   As mentioned before, due to geographical and climate differences in China, each area has its own way of cooking and different eating habits. Northern China has cold weather, and therefore people there eat more hot and spicy foods such as chilies, onions, and garlic. They believe these foods will increase blood circulation and help get rid of the coldness. Generally people from the south like to eat more mild and cooling foods because of the warmer climate. These foods reduce the hotness. This theory is called balancing "Yin and yang".

8   Chinese culture believes there is a positive energy and a negative energy in the universe. "Yin" represents negative energy and "yang" represents positive energy. They have to be equally balanced to create a harmonious and healthy state, otherwise, conflict and disease will be created. There are elements that belong to both "yin" and "yang", meaning some elements of "yin" fall within "yang" and some elements of "yang" fall within "yin". This importance of balancing forces has been a part of Chinese thought for thousands of years. It has become a basic guideline for social, political, medical, and dietary usage[10].

Bitter Melon

9   Foods belonging to the "yin" (also known as "cold" food) are bitter melon, winter melon, Chinese green, mustard green, Chinese cabbage, bean sprout, soybean, mung bean, tulip, water chestnut, cilantro, oranges, watermelon, bananas, coconut, cucumber, beer, ice cream, ice chips, grass jelly, clams, and oysters. These foods cannot be eaten excessively and are thought to cause stomachaches, diarrhea[11], dizziness, weakness, and coldness in the body if done so.

10   Foods that belong to the "yang" (also known as "hot" food) are chili pepper, garlic, onion, curry, cabbage, eggplant, toro, pineapple, mango, cherry, peanuts, beef, turkey, shrimp, crab, French fries, fried chicken, and pizza. Excessive intake of these foods are thought to cause skin rashes, hives, pimples, nose bleeds, indigestion, constipation, redness in the eyes, and sore throat[12]. Both food groups need to be balanced evenly, not taken excessively or deficiently in order to create a harmonious and healthy state.

Red Pepper

Grains and Carbohydrates—Rice, Noodles, Buns

Rice

11   Rice and noodles are a very important part in the Chinese diet. Rice and noodles are equivalent to potato and pasta in the western diet. Handfuls of bite-sized meat and vegetables accompany the rice and noodles. Almost every meal uses rice. The different types of rice are sweet rice, long grain rice, short grain rice, jasmine rice, and brown rice[13]. The different ways to prepare rice are steamed rice, rice soup, fried rice, and pot rice. People living in south China especially consume large amounts of rice. On the north side of China, people consume more noodles or steam buns (bread). Polished rice (white rice) contains 25% carbohydrates and small amounts of iodine, iron, magnesium, and phosphate[14]. For brown rice, the bran[15] part has not been removed from the rice. In the old days, only the poor Chinese people ate brown rice, but now studies show that brown rice actually contains more vitamin B than the polished rice. There are many processes involved before the white rice is ready for the market. Rice is treated most respectfully in China. Every grain of rice represents a hardship of labor. Parents always tell their children to finish every grain of rice in the bowl; otherwise, they will marry someone with a pimple-scarred face.

Noodles

12   Chinese noodles come in different sizes and shapes. They can be cooked in the soup or stir-fried, which is known as "chow mien". Noodles are usually served for breakfast, lunch, or late snacks. During birthday celebrations, noodles are served to symbolize long life. The longer the noodle, the longer the life will be for the birthday person. Accompanying meat and vegetables are chopped up into small pieces and stir-fried or steamed. A dinner meal usually has soup in the middle, surrounded by 3 to 5 main dishes of vegetables, seafood, and poultry dishes.

Buns and Breads

14   Chinese bakeries carry pastries and sweet buns filled with delights such as red bean paste, egg custard[16], BBQ pork, or coconut cream. Families eat them on the run for breakfast, or to curb a midday snack attack[17]. Hong Kong bakeries are known for their wide variety of baked and steamed buns, which may have been influenced by English high tea culture during British rule of the colony. Northern Chinese are known for their fluffy white buns, which may be served in place of rice during meals. In the U.S., we often see these white buns served with Peking Duck.

Proper Food Names

dim sum	点心
snow cabbage	雪里红(一种腌菜)
mustard green	芥菜
cuttlefish jerky	墨鱼干
lotus	莲子
papaya	木瓜
Chinese cabbage	大白菜
bean sprout	豆芽
mung bean	绿豆
water chestnut	荸荠
cilantro	香菜
grass jelly	凉粉
clam	蛤蜊
toro	一种高级牛肉
bok choy	白菜

Notes

1. swimming fish, snappy crabs, and squawking chickens: 鲜活的鱼、爬动的蟹、咯咯叫的鸡(指食材的新鲜)

2. Even prepared foods such as dim sum or BBQ duck for to go orders must gleam, glisten, and steam: 此处 dim sum 指"点心"; BBQ duck 指"烤鸭"; for to go order 指"供外卖的"; gleam,

glisten, and steam 指 "食物新鲜、色泽好且热气腾腾"。

3. texture, flavor, color, and aroma: 食物的色香味形俱全

4. dehydrated: 脱水的(此处指蜜饯类水果，如：dehydrated mango slice 芒果干)

5. replenished and strengthened: 此处指体力可以得到补充和加强。

6. bronchia: 支气管

7. dehydrated tiger testicle increases stamina for men: 吃虎鞭(老虎的睾丸)能增加男性的精力

8. delicacies and tonics: 此处指这些食物不仅是美味的食物，还是强身的补药。

9. **Beijing cuisine, Hunan or Hubei cuisine, Shanghai cuisine, Sichuan cuisine, Cantonese cuisine, Hakka cuisine:** (中国的几大菜系)北京菜、湖南(湖北)菜、上海菜、四川菜、广东菜、客家菜

10. dietary usage: 饮食的功能

11. diarrhea: 痢疾

12. Excessive intake of these foods are thought to cause skin rashes, hives, pimples, nose bleeds, indigestion, constipation, redness in the eyes, and sore throat. 此句大意为：过度摄取此类食物会导致皮疹、荨麻疹、丘疹、流鼻血、消化不良、便秘、红眼症和嗓子疼。

13. sweet rice, long grain rice, short grain rice, jasmine rice, and brown rice: (米的种类)糯米、长粒米、短粒米、香米和糙米

14. iodine, iron, magnesium, and phosphate: 碘、铁、镁、磷酸

15. bran: 糠

16. egg custard: 蛋黄和牛奶调成的一种馅

17. curb a midday snack attack: 此处指上下午的时候当点心吃

● **Reading Comprehension**

1. Directions: *Discuss the following questions with your classmates.*

1) What do Chinese daily meals consist of?

2) What is the function of meat in Chinese dishes?

3) Can you quote an example of "yi xing bu xing" from the passage?

4) Why do people say "Eating is in Canton"?

5) What are the "yin" food and "yang" food according to the passage?

6) What are the equivalents of rice and noodles in Western meals?

2. **Directions:** *Item I is the title of each part of the text. Item II is the idea mentioned in each part of the text. Match the idea with the title.*

Item I	Item II
_____ "Fashion is in Europe, living is in America, but eating is in China."	a. There is a balance in human body and if the balance is upset, diseases will be created.
_____ "Yi xing bu xing."	b. It has a very special meaning on somebody's

_____ Regional Cuisine

_____ Yin Yang foods

_____ Rice

_____ Noodles

_____ Buns and breads

birthday.

c. Freshness plays a very important role in Chinese cooking.

d. It has various stuffing.

e. By eating some part of the animal, the same part of the human body can be gained.

f. It is a very respectful grain not only because it is consumed every day but also because it needs a lot of labor before it is sold.

g. Soup is vital in Cantonese cuisine and it consists of different ingredients and herbs.

Part Three

Topic-related Activities

1. Food for Thought: Digging into Family and Holiday Traditions

Step One

Directions: *Ask students to interview each other about special dishes or traditional food their families prepare for the Spring Festival or other holidays or celebrations.*

Step Two

Directions: *Please work in pairs and match the food in Column A with relevant holidays in Column B.*

Column A	Column B	Column A	Column B
Zong Zi	Mid-autumn Day	Turkey and pudding	Thanksgiving Day
Moon cake	The Double Seventh Festival	Egg	Christmas
Dumpling	The Dragon Boat Festival	Candy	Valentine's Day
Yuan Xiao	The Spring Festival	Turkey and Pumpkin Pie	Easter
Chocolate	The Lantern Festival	Chocolate	Halloween

Step Three

Directions: *Are there any family stories or folklore behind the holidays and the traditional food? Pick one you are interested in and make a presentation about it.*

2. Making Fresh Fruit Platters

Step One

Directions: *Work in groups of 4 or 5. Each group should bring to class different fruits for a fruit* *dinner they designed. One student from the group should introduce the English names of all the fruits to the class.*

Words for reference:

apricot 杏子	fig 无花果	persimmon 柿子
bitter orange 酸橙	litchi 荔枝	navel orange 脐橙
blackberry 黑莓	gingko 白果，银杏	papaya 木瓜
canned fruit 罐头水果	grape 葡萄	pineapple 菠萝
carambola 杨桃	Hami melon 哈密瓜	pomegranate 石榴
cherry 樱桃	hawthorn 山楂	pomelo 柚子，文旦
kiwi fruit 猕猴桃	longan 桂圆，龙眼	red bayberry 杨梅
coconut 椰子	loguat 枇杷	strawberry 草莓
cumquat 金橘	mandarine 柑橘	water chestnut 荸荠
plum 李子	mango 芒果	watermelon 西瓜

Step Two

Directions: *When some students from the group are dealing with different fruits in order to make a fresh fruit platter, one student in the group needs to explain the process to us.*

Words for reference:

chop 切	peel off 削(皮)	carve 雕刻
cut 割	mince 绞	liquidize 榨汁
slice 切片	crosscut 横切	

Step Three

Directions: *After one group has finished their work, the other groups can give comments on the fruit platter by describing the shape, color, tastes, and positions of different fruits. And then a score should be given by the other groups on the fruit platter.*

Words for reference:

方形 square	五边形 pentagon	十字形 cross
长方形(矩形) rectangular	六边形 hexagon	尖角形 angle
菱形 rhombus(diamond)	长方形 rectangle	直线 line
椭圆形 oval	梯形 echelon formation	月牙形 crescent
圆锥形 conical	圆形 circle/round	心形 heart
圆柱形 cylindrical	三角形 triangle	星形 star

Suggested criteria:
　　　　　　　　　1) The appearance of the fruits (3 points)

　　　　　　　　　2) Tastes (2 points)

　　　　　　　　　3) Language of speakers (fluency and correctness) (3 points)

　　　　　　　　　4) Interaction with the audience (1 point)

　　　　　　　　　5) Voice of the speaker (1 point)

　　　　　　　　　Total points: (10 points)

3. Food Myths

Directions: *There are many food myths in the world. For example, the following table shows some Chinese views about bad combinations of foods. That's to say, if we eat the food in Column A together with the food in Column B, we may suffer from the disease in Column C (pork + water chestnut → stomachache). Do you believe in those myths? And do you know any other food myths?*

Column A	Column B	Column C
1. pork	a. water chestnut	A. stomachache
2. beef	b. chestnut	B. vomit
3. lamb	c. watermelon	C. kidney deficiency
4. crab	d. persimmon	D. diarrhea (腹泻)
5. radish	e. agaric (木耳)	E. dermatitis (皮炎)
6. tofu	f. honey	F. deaf
7. potato	g. banana	G. dark speck on face
8. peanut	h. cucumber	H. hurt body

4. Case Study

　　During the Long March, Three Main Rules of Discipline and the Eight Points for Attention were strictly executed. The Red Army (now The People's Liberation Army) was strict with themselves. They neither took a single needle from the people, nor did they give them any trouble. Before the troops moved to the areas of Hui Nationality in Sichuan Province and Ningxia Province, they initiatively disposed of the things related to pigs, like lard, pork, smoked pork and even shoes made from pigskin. When they were in those areas, they didn't eat pork and they didn't even say any words related to pigs. They respected the customs of Hui Nationality, which won them a good impression of the minority nationality.

Notes: The Long March was a strategic operation undertaken from 1934 to 1936 by China's Red Army when being pursued by hordes of Kuomintang troops, moving its headquarters and forces along the Yangtze River to Shaanxi-Gansu Revolutionary Base.

Questions

1. Why did the Red Army dispose of those things related to pigs before moving to the Hui Nationality area?

2. Can you list some other food taboos around the world?

Part Four

Topic-related Information

1. Cuisine of China

In China eating is an art form in its own right. Chinese cuisine is a dominant branch of Chinese culture. It is a perfect fusion of color, shape, appearance and flavour. Delicious and nutritious, food is regarded as the basics of ordinary life. There are eight schools of cuisine, which are popularly known as the ninth art. These include food from Beijing, Guangdong, Sichuan, Jiangsu, Zhejiang, Hunan, Anhui and Fujian.

Beijing dishes are based on imperial court and Shandong cuisine; Beijing food has enjoyed an age-old reputation. The main methods of cooking are deep-frying, sautéing, stir-frying and roasting. Peking Duck is a Beijing favorite. This dish is renowned for its scented, crispy skin and is served with pancakes, which are spread with hoisin sauce and garnished with spring onions. All the ingredients are rolled into a tube and it is a delightful blend of taste and texture, especially the delicious crispy skin. For more exotic fare, stir-fried pigs tripe and chicken gizzard, sautéed fish slices with brewers' rice, pork fillet in brown sauce and sautéed cabbage might become firm favorites.

Guangdong food features a wide range of refined ingredients and quick frying. The dishes are fresh, tender, refreshing and smooth. Guangdong chefs will always try to adapt the dishes according to the season—light flavoring in summer but heavy during winter. Restaurants in Guangdong offer specialties such as smoked pomfret, sweet and sour pork, deep-fried egg jelly wrapped in wheat flour and steamed pomfret topped with scallions and flavored oil. Snake dishes, braised chicken, roast piglet or assorted soups in wax gourds are other dishes worth sampling. Guangdong is also famous for its moon cakes.

Sichuan dishes are noted for their varied and heavy flavors. The eight common seasonings used are pepper sauce, pepper with vinegar,

pepper with fish sauce, chili jam with wild peppercorn, cayenne pepper with wild peppercorn, black pepper with peanut and sesame paste, peppercorn with sesame oil and chili oil—all a little on the hot side, but very tasty. Distinct dishes include pork and chicken cubes with peanuts and chili, and clubbed chicken, which is chicken meat, first pounded and then shredded into floss before eight seasonings are added—a sweet but hot dish. Others include Luyang-style crisp chicken and bean curd.

Anhui specialties feature dishes stewed in brown sauce and most of the cooking a lot of oil and other sauces. Stewed fish belly in brown sauce, stir-fried eel slices, and deep-fried meatballs in plum sauce are the main delicacies offered in many restaurants in here.

Fujian dishes are usually marinated in wine and taste sour with a tinge of sweetness. "Buddha Jumps the Wall" is a famous dish with interesting ingredients. Made from sharks fin, sharks lip, fish maw, abalone, dried scallop, squid, sea cucumber, chicken breast meat, duck chops, pork tripe, pork leg, minced ham, mutton elbow, winter bamboo shoots, mushrooms and others, this lot is then seasoned and steamed separately and then put into a clay jar, mixed with cooking wine and some pigeon eggs. The jar is first covered and put over intense heat and then simmered. Four or five ounces of liquor are added while the ingredients simmer for another five minutes. The result is totally tantalizing.

Hunan curing, simmering, steaming and stewing are the main cooking methods of Hunan food. Hunan dishes are usually tinged with sour and spicy flavors. Fragrant, spicy yet slightly sour Dongan-style fried chicken is one of the main attractions.

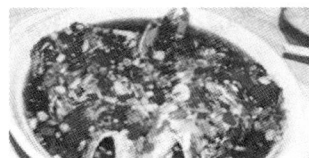

Jiangsu cuisine can be classified into three categories, the Suzhou-Wuxi, Zhenjiang-Yangzhou and Shanghai styles. Suzhou cooking tends to retain the original flavour and stock of the main ingredient and specialties are boat-shaped fried duck, braised pork in fermented bean-curd sauce, fried rolls stuffed with croakers and minced shrimp, stewed bean-curd with shrimp and ginger sauce, five-spiced chicken drumstick and so on. But most of all, one should try the sizzling rice with shrimps! Tender shrimps in tomato sauce, ladled over deep-fried, golden, crispy rice crust... delicious.

Zhenjiang-Yangzhou cooking can best be described as "the soup is crystal clear one can see the bottom of the bowl, while the sauces are so thick that they resemble cream." Among the well-known dishes are boiled bean-curd slices, crab meatballs shaped like lion-heads, butterfly-shaped sea cucumber and silvery carp in the form of lotuses.

Zhejiang food is represented by Hangzhou, Ningbo and Shaoxing styles. Hangzhou dishes are meticulously prepared and therefore are tasty and crispy. Famous features are sweet and sour fish, deep-fried fish-balls; shrimps cooked in Dragon Well tea, and braised pork Dongpo style. Exquisite dishes such as braised fish, braised eel casserole, and fried peanuts with liver moss are popular. Most dishes uses poultry as its main specialty and the dishes are usually crisp, glutinous and palatable.

Medicinal Dishes are considered as food-and-drink therapy and just as vegetarian dishes—they have been in the Chinese culture for a long time. As early as the Warring States Period (475-221 B.C.), China's ancestors realized the importance of the relationship between food and health.

China's master chefs learnt from the theory of traditional Chinese medicine and discovered a set of scientific food therapy. Famous medicinal dishes include Lily Chicken Soup, Pearl Powder Shrimps, Heavenly Carp, Preserved Duck with Bean Sauce and Minced Pork Buns.

As for snack food, China offers a variety of desserts and snacks, which will see you through the day if you do not feel like having an elaborate meal. For breakfast, there are Chinese pancakes, deep-fried twisted dough, glutinous rice balls, creamy soya bean milk, wonton soup, steamed stuffed dumplings, steamed bread with meat fillings, and various types of noodles.

Seasons play a part in the availability of snacks. Fried spring rolls and oysters marinated in wine are for spring, cold drinks and cold noodles for summer, dumplings stuffed with crabmeat and minced pork and sweet potatoes scented with osmanthus flowers for autumn and New Years glutinous rice cakes with braised pork and noodles in mutton gravy for winter.

2. Mealtimes in America

Many meals in America are arranged around popular television shows. People like to eat in front of the TV, not always sitting at a table. They sit in a chair or on a sofa. Cooking in the USA is not just hamburgers, pizza and fast food. However, the American fast food restaurant chains have been very successful at introducing American style fast food around the world. Now people from many lands believe it is what we everyone eat all of the time in the USA.

Most traditional American foods were introduced by the early European immigrants but modified to take advantage of the locally available ingredients. Fried chicken, meatloaf, baked potato, corn, baked beans and apple pie would be considered traditional American dishes.

Regional cooking varies from state to state and is highly influenced by the types of ingredients locally available, as well as the cultural background of the people that settled in the area. New England cooking, native to the northeastern states, was heavily influenced by the cuisine of the original English settlers. Southern cooking has definite African influences. Cajun cooking, from the New Orleans area, is a spicy mixture of Spanish, French and African styles. California cooking is known for the use of fresh fruits and vegetables in interesting combinations with Asian, Mexican and Spanish flavorings.

Breakfast: A typical American breakfast menu includes scrambled or fried eggs or an egg omelet, juice, bacon or sausage, toast, biscuits, or bagels. An alternative American breakfast could be cereal with milk, juice, and toast or pancakes or waffles with syrup and butter, juice, and white milk. Drinks include orange juice, milk, tea or coffee. There are different types of breakfast as follows:

Continental Breakfast—choice of orange, grapefruit, and cranberry juices, sliced fruits and seasonal berries; an assortment of bakery items such as croissants, bagels, muffins, and assorted Danishes; served with jam, cream cheese and butter; freshly brewed coffee, decaffeinated coffee and, iced & herbal teas.

All-American Breakfast Buffet—choice of orange, grapefruit, and cranberry juices, sliced fruits and seasonal berries; an assortment of bakery items such as croissants, bagels, muffins, and assorted Danishes; served with jam, cream cheese and butter; assorted bowls of cereals, granola, and raisins; individual flavored yogurts; farm fresh scrambled eggs; country sausage; three pepper bacon; breakfast potatoes; freshly brewed coffee, decaffeinated coffee and, iced & herbal teas; thick sliced French toast with warm maple syrup.

Lunch: The lunch menu normally involves sandwiches (peanut butter and/or jelly, cheese, bologna, turkey, ham), rolls, hamburgers, hot dogs, pizza, tacos, chicken, salad, fruit (orange, banana, apple, tangerine), milk, soft drink, tea or coffee.

The normal practice in America is to eat the salad before the main course. A wonderful American invention is the salad bar. In restaurants that have these salad bars the waiter does not bring your salad. You go to the salad bar and help yourself, usually to as much as you want. This is normally done after you have ordered your meal; you eat the salad while the main course is being cooked.

There are many different salads, such as: "Grilled Chicken Salad"—mixed greens tossed with warm grilled chicken breast, carrots and tortilla strips in our cider vinaigrette; topped with roasted walnut sauce. "Chicken Tender Salad"—chicken tenders atop mixed greens; avocado, scallions, tomato and shredded Cheddar, tossed in Peppercorn Ranch Dressing; drizzled with barbecue sauce. "Steak Salad"—grilled seasoned beef on mixed young greens with avocado, tomato and fresh mozzarella tossed in Italian vinaigrette.

Sandwiches are also served in many different ways. If you eat out, sandwiches may be as follows: served with crispy seasoned French Fries or mixed young greens or baked potato. Cheeseburger—grilled with your choice of cheese on a toasted sesame seed bun; cooked well done unless otherwise specified; Zone Burger—add seared mushrooms, red peppers, and onions to our Cheeseburger; cooked well done unless otherwise specified; Turkey Burger—grilled all white meat; patty with your choice of cheese on a toasted sesame seed bun.

Dinner: Dinner is normally the largest meal of the day. It normally involves food such as pizza, meat (steak, chicken, fish, pork, turkey) with potatoes and a vegetable (corn, green beans, beans, carrots, spinach, peas, greens, asparagus, cauliflower, broccoli), spaghetti with either tomato or meat sauce, lasagna, tacos, and dessert (cake, cookies, pies, ice cream, and candy). Dessert is served after the main meal—triple chocolate cake, All-American Apple Pie, rum carrot cake, Sudden Death Brownie, chocolate chip cookie sundae, berries and sorbet. Turkey is a traditional food for Thanksgiving meals.

Hyperlinks

[1] http://www.faqs.org/nutrition/Ome-Pop/Popular-Culture-Food-and.html

[2] http://chinesefood.about.com/

[3] http://www.chinesefood-recipes.com/

[4] http://allrecipes.com/Recipes/World-Cuisine/Main.aspx

References

[1] Mark Kurlansky. The Food Chains That Link US All. *Time*[J], June 13th, 2007

[2] http://www.learnenglish.de/culture/foodculture.html

[3] http://ethnomed.org/ethnomed/cultures/chinese/chinese_food.html

[4] http://218.25.62.221/english/english_list.asp?id=92

[5] http://english.cersp.com/ziyuan/jiaoan/200610/1083.html

Unit 10

Common Activities

Part One

Lead-in

That which one cannot experience in daily life is not true for oneself.

—Lawrence (Britain)

日常生活中经历不到的事，对人们来说是不真实的。

——劳伦斯(英国)

Common activities refer to "the things we normally do in daily living including any daily activity we perform for self-care, work, homemaking (such as cooking, cleaning, shopping, personal banking, health-care of family members), and leisure." They are activities full of humane values. On one hand, daily activities provide people with the perpetual structure of communication and feelings in a long and stable way; on the other hand, people can establish some kind of resembling intrinsic quality in the limit of daily activities. They play a basic role in existence and development of human beings.

Part Two

Reading Passages

In-Class Reading

Warm-up questions:

1. Where do you usually shop? Please make a comparison of the ways that people shop in their daily life.

2. What are the payment options in China?

Shopping

1　　Shopping is a large part of American life. The shopping choices in the Argonne area[1] are many. The nearest stores are north of the Laboratory[2] along 75th Street. Stores are located almost continuously for several miles from Kingery Highway on the east to Janes Avenue, west of Interstate 355[3]. In addition there are many malls and **clusters** of stores further north along 63rd Street and on Ogden Avenue. Store hours vary, but are usually 9:00 or 10:00 a.m. to 9:00 p.m. Large food stores remain open longer and several supermarkets are open 24 hours a day. The Newcomers Assistance Office has several pages of information available on local shopping with locations and directions.

2　　An important thing to learn about shopping in America is that a wide range of prices can be charged for the same or **comparable** merchandise. This includes all available goods, but especially clothing, food, electronics, furniture and house wares. Many supermarket advertisements are included in the Sunday and Wednesday editions of Chicago newspapers. These **itemize** the many sale items being offered that week that are often well below the normal price. All stores regularly hold sales at which merchandise is sold at a lower price. If you have the option to wait, you can save considerable amounts of money as the item you require may be offered at a reduced price.

3　　Stores usually allow you to return purchased merchandise if the item has not been used or damaged. You will have to give a reason for the return, such as it doesn't work, wrong size, color not right, etc. Some stores, especially smaller ones, may have a time limit for returns. You must have the original purchase receipt to obtain a refund. Merchandise purchased at a "sale" price may not be returnable. Also some stores now charge a restocking fee[4] on returned items.

Supermarkets

4　　The Chicago area is rich in ethnic diversity. Food stores offering the specialties of many nations can be found in the city and its

surrounding communities. The area near Argonne has many stores specializing in Asian and South Asian products, as well as those from Mexico which reflects the population of many families of **Chinese**, **Filipino**, Indian and **Hispanic** heritage here. The major supermarket chains in the Chicago area all carry a large selection, including many international foods. Most have fresh fish departments and full service pharmacies selling both prescription and non-prescription drugs. In addition, each Jewel, Dominick's, Cub and Meijer store[5] has a large non-food section which carries cosmetics, toys, school and office supplies and household goods.

Shopping Centers

5   A shopping center is a collection of stores and shops offering a wide variety of products and services. Many small shopping centers have self-service[6] **laundromats**, dry cleaners, barbers, and hairdressers. The large shopping center (or mall) sits in the middle of a gigantic parking lot and can cater to the needs of thousands of people at once. It features two to four large department stores plus many smaller shops and restaurants. There are several malls within a thirty-minute drive of Argonne:

- Yorktown Center—at Highland & Butterfield Roads, Lombard
- Oakbrook Center—22nd Street & Kingery Highway , Oakbrook
- The Promenade at Bolingbrook , E Boughton Rd & Janes Ave , Bolingbrook
- Westfield Shopping town at Fox Valley—Route 59 & New York Ave , Aurora

Discount/Outlet Stores

6   Although the traditional department stores and smaller, individually owned stores may charge fixed prices, often the same items can be bought for less at discount stores. This is particularly true for electrical appliances, clothes, hardware, and house wares. Although these discount stores provide little in the way of personal service, they sell items at prices 20% or more less than those of conventional stores. Be careful when **patronizing** a discount store because some stores advertise "discounts" that may not be much of a savings and the merchandise may be of an inferior quality. Outlet stores offer merchandise from one company directly from the factory often at a reduced price. The closest outlet mall is Chicago Premium Outlets on I-88 at Farnsworth Ave in Aurora.

Payment Options

7   You can pay for any item at a store with cash. As most Americans do not carry much cash with them the most common form of payment is with a credit card, debit card[7] or check. Other options include:

8   **Store Specific Charge Accounts:** At some stores, you can arrange to make your purchases on credit by applying for a store credit card. The store will send you a bill or statement once a month. There is no charge for this service if you pay the

total amount of the bill within 30 days; otherwise, customers are charged interest on the unpaid balance similar to other major credit cards such as MasterCard[8]. Often you can save a certain percentage on all purchases using the special store charge card when opening the account and on special days throughout the year.

9   **Lay-Away Buying**: Some stores will hold an item for you until total payment has been made. You make arrangements with the store, according to their layaway policy, on how many payments must be made before total payment is completed so that you may take possession of the article.[9] You do not pay interest on lay-away buying.

10   **Installment Buying**: This is a method of paying for an item over an extended period of time. Payments are made in equal monthly amounts; a service charge, interest on the unpaid balance, is added monthly to the bill. Installment buying can add as much as 21% additional cost per year to the item purchased, but it does allow you to have immediate possession. Be cautious with offers of "do not pay for 12 months" as there are often hidden costs in using such a service and severe penalties for a missing or late payment.[10]

New Words and Expressions

cluster	*n.*	a group of things of the same kind that are very close together 群，组
comparable	*a.*	similar to something else in size, number, quality, etc, so that you can make a comparison 同类的
itemize	*v.*	make a list and give details about each thing on the list 列出清单
Filipino	*a.*	from or relating to Philippines 菲律宾的
Hispanic	*a.*	from or relating to countries where Spanish or Portuguese are spoken, especially ones in Latin America 西班牙的
laundromat	*n.*	a self-service laundry 自助洗衣店
patronize	*v.*	visit a shop 光顾，惠顾

Notes

1. Argonne area: 阿贡地区
2. Laboratory: 文中指美国阿贡国家实验室(Argonne National Laboratory)
3. **Interstate 355:** also known as the Veterans Memorial Tollway, an interstate highway and tollway in the western and southwest suburbs of Chicago, Illinois, U.S.
4. restocking fee: amount charged by a seller for accepting a returned merchandise and paying a refund 退货费用
5. Dominick's, Cub and Meijer store: 商店名称
6. **self-service**: a self-service restaurant, shop, etc., is one in which you get things for yourself and then pay for them.
7. **a debit card:** (also known as a bank card or check card) a plastic card which provides an

alternative payment method to cash when making purchases

8. **MasterCard:** 万事达信用卡

9. You make arrangements with the store, according to their layaway policy, on how many payments must be made before total payment is completed so that you may take possession of the article. 此句意为：根据"分期累计预付购物政策"，商家和客户约定，客户分几次付清货款后，最终拥有该产品。

10. Be cautious with offers of "do not pay for 12 months" as there are often hidden costs in using such a service and severe penalties for a missing or late payment. 此句意为：商家提出 12 个月内无须付款的时候要当心，因为采用分期付款这种方式会有隐藏的费用，如果顾客不付款或者逾期付款的话，就会受到重罚。

● **Reading Comprehension**

1. Directions: *Discuss the following questions with your classmates.*

1) What are the store hours in Chicago according to the passage?

2) How could you return purchased merchandise?

3) Why should we be careful when we purchase the product at the discount store?

4) What are the payment options in Chicago? What about China?

5) What is the advantage of paying for the item with a store credit card?

6) What's the difference between lay-away buying and installment buying?

2. Directions: *Read the following statements carefully, and decide whether they are true (T) or false (F) according to the text.*

_____ 1) You may find the information of sale items in the editions of Chicago newspapers.

_____ 2) Stores usually allow you to return any purchased merchandize if the item has not been used or damaged.

_____ 3) Discount stores usually offer merchandise from one company direct from the factory at a reduced price.

_____ 4) You do not have to pay interest on installment buying.

_____ 5) If you do not pay for the item within the time limit when using the service of installment buying, you will be severely punished.

● **Discussion**

Please make a comparison between Chinese and Americans from the perspective of their shopping habits, and payment options.

After-Class Reading

Passage One

Warm-up questions:

1. Do you have a bank card or credit card? How do you apply for it?

2. Where and how do you use your bank card or credit card? Do you have any such experience? Do you have any trouble in using your bank card or credit card?

No More Sneaky Fees

1   Think you've never been charged a sneaky fee by your bank, broker, credit-card issuer or cell-phone provider? Then you haven't looked at your bills very closely. The Internet has made it easy to compare shops with a few clicks, so companies find it tougher to raise prices. As a result, they've taken to boosting revenue by adding fees on the back end. In 2007, Americans paid almost $30 billion in fees to credit-card issuers, reports R. K. Hammer, a bankcard advisory firm. "Companies figure they'll throw in as many fees as they can and a large percentage of people won't complain," says Bob Sullivan, author of *Gotcha Capitalism*[1].

2   Don't be one of them. If your bank, for example, suddenly slaps a $5 monthly fee on your checking account, you're not necessarily bound to pay it. In fact, you can save thousands of dollars a year if you pick your battles and fight smart. Sullivan has his own methods:

Call during Business Hours

3   Few managers are available on weekends, and you won't get the cream of the crop[2] among lower-level representatives. At Gethuman.com[3], you can find codes that let you avoid using company phone trees.

Do Your Research and Flex Your Muscle

4   Tabulate how much money you've spent with the company, which can boost your bargaining power. If you think you've been treated unfairly, don't hesitate to say you're considering a letter to the state attorney general[4].

Don't Waste Your Time

5   A $2 fee may get your goat[5], but you can't afford to fight every charge. Your chances of winning are directly correlated to how much power you have. With financial services, such as banking and credit, "consumers ultimately hold all the power because they can vote with their feet[6]," says Greg MeBride, of Bankrate.com[7]. In fact, a survey for Sullivan's book found that customers who complain to credit-card companies get results 65% of the time.

6   This month, we show you how to avoid the most annoying fees—and save $5,000 (or more) a year.

Bank Accounts and Credit Cards

7   When Ilana Matfis moved from Sharon, Mass., to San Francisco, she figured that ordering new checks from Bank of America would be a snap. But when the new set arrived "they'd spelled San Francisco wrong," recalls Matfis, 25.

8   After misspelling Matfis's name on the second order of checks, the bank finally got it right—then sent her a tab for all three sets. "The charges were only about $10 each time, but I had to dispute them on principle," says Matfis. A customer-service representative in San Francisco refused to issue a refund. So she called her branch back in Sharon, where an employee remembered ordering the first batch of checks and agreed to remove all the charges.

9   There's little hope of restitution for some fees, such as the $3 to $5 you'll pay to withdraw cash from an out-of-network ATM[8], so it pays not to stray. Or open an account with a bank that reimburses ATM fees.

10   McBride says that as long as your account isn't paying interest, you should be able to qualify for free checking. If your bank balks, head elsewhere.

11   Also worth the haggle are fees for receiving canceled checks with your monthly statement (up to $3); getting a replacement ATM card ($5); making too many monthly transfers (up to $10); or using a live representative instead of the phone tree (up to $2).

12   The best way to avoid the dreaded insufficient-funds fee—which averages $28 for the first overdraft or bounced check[9] and may increase as offenses pile up—is to balance your account regularly. As an alternative, link your checking account[10] to a savings account[11] so that overdrafts are covered by your own funds. Expect to pay $5 to $10 for triggering the service, but you'll avoid interest charges on an overdraft line of credit.

13   The success rate for challenging credit-card fees is higher than with bank-account fees. Even supposedly nonnegotiable charges, such as late-payment fees, aren't set in stone[12]. "If you're a good customer, you can probably get late fees removed once a year," says Bill Hardekopf, of Lowcards.com.[13] The tardy payment may still tarnish your credit score, but you'll be as much as $39 richer.

14   Other fees worth a phone call: the 3% many card issuers charge to transfer a balance; the fee of up to $5 for a duplicate copy of a bill; and the fee of as much as $25 to rush you a replacement card.

15   Companies have to notify you when they add a new fee, but "it might come in a white envelope that looks like junk mail," says Hardekopf. Sign up for electronic delivery to stay on top of sneaky maneuvers.

Stocks and Mutual Funds

16   Making a buck on your investments is tough enough without watching your profits nibbled away by fees that are pesky at best and punitive at worst. The best way to avoid them is to deal

with firms that offer the best value for the services you want.

17   Lance Cashion saved $3,200 in commissions over the past year by using a broker that's in sync with his investing strategy. Cashion, a 33-year-old technology executive at an insurance firm, frequently trades stocks and options. But the fees at TD Ameritrade[14] "were killing me," he says. TD Ameritrade charges $9.99 per online stock trade, and $9.99 for an options trade plus 75 cents per contract.

18   So last year Cashion made the switch to Zecco Trading[15], which offers ten free stock trades per month on accounts with $2,500 or more and charges $4.50 per stock trade thereafter. For options, Zecco charges $4.50 per online trade plus 50 cents per contract. "I'm going to go wherever the free trades are," says Cashion, who lives in Fort Worth.

19   But commissions aren't everything. Cashion and his wife, Kathryn, keep their retirement assets with TD Ameritrade because they like the firm's service.

20   Online brokers now charge an average of $10 per stock trade, says Adam Honoré, of Aite Group[16], a financial research firm. That's considerably less than the $30 or more that full-service brokers charge for an online stock trade. If you don't need the extra attention, don't pay for it.

21   Buy-and-hold investors should avoid brokers that charge an inactivity fee. E*Trade (Financial Corporation), for example, slaps a fee of $40 per quarter on account holders who don't make any trades.

22   Investors with smaller balances should also mind account minimums. Vanguard[17], for instance, has a well-earned reputation for low-cost mutual funds. But it charges an annual service fee of $20 for each fund with an account balance of less than $10,000. You can avoid the charge by signing up for electronic delivery of your statements.

23   To encourage customers to use electronic statements, some firms charge for a paper trail. TD Ameritrade bills customers $2 per month for paper statements.

24   Transfer fees can hamstring you if you want investment options that aren't on your firm's menu. Charles Schwab[18] charges $25 to move part of your balance to another firm and $50 to move the entire amount.

25   Most broker fees are clearly listed on a brochure. One glaring exception is the 12b-1 fee[19], which is really a sales charge in disguise. Funds may tack on the fee—up to 1% of your investment—to their expenses, supposedly to cover marketing and distribution costs. It's actually used primarily to pay brokers or advisers who sell you the fund.

—Kiplinger

Notes

1. Gotcha Capitalism: It is a book written by Bob Sullivan in the year 2007. The book primarily serves two purposes: (1) expose the various fees; and (2) provide tips and strategies for fighting back on these fees.

2. the cream of the crop: 精英，优秀人才

3. Gethuman.com: a website providing database of bypass phone systems, on which you can talk to a live person and share customer help tips

4. the state attorney general: 州首席检察官

5. get your goat: [俚语]惹火

6. vote with feet: 用脚投票(意指：客户对你满意了，就会走到你身边，而不是竞争对手的身边)

7. Bankrate.com: a website which provides mortgage loan rate quotes for home loans, mortgages, home equity loan, auto loans, and the best credit cards

8. **ATM:** automated teller machine 自动存取款机

9. **bounced check:** 被拒付的支票

10. **checking account:** 支票户头

11. **a savings account:** 储蓄账户

12. set in stone: 一成不变

13. Lowcards.com: a website for credit card information including thousands of credit card offers and rates to find the best credit cards

14. TD Ameritrade: one American bank

15. Zecco Trading: a company providing online stock exchange service

16. Aite Group: a research and advisory firm focused on business, technology and regulatory issues and their impact on the financial services industry

17. Vanguard: a client-owned investment management company

18. Charles Schwab: a leading provider of investment services including online investing, financial advice and banking solutions

19. 12b-1 fee: an extra fee charged by some mutual funds to cover promotion, distributions, marketing expenses, and sometimes commissions to brokers

● **Reading Comprehension**

1. Directions: *Discuss the following questions with your classmates.*

1) What does "if you pick your battles and fight smart" mean in the second paragraph?

2) According to Bob Sullivan, what are the tactics that can help save thousands of dollars a year?

3) What are the fees that are worth the haggle?

4) What is the best way to avoid the dreaded insufficient-funds fee?

5) How did Lance Cashion save $3,200 in commissions over the past year?

6) How can one avoid the charge of an annual service fee of $20 with Vanguard?

2. Directions: *Match the corresponding information of Column B with the information of Column A with a line.*

Column A	Column B
Gethuman.com	has a well-earned reputation

Lowcards.com	offers 10 free stock trades per month on accounts with $2,500 or more
TD Ameritrade	charges $9.99 per online stock trade
Zecco trading	removes your late fee once a year
Aite group	is a financial research firm
Vanguard	has codes letting you avoid using company phone trees

Passage Two

Warm-up questions:

1. Do you often see the doctor? Do you know any differences between China and any western countries in seeing a doctor?

2. What do you know about Chinese health insurance plans? Have you ever purchased any healthcare insurance?

How Deductibles and Co-pays Work

Introduction to How Deductibles and Co-pays Work

1   Health-care costs have gone up for the sixth year in a row[1], increasing at rate higher than inflation. Those who can still afford health care are often finding that their benefits are being trimmed[2] while their co-pays and deductibles are increasing. With these growing costs is the growing importance of getting the most out of your health-care coverage[3]. Unfortunately, health-care policies are often complicated and confusing, filled with jargon[4] that can confuse anyone without a law degree.

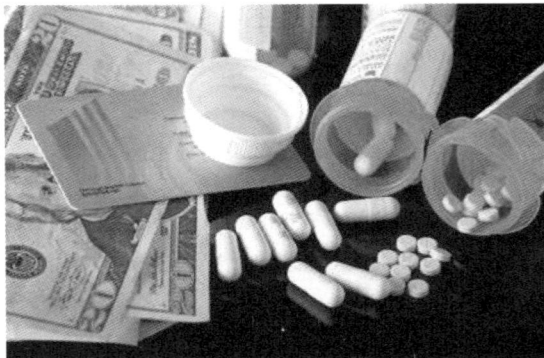

2   So let's start with a few basic terms: a co-payment and a deductible. Once we decipher[5] what they mean, we will attempt to explain how they are used in different types of health insurance plans. Perhaps a little bit of knowledge will save you some health-care cash.

3   A co-payment, or co-pay, is the flat amount[6] you pay at the time of a medical service or to receive a medication. Each health insurance plan establishes these fees up front[7]—they are often printed on your health insurance card. Insurance companies use these co-pays in part to share

expenses with you. In addition to cutting a small portion of the costs, the co-pay is also used to prevent people from seeking care for every trivial medical condition they might encounter[8].

4　In this way, co-pays can save an insurance company a substantial amount of money. However, while the co-pay has been found to lower costs by making people think twice before running to the doctor over a case of the sniffles, they might also prevent people from seeking necessary medical attention. For example, a person with a chronic condition may need to see four doctors over the course of a month, all of which require a $25 co-pay. However, if that patient cannot afford $100 each month, he or she will most likely skip one, if not all, of those appointments. Co-pays can often total hundreds of dollars each month if you have several health ailments[9]. In these cases, many patients begin to pick and choose which medications they deem necessary, making for a potentially dangerous situation. But most would say that the alternative—no health insurance—would be worse.

5　Now that we've defined co-pay, let's move on to the deductible.

Deductibles

6　A deductible is a fixed amount of money you have to pay before most, if not all, of the policy's benefits can be enjoyed. However, in many health insurance policies, you can use some services, like a visit to the emergency room or a routine doctor's visit, without meeting the deductible[10] first. These services will vary with each type of plan.

7　A deductible amount is calculated yearly, so you have to meet a new deductible for each year of the policy. Before you meet this amount, you are required to pay for health care. Once you meet this deductible, however, the health insurance benefits kick in[11], and you're then responsible only for paying monthly premiums[12] and coinsurance if applicable. Deductible amounts vary by plan and can be separated into individual or family deductibles. In general, a family deductible is double an individual deductible, but it can include several members of a family.

8　A plan with a high deductible will have a low monthly premium, and vice versa. If you are relatively healthy, a smart rule of thumb when buying a policy is to pick a high deductible to lower your monthly premium costs[13]. If all goes well for your health that year, you won't spend much money on health-care expenses, and your monthly premium costs will be very low.

9　But if something catastrophic occurs, your initial expenses will be high. This is because your entire deductible has to be met before your insurance company will cover many of the services you will likely need, including hospital stays[14].

10　A deductible is also considered an out-of-pocket expense[15] and can help you meet your out-of-pocket expense maximum. An out-of-pocket expense maximum, or cap[16], is the amount you need to meet for the insurance company to pay 100 percent of your health expenses. Normally, your deductible and coinsurance can be applied toward this maximum amount. Your co-payments or monthly insurance premiums are not included in this cap.

11　Now that both the co-payment and the deductible have been defined, let's find out how they vary with different plans.

Deductible and Co-pay Types

12　Health-care services and fees can vary greatly. There are many plans out there, but we'll narrow them down[17] to two main types: **fee-for-service** plans and **managed health-care** plans. A fee-for-service plan is what most Americans think of as traditional health insurance. The deductibles and co-pays for this type of plan are generally higher than those of a managed health-care provider. These fees can add up over the course of a year, but they also buy more options. Under a fee-for-service plan, you're free to choose your own doctors, usually don't need a referral[18] to see a specialist, and can choose your hospital.

13　These types of plans usually have out-of-pocket expense caps. Once you reach the cap, a basic plan will cover doctor's visits and hospital stays, along with all the attendant expenses, like X-rays, medications, treatments and surgery. Major plans pick up where basic plans leave off[19]—they are usually best for those with yearly medical bills exceeding $250,000.

14　If you receive health insurance through your employer, it's most likely a managed health-care plan. Managed care plans include **health maintenance organizations** (HMOs), **preferred provider organizations** (PPOs) and **point-of-service plans** (POS). A managed health-care plan is the best way for insurance providers to control their costs, so they can offer much lower co-pays and deductibles.

15　Of the three main types of managed health-care plans, HMOs are by far the cheapest and most restrictive. An HMO arranges a provider network by gathering contractual agreements with specialists, general practitioners[20], hospitals and other health-care professionals—you can receive treatment from this network alone. You have to choose a primary care physician (PCP) who authorizes and coordinates your health-care needs by working within the network. As long as you stay within this network, co-payments and deductibles are kept to a bare minimum[21].

16　A PPO operates under the same guidelines as an HMO, but it casts a much wider net, and you don't have a PCP acting as an intermediary for your health care. With a PPO, you can choose from within the network of providers for smaller co-pays and deductibles, or pick an out-of-network provider for a substantially higher price.

17　·A POS plan is a fusion of these two managed health-care models. It is sometimes referred to as an "open-ended HMO" because you can choose either the HMO or PPO model whenever you need health care. Because of this, your co-pays and deductibles can vary from treatment to treatment, doctor to doctor and month to month.

Notes

1. the sixth year in a row: 连续第六年
2. trim: cut down to required size or shape 削减

3. With these growing costs is the growing importance of getting the most out of your health-care coverage. 此句大意为：随着医疗成本的日益增长，如何最有效地利用医疗保险变得越来越重要。

4. jargon: the language, esp. the vocabulary, peculiar to a particular trade, profession, or group 行话；暗语

5. decipher: to discover the meaning of 解开(疑团)

6. flat amount: 固定金额

7. up front: 预先

8. In addition to cutting a small portion of the costs, the co-pay is also used to prevent people from seeking care for every trivial medical condition they might encounter. 此句大意为：除了能够减少部分医疗费用外，"共同支付"还可以防止人们一遇到小毛病就看医生。

9. ailments: a physical or mental disorder, especially a mild illness (不严重的)疾病

10. meet the deductible: 满足扣除额

11. kick in: become operative; take effect 起作用，生效

12. premium: the amount at which a securities option is bought or sold 保险费

13. If you are relatively healthy, a smart rule of thumb when buying a policy is to pick a high deductible to lower your monthly premium costs. 此句大意为：如果你相对比较健康，一个很好的经验是购买高起付线的医疗保险政策，以减少每月的保险费用。

14. hospital stays: 住院

15. an out-of-pocket expense: 实际现金支出

16. cap: an upper limit 最高限额

17. narrow down: become more focused on an area of activity or field of study 减少，缩小

18. **referral:** the process of directing or redirecting (as a medical case or a patient) to an appropriate specialist or agency for definitive treatment 转诊

19. Major plans pick up where basic plans leave off…: 主要医疗保险计划可以补充基本医疗保险计划没有涵盖的费用……

20. **general practitioner:** a physician whose practice consists of providing ongoing care covering a variety of medical problems in patients of all ages, often including referral to appropriate specialists, also called *family doctor* 全科医生

21. **a bare minimum:** the smallest possible quantity or the least fulfilling, but still adequate, condition that is required, acceptable, or suitable for some purpose 最低限度

● **Reading Comprehension**

1. **Directions:** *With detailed analysis, the author explains to us how the American health insurance system works. Read the passage carefully to find out what are included in the system and how they differ from each other.*

2. **Directions:** *Read the following statements carefully, and decide whether they are true (T) or false (F) according to the text.*

_____ 1) A deductible is the flat amount you pay at the time of a medical service or to receive a medication.

_____ 2) While the co-pay has been found to lower costs of insurance company by making people think twice before running to the doctor over a case of the sniffles, they might also prevent people from seeking necessary medical attention.

_____ 3) The deductibles and co-pays for a fee-for-service plan are generally lower than those of a managed health-care plan.

_____ 4) Insurance providers usually offer much lower co-pays and deductibles to those who purchase a managed health-care plan.

_____ 5) When you choose PPO model, you'll have to pay a much higher price if you pick an out-of-network provider.

_____ 6) With an HMO, your co-pays and deductibles can vary from treatment to treatment, doctor to doctor and month to month.

Part Three

Topic-related Activities

1. Team Project

Directions: *Form a group of four or five students. One student serves as a psychiatrist in a care-center. The others act as patients at different age. The psychiatrist listens to their problems carefully and gives advice.*

2. Group Work

Directions: *Have you accepted any credit cards? What are the advantages and disadvantages of using credit cards? What kind of payments do you prefer? Please discuss these questions with your classmates.*

Suggested words and expressions:

Peony Card 牡丹卡	Dragon Card 龙卡
Money-link Card 银联卡	The Great Wall Card 长城卡
Kins Card 金穗卡	golden card 金卡
ordinary card 普通卡	annual commission 年费
card holder 持卡人	issuing bank 发卡行
withdrawal record 取款记录	deposit book，passbook 存折
overdraft, overdraw 透支	debit card 借记卡
credit card 贷记卡(信用卡)	bank card 银行卡

Visa 维萨卡   MasterCard 万事达卡

American Express 美国运通卡

3. Role Play

Directions: *Make a dialogue with your partner based on the situations given below and act on it.*

1) Your friend would like to open an online shop, but he is not sure what items to choose.

2) Mary has purchased an expensive watch from the thrift shop, and after 30 days, it stops working. You have the receipt and want the store to repair or replace it.

3) Ask a salesperson to help you select a shirt for your friend. Be sure to describe your friend carefully and tell the salesperson the style and color of the shirt you are looking for.

4. Case Study

Directions: *Please read the features of Bank of America in the following. Identify different features from those of Chinese banks and discuss with your partners.*

1) There are different bank accounts you can open with Bank of America, such as Checking Account, Savings Account, Certificate of Deposit, IRA (Individual Retirement Account), etc.

2) With Checking Account, usually there is no interest in this account, but one can deposit money in and withdraw money from this account freely.

3) With Savings Account, usually there is interest, but one needs to pay his service fees under certain circumstances while using it.

4) Certificate of Deposit is a bank account with which one can deposit money for a period of time and gain interest out of it.

5) IRA (Individual Retirement Account) is an account in which one can deposit money saved for retirement by providing tax benefits.

Part Four

Topic-related Information

1. Introduction to Banks of a Great Variety

1) Banks

Central bank, reserve bank: A country's central bank maintains the stability of its national currency. In the United States, the Federal Reserve functions as the central bank and acts as a last-resort lender to failing financial institutions. The Fed was created in 1913 to provide financial stability in response to the Panic of 1907[1].

Commercial bank: A commercial bank, also known as a business bank, takes deposits and gives loans, mostly to corporations. After the Great Depression, Congress required that commercial and investment banks be separate with the Glass-Steagall Act[2]; that restriction no longer applies today. Bank of America is currently the largest commercial bank in the United States.

Investment bank: An investment bank raises money by selling securities to companies and to the government. They also provide advice to corporations about mergers and buyouts. Goldman Sachs and Morgan Stanley are the two largest investment banks in the United States.

Retail bank: A retail bank deals directly with consumers instead of companies or other banks. (The latter business is conducted by a commercial bank.) A retail bank primarily handles savings and checking accounts, mortgages, and personal loans.

Universal bank: A universal bank participates in the banking activities of a commercial bank and an investment bank. Bank of America is a universal bank—in addition to being the leading commercial bank, it is also an investment bank.

2) Other Financial Institutions

Savings-and-loan association: A savings-and-loan association primarily accepts deposits from consumers and makes mortgage loans. During the savings-and-loan crisis of the late 1980s and early 1990s, the number of such associations declined by 50 percent after the housing market experienced a downturn.

Clearing house: A clearing house is a private company or a part of a bank that helps settle transactions. For example, it might ensure that a checking account has sufficient funds for a certain debit card transaction before the money goes through. LCH.Clearnet[3], Europe's largest clearing house, declared Lehman Bros.[4] in default and suspended the bank from operating in the London market.

Brokerage firm, securities firm: A brokerage firm acts as a mediator between a buyer and a seller of stocks or securities. When someone wants to buy something in the stock market, they usually go through a brokerage firm, such as Wachovia Securities[5]. While brokerage firms aren't insured under any federal agency, they can register to be insured under the Securities Investor Protection Corp., which was created by Congress in 1970.

Notes

1. **the Panic of 1907:** also known as the 1907 Bankers' Panic, a financial crisis that occurred in the United States when the New York stock exchange fell close to 50% from its peak the previous year

2. **the Glass-Steagall Act:** Two separate United States laws are known as the Glass-Steagall Act. Both bills were sponsored by Democratic Senator Carter Glass of Lynchburg, Virginia, a former Secretary of the Treasury, and Democratic Congressman Henry B. Steagall of Alabama, Chairman of the House Committee on Banking and Currency. The first Glass-Steagall Act was passed in February 1932 in an effort to stop deflation and expanded the Federal Reserve's ability to offer rediscounts on more types of assets such as government bonds as well as commercial paper. The second Glass-Steagall Act was passed in 1933 in reaction to the collapse of a large

portion of the American commercial banking system in early 1933.

3. LCH Clearnet: known as London Clearing House

4. Lehman Bros.: Lehman Brothers was a global financial-services firm that, until declaring bankruptcy in 2008, did business in investment banking, equity and fixed-income sales, research and trading, investment management, private equity, and private banking. It was a primary dealer in the U.S. Treasury securities market. Its primary subsidiaries included Lehman Brothers Inc., Neuberger Berman Inc., Aurora Loan Services, Inc., SIB Mortgage Corporation, Lehman Brothers Bank, FSB, Eagle Energy Partners, and the Crossroads Group. The firm's worldwide headquarters were in New York City, with regional headquarters in London and Tokyo, as well as offices located throughout the world.

5. Wachovia Securities: Wachovia Securities was the trade name of Wachovia Corporation's retail brokerage and institutional capital markets and investment banking subsidiaries.

2. Stores and Shopping

1) Farmers Markets

Farmers markets are open for business in communities all across the United States. Many communities host outdoor farmers markets once or twice a week during the summer, while indoor farmers markets in larger communities can operate all year long. The farmers market will usually be set up in a park, parking lot, or yard of a school or library. Local entertainers and musicians may perform, and the farmers market may function as a convivial community meeting place. The idea of the farmers markets is that local producers of fruits and vegetables will bring in and sell their fresh produce without having to go through cumbersome distribution chains, selling directly to the consumer. The products available at a typical farmers market will vary through the season. In addition to fruits and vegetables, many farmers markets have tables offering jams and preserves, honey, baked goods and other specialty food items.

2) Convenient Retail Food

For quicker food purchases, Americans rely on convenience stores and delicatessens. These stores offer fewer products, rarely have specials and are more expensive than supermarkets. They offer quick service and long hours. Delicatessens usually make sandwiches and offer prepared foods ready to heat and serve that are purchased by the pound.

3) Specialty Food Stores

Urban areas may have old style food stores that sell just one type of item: fruit stands, butchers, cheese stores, fish stores, etc. Many of these establishments are in ethnic areas and serve particular ethnic groups. Specialty and gourmet shops can be found in major cities and shopping centers. Food here is high quality and expensive, often hard to find or imported.

4) Shopping Malls

Not Just for Shopping: A shopping mall is an enclosed shopping area, often strikingly designed to be a safe, pleasant place for the entire family to shop. There are some shopping malls in the inner cities, but usually you drive to a mall in the outer areas or suburbs, and park your car in a lot that may be as big as an airfield. You will spend several hours here.

Uniformity: You can go into a mall anywhere in the United States and find exactly the same thing. The mall will have a few major department stores and hundreds of small specialty shops. The vast proportion of these specialty shops will be chain or franchise stores which will have identical signs and identical goods at identical prices anywhere you find them. The mall might have a movie theater complex that may offer up to a dozen different films in separate theaters.

Promotions: Malls often feature various promotions or theme events. Merchants selling a certain type of product or handicraft will set up temporary stands in the aisles. Because the mall is such an important part of American life, a great deal of socializing goes on there. Teenagers go to the shopping mall just to meet each other.

5) Strip Shopping Centers

Strip shopping centers are smaller than shopping malls and are rarely enclosed. Their largest stores are discount or drug stores or supermarkets, with a few specialty stores. They are located on major roads with parking areas in front. In some suburban areas, strip shopping centers can adjoin each other making for non-stop stores for miles on end. Americans do a great deal of their average everyday shopping in strip shopping centers.

6) Category Killers

The term Category Killer refers to a type of retailer or chain of stores that is so big that it kills the category for everyone else. On the Internet, both eBay and amazon.com act as category killers. The term is usually used to refer to big box stores, for example electronics giant Best Buy. The huge home and building centers The Home Depot and Lowe's put many small hardware stores out of business, while local toy stores have had a hard time competing with giant Toys-R-Us. Book chains such as Barnes and Noble and Borders have had a similar effect on smaller bookstores. Other examples include PetSmart and Petco for pet products and Bed Bath & Beyond for home products.

7) Catalogue and Internet Shopping

Catalog and mail order shopping is a major component of the American consumer system. Thousands of companies put out catalogs specializing in anything you can imagine. If you subscribe to any major national magazine, your name and address will be sold to catalog houses and you'll receive plenty of catalogs of all types. You can also request to be put on catalog mailing lists. Catalog shopping is quiet and convenient. The best catalog companies allow you to return goods you don't like and bend over backwards to give you good customer service. With catalogs, however, you will often pay more. The products advertised in the catalogs look wonderful and are beautifully described, but in general you should only use catalogs if you simply don't have the time and energy to touch and feel the items in a real store, or if the item you want is hard to find.

Internet shopping is becoming more prevalent daily in the United States. The big catalog companies are all flocking to the Internet, while other companies such as bookseller Amazon.com sell only on the Internet.

8) Street Vendors and Flea Markets

Street vendors and flea markets can be excellent sources of goods, but of course, quality can vary. Flea markets don't sell insects; the term refers to an organized group of individual sellers, perhaps moving from one place to another, who will sell under a tent or in a parking lot. Most flea market and street sellers operate as part of the underground economy on a strictly cash basis, often neglecting to charge you sales tax. While many offer genuine bargains, some sell damaged or inferior goods, and there is always the chance that the product is inexpensive because it has been stolen. You'll have to use your judgment.

9) Thrift Shops

Thrift shops or second-hand shops are usually small, permanent stores run by hospitals, churches, or other charitable organizations. Sometimes you will find a thrift shop run by an individual for profit. You can find wonderful deals in a thrift shop, such as old-fashioned linens and cookware, but because you're buying used goods, you must inspect items carefully to see what condition they are in and whether they work properly. Look at the price tag. Prices in a thrift shop vary widely, especially when the shop owner doesn't know what it is he or she is putting a price sticker on.

If you think an item is priced too high, you can try to negotiate a price with the cashier or the owner. Just keep in mind that, in the smallest stores, the cashier and the owner may be one and the same.

Some thrift shops will buy used goods from you to resell, while others will let you trade items against the cost of goods from the store. Others only accept cash for their wares and sell only items that were donated, either directly to the store or through a charity.

If your item sells, the shop owner takes a percentage of the profit or charges a small fee, and gives the rest to you. If a consigned item does not sell within a certain period of time, you take it back. Just remember that most thrift stores will not accept items in return once they are purchased. It can be challenging to strike a balance between careful consideration and not missing out on that one-of-a-kind item you may never see for sale again.

10) Yard and Garage Sales

Yard, garage, tag, moving and apartment sales all refer to essentially the same thing: a private individual selling personal belongings from their own home. The goods for sale are typically displayed outside, either in the yard, garage, or driveway. Items may also be displayed inside the house or apartment if no outside space is available. Sellers advertise by posting small signs on neighboring streets, directing buyers to the seller's home. Sometimes the signs also describe what sort of items will be available for purchase.

Yard sales are most often held in the summer when weather is conducive to outdoor displays. Purchases are made with cash. Since the seller has to make change out of their own pocket, small bills (such as $1 or $5) are always appreciated and large bills (such as $50 or $100) may not be accepted.

3. Tax Refund

When shopping in the European Union, shoppers must pay a sales tax (known as VAT) on most goods. This VAT is already included in the sales price and the rate of VAT varies from one country to another. By law, non-EU residents are entitled to reclaim the VAT paid on items purchased but exported from the EU.

Procedures

1) Refund Check: Ask the shop staff for a Refund Cheque when paying for your purchases.

2) Custom Stamps: Show your purchases, receipt and passport to Customs when leaving the country, or at the final point of departure when leaving the European Union, and have your Refund Cheque stamped.

3) Refund Office: Show the stamped Refund Cheque, passport and credit card at a nearby Refund Office and ask for an Immediate Refund on your credit card. Alternatively the Refund can be paid in cash.

Hyperlinks

[1] http://www.bankofamerica.com

[2] http://www.citibank.com/us/index.htm

[3] http://www.cibc.ca

References

[1] http://www.bankofamerica.com

[2] http://en.wikipedia.org/wiki/Central_bank

[3] http://en.wikipedia.org/wiki/Savings_and_loan crisis

[4] http://www.dep.anl.gov/newcomers/shopping.htm(inclass reading)

[5] http://www.lifeintheusa.com/services1/index.html

[6] http://health.howstuffworks.com/deductible-copay.htm

[7] http://en.wikipedia.org/wiki/Debit_card

[8] http://health.howstuffworks.com/deductible-copay.htm

[9] Kiplinger. No More Sneaky Fees. *Personal Finance*[J], 2008(7)

Unit 11
Movie

Part One
Lead-in

The script is what you've dreamed up—this is what it should be.

The film is what you end up with.

—George Lucas (America)

梦想开始于剧本，而终结于电影。

——乔治·卢卡斯（美国）

Movie, an important source of popular entertainment, is undoubtedly the most influential art form in the 20th century. From the early days of Hollywood to the high-tech cinema of today, the silver screen has projected our dreams and fantasies, presented both glamour and works of social conscience and served as our collective memory.

Part Two

Reading Passages

In-Class Reading

Warm-up questions:

1 Have you heard about the Academy Awards or the Oscars? Do you know anyone who has won an Oscar? Who is he or she?

2. Do you know any famous black actors or actresses? Can you say something about them?

Colorblind at Last?

1   Black Hollywood has been keeping a secret. For decades, African-Americans had been so consistently overlooked by the Academy Awards[1] that a private group began sponsoring the "Black Oscars." Every year, on the night before the actual Oscars, members of the community—including James Earl Jones, Whitney Houston, Samuel L. Jackson and Will Smith—gather at a Beverly Hills hotel[2] to honor their own. "Everyone has on their **tuxes**, and you see all these people you want to work with who are cheering you on," says Malcolm D. Lee, director of "Undercover Brother" and cousin of Spike Lee. "It's a great feeling, and intimate—nice."

2   But on March 24, 2002, Halle Berry crossed the stage at the Kodak Theatre[3] to become the first African-American woman to win an Oscar for best actress. (She also set the record for most tears shed during an acceptance speech.) Minutes later, Denzel Washington took the best-actor award, the first black man to do so in 38 years. It was, by any measure, historic. Since 2002, 11 black actors have earned Oscar nominations. Jamie Foxx and Morgan Freeman have both won, and at least one black actor has been nominated every year. This year a **record-breaking** five—Forest Whitaker, Jennifer Hudson, Eddie Murphy, Will Smith and Djimon Hounsou—will be walking the red carpet on Feb. 25. "I certainly always hoped I'd see this day," says Sidney Poitier, the first African-American man to win best actor. "I would have thought it would have occurred sooner."

3   Yet breaking the color barrier hasn't exactly been met with **unmitigated** joy in black Hollywood. The decades of exclusion have left a scar of **skepticism**. "I'm pleased all this is happening, but I hope and pray

it's not just a phase," says Louis Gossett Jr., who won the 1982 best-supporting-actor Oscar for "An Officer and a Gentleman" —and never got another role of that **stature**. History **is peppered with** bursts of **high-profile** work for black actors that **blazed out** just as fast.[4] Angela Bassett couldn't find work for a year after being nominated for "What's Love Got to Do with It." In the early '70s, Diana Ross, Cicely Tyson and Diahann Carroll all earned best-actress nominations—and then no African-American woman was nominated in that category again for more than a decade. Even Washington questions the long-term impact of his own win. After Foxx won the 2004 best-actor Oscar, Washington told *Newsweek*[5], "Who knows what it means for the future? I think we have to take it for just what it is—African-Americans winning awards. Beyond that, we have to wait and see."

4   What's most startling is that the 2002 Oscars have left a bitter **aftertaste** because of the kinds of roles that **score**d Washington and Berry their statues.[6] He played a corrupt cop in "Training Day"; she starred as a woman who falls in love with a racist in "Monster's Ball." A segment within black Hollywood believes that white Academy voters reward black actors for roles that reinforce stereotypes—the angry black man, the noble slave, the **sexualized** black woman—rather than challenge them. "There's a sense that in order to be embraced by the white community, you probably did something that violates your integrity within the black community," says actress Kerry Washington, who stars opposite Whitaker in "The Last King of Scotland." For black actors, succeeding in Hollywood comes at a price. "The playing field is not even, but I don't know that it's as evil as everyone likes to think it is," says Antoine Fuqua, who directed "Training Day." "People make films about what they experience, about what they know, and the film business was created by people that weren't African-American."

5   It would be unfair to leave the impression that African-Americans don't value the recognition and their increasing power within the industry. The success of Will Smith's "The Pursuit of Happiness"—a serious drama that has **grossed** more than $200 million worldwide and earned him his second Oscar nomination—is a milestone. "That movie is a story about determination and the American Dream," Lee says. "And it has nothing to do with being black." No one doubts that there's more, and better, work available now for actors of color than at any time in American history. In addition to the five black actors nominated this year, there's a Japanese actress and a Mexican actress, plus one Latino director. That's not **altruism**— it's business. The majority of theatrical revenue on studio films now comes from foreign box office, not domestic. And young audiences—the movie industry's bread and butter—care much less about race than their parents do. "We read trend reports that high-school and junior-high kids are much more comfortable in a **multiracial** world," says Stacey Snider, CEO of DreamWorks[7],

which released "Dreamgirls." "That has to have an impact, not just on music and fashion, but on movies as well."

6   But rewriting history isn't easy. Actresses still haven't benefited much from Berry's win—no black woman has been nominated for best actress since she won. "We still don't have a female African-American superstar," says black-film historian Donald Bogle. "There's not even a female equivalent for Samuel L. Jackson or Morgan Freeman." The next generation of men, however, has flourished. Five men have gotten lead Oscar nods since 2002. "Ten years ago, Denzel was the only black actor who could get a lead in a quality movie," says John Singleton, who directed the landmark film *Boyz n the Hood*. "Now, actors like Terrence Howard can get an Oscar nod with their first starring role." That change, Singleton says, will not be undone. "There's no going back to the back of the bus."[8] He may be right. Perhaps the biggest indicator that the world has changed is that the Black Oscars have been canceled. After being a necessity for more than 25 years, they have succeeded by becoming redundant. "We only had the event to acknowledge those who weren't being acknowledged," says a member of the **(secretive)** Friends of the Black Oscars board. That's no longer the case. "This year, the Black Oscars will be at the Kodak."

—Sean Smith and Allison Samuels

New Words and Expressions

aftertaste	*n.*	a taste that stays in your mouth after you have eaten or drunk something 回味，余韵
altruism	*n.*	consideration of the happiness and good of others before one's own; unselfishness 利他主义，利他
gross	*v.*	gain an amount as a total profit, or earn it as a total amount, before tax has been taken away (税前)赚得……总收入
high-profile	*a.*	attracting a lot of public attention, usually deliberately 高姿态的；立场明确的；备受瞩目的
multiracial	*a.*	including or involving several different races of people 多民族的
record-breaking	*a.*	a record-breaking number, level, performance, or person is the highest, lowest, biggest, best, etc. of its type that has ever happened or existed 破纪录的
score	*v.*	be very successful in something you do 成功做成某事
secretive	*a.*	keeping one's thoughts, intentions, or actions hidden from others 秘密的，偷偷摸摸的
sexualize	*v.*	be made to have sex with sb. 使有性关系
skepticism	*n.*	an attitude of doubting that particular claims or statements are true or that something will happen 怀疑论

stature	*n.*	the degree to which someone is admired or regarded as important stature 声望，地位
tux	*n.*	a man's jacket that is usually black, worn on formal occasions 男士无尾半正式晚礼服
unmitigated	*a.*	completely bad or good 绝对(坏)的或完全(好)的
be peppered with		include large numbers of sth. 充满
blaze out		burn very brightly 熊熊燃烧

Proper Film Names

An Officer and a Gentleman	《军官与绅士》
Boyz n the Hood	《街区男孩》
Dreamgirls	《梦幻女郎》
Monster's Ball	《死囚之舞》
The Last King of Scotland	《末代独裁》
The Pursuit of Happiness	《当幸福来敲门》
Training Day	《训练日》
Undercover Brother	《卧底兄弟》
What's Love Got to Do with It	《与爱何干》

Proper Names

Angela Bassett	安吉拉·贝塞特(美国女演员)
Antoine Fuqua	安东尼·福奎阿(美国导演，代表作有《亚瑟王》、《训练日》)
Cicely Tyson	西西莉·泰森(美国女演员)
Denzel Washington	丹泽尔·华盛顿(美国男演员，代表作有《费城故事》、《马尔科姆·X》、《人骨拼图》和《飓风》等)
Diahann Carroll	戴安·卡罗尔(美国女演员)
Diana Ross	戴安娜·罗丝(美国女演员)
Djimon Hounsou	吉蒙·休斯(美国导演)
Donald Bogle	唐纳德·伯格(美国黑人电影历史学家)
Eddie Murphy	艾迪·墨菲(美国导演)
Forest Whitaker	福里斯特·惠特克(美国导演)
Halle Berry	哈莉·贝瑞(美国女演员，代表作《死囚之舞》、《谁与争锋》、《X战警》、《剑鱼行动》等)
James Earl Jones	詹姆斯·厄尔·琼斯(美国男演员)
Jamie Foxx	杰米·福克斯(美国男演员)
Jennifer Hudson	詹妮弗·哈德森(美国女演员)

John Singleton	约翰·辛格顿(美国导演)
Kerry Washington	凯丽·华盛顿(美国女演员)
Louis Gossett, Jr	小路易斯·格赛特(美国男演员)
Malcolm D. Lee	马尔科姆·李(美国导演)
Morgan Freeman	摩根·弗里曼(美国男演员，代表作有《为戴西小姐开车》、《光荣》、《百万宝贝》等)
Samuel L Jackson	塞缪尔·杰克逊(美国男演员，代表作有《低俗小说》、《星战前传》等)
Sidney Poitier	西德尼·波蒂埃(美国演员，代表作有《原野百合花》等)
Spike Lee	斯派克·李(美国导演，代表作有《内部人士》等)
Stacey Snider	史黛西·施奈德(梦工厂公司 CEO 兼联合主席)
Terrence Howard	特伦斯·霍华德(美国男演员)
Whitney Houston	惠特尼·休斯敦(美国女演员)
Will Smith	威尔·史密斯(美国男演员，代表作有《全民公敌》等)

Notes

1. **The Academy Awards/ the Oscars:** 奥斯卡金像奖

   The Academy Awards, popularly known as the Oscars, are presented annually by the Academy of Motion Picture Arts and Sciences (AMPAS) to recognize excellence of professionals in the film industry, including directors, actors, and writers. The formal ceremony at which the awards are presented is among the most prominent and most watched film awards ceremonies in the world.

2. Beverly Hills hotel: 贝弗利山酒店

3. Kodak Theatre: 柯达剧院

   The Kodak Theatre is a live theatre in the Hollywood and Highland retail, dining, and entertainment complex on Hollywood Boulevard and North Highland Avenue in the Hollywood district of Los Angeles. Since its opening on November 9, 2001, the theatre has been the home of the annual Academy Awards Ceremonies (The Oscars), which were first held there in March 2002, and is the first permanent home for the awards.

4. History is peppered with bursts of high-profile work for black actors that blazed out just as fast. 此句大意为：在历史上有很多这样的例子，即有些黑人演员在短时间内备受瞩目，然而这样的瞩目往往转瞬即逝。

5. *Newsweek*:《新闻周刊》

   Newsweek is an American weekly newsmagazine published in New York City. It is distributed throughout the United States and internationally. It is the second largest news weekly magazine in the U.S., having trailed *Time* in circulation and advertising revenue for most of its existence, although both are much larger than the third of America's prominent weeklies, *U.S. News &*

World Report. Newsweek is published in four English language editions and 12 global editions written in the language of the circulation region.

6. What's most startling is that the 2002 Oscars have left a bitter aftertaste because of the kinds of roles that scored Washington and Berry their statues. 此句大意为：华盛顿和贝利在获奖影片中所扮演的角色是典型的黑人角色，因此 2002 年的奥斯卡给人们留下了一丝苦涩的回味，这一点非常令人吃惊。

7. **DreamWorks:** 梦工厂

DreamWorks, LLC, also known as DreamWorks Pictures, DreamWorks SKG, or DreamWorks Studios is a major American film studio which develops, produces, and distributes films, video games, and television programming. It has produced or distributed more than ten films with box-office grosses totalling more than $100 million each. Its most successful title to date is *Shrek 2.*

8. There's no going back to the back of the bus. 本句话中的 the back of the bus 象征着种族隔离，这源自于美国历史上有名的抵制公车事件。1955 年 12 月 1 日，阿拉巴马州蒙哥马利，一位名叫罗沙·帕克斯 (Rosa Parks) 的非裔美国妇女，因为拒绝让座位给白人，违反当地法律而被逮捕。因为该州法律规定当公车满座时，黑人必须让位给白人。此外，黑人也只能坐在公车的后半部。事件发生之后不久，蒙哥马利郡的黑人社区开始了一场罢公车运动 (Bus Boycott)。

● **Reading Comprehension**

1. Directions: *Discuss the following questions with your classmates.*

1) What does the title of the article suggest?

2) What is the "Black Oscars"? And what happened to the "Black Oscars" in the end?

3) What happened at the Kodak Theatre in 2002, which was considered a big event for all the black actors and actresses in America?

4) What is the stereotype of the role that characterizes the black people in the Award-winner films, and what does that suggest?

5) What price should black people pay in order to be recognized by the white people?

6) What is the present situation for the black actresses? And how about the black actors?

2. Directions: *The following table is a list of the blacks who have won the Academy Awards in chronological order. Fill in the blanks with appropriate content based on the information given in the passage.*

Year	Name	Film	Role	Winning Role
1939	Hattie McDaniel	*Gone with the Wind*	Mammy	Best Supporting Actress
1963	Sidney Poitier	*Lilies of the Field*	Homer Smith	1) _____
1982	Louis Gossett, Jr.	2) _____	Gunnery Sergeant Emil Foley	Best Supporting Actor
1989	Denzel Washington	*Glory*	Pvt. Trip	Best Supporting Actor
1990	Whoopi Goldberg	*Ghost*	Oda Mae Brown	Best Supporting Actress
1996	Cuba Gooding, Jr.	*Jerry Maguire*	Rod Tidwell	Best Supporting Actor
2002	3) _____	*Monster's Ball*	Leticia Musgrove	Best Actress
2002	Denzel Washington	4) _____	Alonzo Harris	Best Actor
2004	Jamie Foxx	*Ray*	Ray Charles	5) _____
2004	6) _____	*Million Dollar Baby*	Eddie Scrap-Iron Dupris	Best Supporting Actor
2006	Forest Whitaker	*The Last King of Scotland*	Idi Amin	Best Actor
2006	Jennifer Hudson	*Dreamgirls*	Effie White	Best Supporting Actress

● **Discussion**

1. Martin Luther King, Jr and Rosa Parks were both famous people in the Civil Rights Movement of America. What do you know about them and what difference did they make in American Civil Rights Movement to your knowledge? Search the relevant information on the Internet and then discuss with your classmates.

2. What is the American Dream? Can you tell a few stories of some people who have realized their American dreams, especially those of some black people?

After-Class Reading

Passage One

Warm-up questions:

1. Do you like watching romantic movies? Why or why not?

2. Can you name some impressive romantic movies of Hollywood?

Who Killed the Love Story?

1   Somewhere in the outer reaches of outback Australia[1], a place where there are few paved roads and, since it's winter, the temperature gets to only 98°F (37°C), Nicole Kidman is trying to fall in love. This is an incredibly risky thing to do. Not because it's difficult: the object of her affection is Hugh Jackman, a broad-shouldered swoony hunk of the old school[2]. And not because a lot of her needs—Chanel, lip gloss, salad—aren't available in nearby Kununurra[3], and the nearest big town is about 350 miles (560 km) away. It's because Kidman & Jackman are making a big, $130 million—plus historical romantic drama, that anyone hardly makes anymore.

2   The most successful movie of all time by almost any standard, *Titanic*, will be 10 years old this year. It made roughly $600 million in the U.S. and won 11 Academy Awards. That same year, *As Good as It Gets, My Best Friend's Wedding* and *Good Will Hunting*, all of them romantic to the core, were among the top 10 box-office draws. Since then, however, not one romantic drama has cracked that list. The only love story this century to be among the five highest-grossing movies[4] of its year was *My Big Fat Greek Wedding*.

3   Is it finally over between us and romance? After decades as one of cinema's favorite subjects and centuries as the engine of novels and songs, romance faces a cold shoulder as a subject worthy of our attention. Is it that several decades of sexual liberation[5] and feminism[6] and a decade of Internet dating have fundamentally altered the strength or chemistry of the traditional love story? Or is it more that romance has had its power drained by an industry that is increasingly geared toward films that gush rather than trickle money?[7] Who killed the great American love story?

4   Talk to a romance fan, and you'll find she is one unfulfilled woman. "I love romance, but intelligent romantic movies, either dramatic or humorous, are few and far between," says Lisa

Salazar, 45, a divorced Houston attorney who likes movies enough to have seen 92 last year and maintains a little blog sharing her opinions. She's not the only one. "I asked my friend Alyssa for some advice on romance, and she said that she sticks to the classics," says Genna Gallegos, "She's a huge fan of Audrey Hepburn films." Alyssa and Genna are 17 years old. When teenagers, the sweetest fruit on capitalism's vine, have to use a half-century-old product because they can't find a more recent model that works for them, there is something seriously wrong with an industry.

5   But everyone in that industry, apparently, is dying to make a romantic movie. "I've always really wanted to make a successful love story. I think a lot of us in this business do," says John Davis, who has produced more than 80 movies, most recently Norbit. "It's hard. It's hard to find really great unique stories. And it's very, very hard to get the studios to want to finance them."

6   Not us, say the studios. "I think actors and filmmakers are a little more cautious of it than studios are," says New Line's[8] head of production, Toby Emmerich. "I get the sense that actors, stars you really want to be in business with, are interested in things that are a little edgier, that are a little more subversive."[9]

7   New Line is distributing the filmed version of Gabriel García Márquez's novel *Love in the Time of Cholera*, and since Latin female stars have higher wattage than ever, it would seem good timing. But you won't find one of them in this movie. And not just because of the budget. It used to be that playing a romantic lead was a rite of passage for any actor who wanted be on the A list. But in a world concentrated on details of what sweatpants and cereals celebrities choose, it's hard for actors to get people to pin their romantic dreams on them. And there have been so many romantic duds that it's a risk they will take only for a great script.[10] Kidman and Jackman were lured into Australia because it's co-written and directed by Baz Luhrmann, who is an Oscar and Golden Globe-nominee.

8   Ah, the story. Love stories are old. They're universal. Nearly everyone has one, which makes them nearly impossible to write well. This summer has brought us *I Now Pronounce You Chuck & Larry*, in which Adam Sandler pretends to marry his firefighter buddy for health-insurance reasons; *No Reservations*, in which two competitive chefs fall in love; and *Becoming Jane*, in which Jane Austen has to choose between love and proper behavior; *Coming in September is Good Luck Chuck*, in which every girl Chuck sleeps with goes on to marry the next guy she meets. All of them, except the Austen, are what's known in the romance-novel business as HEAs (happily-ever-afters).[11] "Romantic comedies are backbreaking to write because they have to be fresh," says Mike Newell, director of *Four Weddings and a Funeral* and the upcoming Love in the *Time of Cholera*. "I've yet to find another one which was surprising enough to do."

9   But it's not just familiarity that breeds contempt for love stories. It may be actually getting harder to get people to believe in them, acknowledges Richard Curtis, writer of such romances as *Four Weddings and Notting Hill*, because our expectations have changed. "If you write a story about a soldier kidnapped a pregnant woman and finally shot her in the head, it's called extremely

realistic, even though it's never happened in the history of mankind," he notes. "Whereas if you write about two people falling in love, which happens about a million times a day all over the world, for some reason or another, you're accused of writing something unrealistic and sentimental."

10　But there is an even graver enemy than familiarity and changed anticipation. It's an old affliction she has never truly destroyed: money. On its first weekend, *Titanic* made about $28 million. Nothing special. It didn't hit $150 million for 14 days, which, considering what Paramount[12] had spent on it, was agonizingly slow. It wasn't until two months into the movie's release, when most movies are sputtering out, that *Titanic* proved its mettle.[13] *My Big Fat Greek Wedding*, started even smaller. Romantic movies don't open well. The one with the highest opening weekend is *Will Smith's Hitch*, which, at $43 million, is considered an underperformance for him.

11　Why should that matter? It's all legal currency, no? Well, no. Not to Hollywood. Studios make most of their box-office money in the first 10 days of a movie's release, when they take in 90% of the movie's profits and the cinema owners, or exhibitors, get the rest. After two weeks, they generally split the proceeds 70/30 and then down from there.[14] *Spider-Man 3,* the most successful movie in America so far this year, made 45% of its profits to date on the first weekend. *Titanic*, by contrast, made 5%. The studios don't just want money, they want it fast. Spidey fast. Otherwise the guy who sells the popcorn and makes sure the toilets are clean gets too much of it.

12　Opening a movie big is not rocket science. It involves spending a lot of money on special effects and on preopening publicity. But even more, it involves appealing to the type of people for whom seeing a movie the first weekend is important: young men. Thus there are a lot of movies—this is not sexist, it's just business—about superheroes, things blowing up and terrifying ordeals at the hands of psychos.[15] To be fair, research shows young women also enjoy the last. Then the guys—or girls—can attain some social status from being able to discuss the cool scenes. Nobody goes to work or class the next day and says, "You gotta go see that awesome broken heart!"

—Belinda Luscombe

Proper Film Names

As Good as It Gets	《尽善尽美》
Becoming Jane	《成为简·奥斯汀》
Catch and Release	《捉放爱》
Good Luck Chuck	《幸运库克》
Good Will Hunting	《心灵捕手》
Hitch	《全民情敌》
I Now Pronounce You Chuck & Larry	《我盛大的同志婚礼》
In the Land of Women	《女人领地》

Love in the Time of Cholera	《霍乱时期的爱情》
My Best Friend's Wedding	《我最好朋友的婚礼》
My Big Fat Greek Wedding	《我的巨型希腊婚礼》
No Reservations	《美味关系》
Norbit	《我老婆是巨无霸》
Notting Hill	《诺丁山》
The Ex	《快行道》

Proper Names

Adam Sandler	亚当·山德勒(美国男演员)
Audrey Hepburn	奥黛丽·赫本(美国女演员)
Baz Luhrmann	巴兹·鲁曼(澳大利亚导演、制片人)
Gabriel García Márquez	加夫列尔·加西亚·马尔克斯(哥伦比亚作家、记者；拉丁美洲魔幻现实主义文学的代表人物)
Hugh Jackman	休·杰克曼(澳大利亚男演员)
John Davis	约·戴维斯(美国制片人)
Mike Newell	迈克·纽威尔(英国导演，代表作有《哈里·波特》)
Nicole Kidman	妮可·基德曼(澳大利亚女演员)
Toby Emmerich	托比·艾莫里契(美国制片人、编剧)
Will Smith	威尔·史密斯(美国男演员)

Notes

1. Somewhere in the outer reaches of outback Australia: 在澳大利亚偏僻小镇外围地区的某个地方
2. Hugh Jackman, a broad-shouldered swoony hunk of the old school: 休·杰克曼，一个身材魁梧、对女性富有令人晕眩的吸引力的单身汉
3. Kununurra: 澳大利亚库能诺拉峡谷

   Kununurra is a town in far northern Western Australia located at the eastern side of the Kimberley Region (金伯利地区) approximately 37 kilometres from the Northern Territory. Kununurra has a "Celebrity Tree Park" with many trees planted by famous people. The town has many local attractions, including waterfalls, gorges and ranges. It was voted the second best town to live in in Australia for outdoor adventure by *Outdoor Australia* magazine in the March/April 2007 edition.
4. highest-grossing movies: 获利最高的影片
5. **sexual liberation:** 性解放运动

   The sexual revolution refers to the well documented changes in social thought and codes of behaviour related to sexuality throughout the Western world from the 1960s into the early 1970s.

6. **feminism:** 女权运动

Feminism comprises a number of social, cultural and political movements, theories and moral philosophies concerned with gender inequalities, and more rights for women.

7. Or is it more that romance has had its power drained by an industry that is increasingly geared toward films that gush rather than trickle money? 此句意为: 或者更主要的原因是因为电影产业越来越青睐那些能够迅速而不是慢慢收回投资的影片而导致爱情电影产量减少了？ gear 在句中意为 "以……为驱动"; drain 在句中意为 "减少"。

8. New Line Cinema: 新线电影公司

New Line Cinema, founded in 1967, was one of the major American film studios. Though it initially began as an independent film studio, it became a subsidiary of Time Warner(时代华纳).

9. I get the sense that actors, stars you really want to be in business with, are interested in things that are a little edgier, that are a little more subversive. 此句意为: 我的感觉是, 那些你确实非常想合作的演员或明星们感兴趣的是有点新潮的、颠覆性题材的影片(而不是浪漫的爱情故事)。

10. And there have been so many romantic duds that it's a risk they will take only for a great script. 此句意为: 已经有这么多爱情电影票房惨淡的例子, 仅仅因为一个好剧本而接拍确实冒很大风险。dud 此处意为 "失败"。

11. "HEAs (happily-ever-afters)": 此处意为 "有情人终成眷属"。

12. Paramount: 派拉蒙影业(美国电影制片公司)

13. It wasn't until two months into the movie's release, when most movies are sputtering out, that *Titanic* proved its mettle. 此句意为: 直到影片上映两个月之后, 《泰坦尼克号》才显示其巨大的后劲, 大部分影片在这个时候都快要下档期了的时候。sputtering out 此处意为 "下档期"; mettle 此处意为 "后劲"。

14. After two weeks, they generally split the proceeds 70/30 and then down from there. 此句意为: 两周之后, 他们通常将利润七三分, 越往后制片方分的就越少。.

15. Thus there are a lot of movies—this is not sexist, it's just business—about superheroes, things blowing up and terrifying ordeals at the hands of psychos. 此句意为: 因此许多影片涉及超级英雄、爆炸场面, 以及深受精神病患者折磨的可怕经历。(这么多影片针对年轻男性观众群,)但这并非是性别歧视, 而只是商业运作。

● **Reading Comprehension**

1. **Directions:** *Try to find out the reasons for the killing of the great American love stories in the passage and then discuss with your partner which reason you think would be the most important one?*

2. **Directions:** *Discuss the following questions with your classmates.*

1) Why does the author say that the Kidman-Jackman's love story is an incredibly risky thing?

2) What does "the sweetest fruit on capitalism's vine" (Line 7, Para. 4) probably mean?

3) What are actor's and filmmaker's attitudes toward romantic movies according to studios?

4) Why nowadays would no actors like to play a romantic lead anymore?

5) Why is writing love stories a backbreaking thing for scriptwriters?

6) How do studios and cinema owners share the box-office money?

7) Why isn't opening a movie big considered to be rocket science?

8) Why don't American young men and women like watching broken-hearted romantic movies?

Passage Two

Warm-up questions:

1. What do you know about the Cannes Film Festival?

2. Can you name some Chinese movies that have won prizes in the Cannes Film Festival?

3. Do you know any Chinese directors, actors or actresses who have ever won prizes in the Cannes Film Festival?

Cannes' Affection for Films from China

1　　The Cannes Film Festival[1] was established in 1939 and gradually became one of the most prestigious film competitions around the globe. Being well known for a strong artistic and independent temperament, each year it attracts the attention of a large number of filmmakers from all over the world. As a country introduced to the film industry in the late 19th century, China is no exception.

History

2　　The Cannes International Film Festival began in the summer of 1939. Owing to World War II and financial difficulties, it stagnated for some time and didn't become a yearly event until 1969. The first time a film made in China embraced Cannes was in 1959 when *Slut and Saint* (Dangfu Yu Shengnu) directed by the Taiwan-based drama patriarch Tian Chen made its debut.[2] The movie describing the legendary experiences of a woman during the War of Resistance Against Japanese Aggression (1937-1945) became China's first attempt to compete for the prestigious Palme d'Or[3] for Best Film.

3　　In 1975, a Chinese Kung-fu film, directed by new martial arts[4] representative Hu Jinquan, took the limelight at the festival. *Sha Nu*, an outsider grabbed the Technical Jury Prize[5], only inferior to the Palme d'Or and the Grand Jury Prize[6]. More or less, this "extraordinary" filmic experience reminds people of another film, *Crouching Tiger, Hidden Dragon* (Best Foreign Language Film[7], 2002 Oscar Academy Awards) filmed by Taiwan director An Lee in 2001. Sha Nu was to efficiently promote Chinese martial arts[8] to the world.

4   The Taiwan-based director Bai Jingrui made Cannes know that China's films were not all about martial arts. His film *Girl Friend*, or *Nu Peng You* (1974) transformed foreign misunderstanding of China's films equal to action and costume drama[9] at the 1975 Cannes Film Festival.

5   Films from the mainland went to Cannes for the first time since the founding of New China, in 1979. Director Xie Tieli brought a film he made 16 years before, called *The Early Spring* (1963), portraying an increasingly open Chinese world on film. After that, many films participated in the varied exhibitions at the film festival, such as *Uproar in Heaven* (animation 1961, 1964), *Nezha Conquers the Dragon King* (animation 1979), and *The Little Street* (1981). It wasn't until 1983 that the organizing committee selected Cen Fan's *The True Story of Ah Q* (1983) as one of the feature films[10] in competition.

Intimate Contact with Cannes

6   The so-called fifth generation of Chinese directors made the world look up and watch Chinese film in a totally new and different light. It can be argued that mainland film was inferior to that of Hong Kong and Taiwan in both outline and cinematography in the early 1980s. However, by the late 1980s, the first group of film graduates after 1976 helped Chinese film to take on an entirely different look through use of the techniques and styles of Western cinematography alongside the original "Chinese" narrative.

7   Once talking of the relationship between Cannes and China, it is impossible then to neglect the well-known director, Chen Kaige. Chen appeared in Cannes for the first time in 1987. Before that, he gained a reputation with *Yellow Earth* (1986) and *The Big Parade* (1986). He competed with the controversial *King of the Children* (1987). Despite failing to win a prize, his unique cinematography, totally different from anything seen in Chinese film before, surprised festival critics. Apart from its impressionistic landscape, the plot catered to Cannes' tastes with a grim realist dark movie.

8   Thereafter, Chen made *Life on a String* (1990) but was again rejected by Cannes judges as it was considered surprisingly mediocre. But soon Cannes became warmly to Chen again and in May 1993, Chen Kaige snatched the Golden Palm (Palme d'Or) with the epic *Farewell My Concubine* (1993) and the film became a milestone for Chinese-language film. However, *Temptress Moon* (1996) and *The Emperor and the Assassin* (1999) frustrated Chen after he reached the zenith of his career in the early 1990s.

9   Zhang Yimou, another prominent fifth generation director, has produced a mixed reaction at

Cannes. As a "professional award-winner", the cold reception he received repeatedly at Cannes really embarrassed him while he had three films competing at the Festival. The first was Ju Dou (1990), and he returned depressed. The second, *To Live* (1994), missed the Palme d'Or but won the Grand Jury Prize and the Best Actor Award as compensation. In 1995 Zhang's highly anticipated *Shanghai Triad* (1995) won only the Technical Grand Prize. His "intimacy" with Cannes finally drew to an end when he "fell out" with the organizing committee for *Not One Less* (1999).

10　Perhaps only at Cannes could it have been possible that comedy clown actor Ge You be nominated and win the Best Actor Award. It expressed the different values of the festival. At Cannes, good-looking Hollywood superstars and the heavily invested scenes are meaningless. The fact that Ge You won the award made many filmmakers take for granted that they had learned what to do next. They followed his trace, but apparently learned nothing. One important thing they might have forgotten was that for Cannes, individuality is top priority.

11　Compared with the ordinary looking Ge You, the most popular Chinese actress at Cannes, Gong Li, is a beauty. Although not winning any award of her own, Gong still captured many foreign hearts for her five competition films. In 1997, together with the Malaysian film star Michelle Yeoh, Gong Li served as a jury member, becoming one of the few major league film actresses in the history of Cannes to do so. Chinese actress and frequent visitor to Cannes, Hong Kong-based superstar Maggie Cheung, [lead in *In the Mood for Love* (2000)] is an actress who has refused to join in the star-studded[11] film celebrations at the festival.

12　Besides, Hong Kong-based Wong Kar-Wai [director of *Happy Together* (1997) and *In the Mood for Love* (2000)] as well as Taiwan-based Hou Hsiao-hsien [director of *Millennium Mambo* (2001) and *A City of Sadness* (1989)] and Edward Yang [director of *Yi Yi* (2000) and *Duli Shidai* (1994)] all have their own place in the history of the Cannes Film Festival. Through Cannes, they have grown gradually popular with filmgoers all over the world.

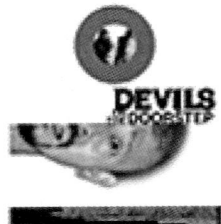

13　What is it about Cannes that fascinates filmmakers from various countries? Is it for its avant-garde[12] and original nature? It seems likely that it may have a similar impact on the next generation of Chinese directors even more. Following Cannes introduces the future greats in the world of film. Today, more and more young and independent Chinese directors display their remarkable filmic skill and talent for story telling at Cannes, including Lou Ye [*Suzhou River* (2000) and *Purple Butterfly* (2003)], Jia Zhangke [*Unknown Pleasures* (2002)], Jiang Wen [*Devils on the Doorstep* (2000)], and so on. On the extensive stage that Cannes offers, no effort is spared in showing the world a more real and vivid China.

Proper Film Names

A City of Sadness	《悲情城市》
Crouching Tiger, Hidden Dragon	《卧虎藏龙》
Devils on the Doorstep	《鬼子来了》
Duli Shidai	《独立时代》
Farewell My Concubine	《霸王别姬》
Girl Friend	《女朋友》
Happy Together	《春光乍泄》
In the Mood for Love	《花样年华》
Ju Dou	《菊豆》
King of the Children	《孩子王》
Life on a String	《边走边唱》
Millennium Mambo	《千禧曼波》
Nezha Conquers the Dragon King	《哪吒闹海》
Not One Less	《一个都不能少》
Purple Butterfly	《紫蝴蝶》
Sha Nu	《侠女》
Shanghai Triad	《摇啊摇，摇到外婆桥》
Slut and Saint	《荡妇与圣女》
Suzhou River	《苏州河》
Temptress Moon	《风月》
The Big Parade	《大阅兵》
The Early Spring	《早春二月》
The Emperor and the Assassin	《荆轲刺秦王》
The Little Street	《小街》
The True Story of Ah Q	《阿 Q 正传》
To Live	《活着》
Unknown Pleasures	《任逍遥》
Uproar in Heaven	《孙悟空大闹天宫》
Yellow Earth	《黄土地》
Yi Yi	《一一》

Proper Names

Bai Jingrui	白景瑞(中国台湾导演)
Cen Fan	范岑(中国大陆电影导演，代表作有《蝴蝶梦》)
Chen Kaige	陈凯歌(中国大陆第五代导演中的领军人物之一)
Edward Yang	杨德昌(中国台湾著名导演)

Hou Hsiao-hsien	侯孝贤(中国台湾著名导演)
Hu Jinquan	胡金铨(中国香港导演)
Jia Zhangke	贾樟柯(中国大陆第六代导演)
Jiang Wen	姜文(中国大陆著名演员、导演)
Lou Ye	娄烨(中国大陆第六代导演)
Maggie Cheung	张曼玉(中国香港著名电影女演员，代表作有《阮玲玉》、《2046》)
Michelle Yeoh	杨紫琼(中国香港著名女演员，代表作有《宋家皇朝》、《卧虎藏龙》)
Tian Chen	田琛(中国台湾导演)
Wong Kar-Wai	王家卫(中国香港著名导演，代表作有《旺角卡门》、《阿飞正传》)
Xie Tieli	谢铁骊(中国大陆电影导演，代表作有《暴风骤雨》、《早春二月》)

Notes

1. **The Cannes Film Festival:** 戛纳电影节

    Founded in 1939, it is one of the world's oldest, most influential and prestigious film festivals alongside Venice and Berlin. The private festival is held annually (usually in the month of May) at the Palais des Festivals et des Congrès, in the resort town of Cannes, in the south of France.

2. The first time a film made in China embraced Cannes was in 1959 when *Slut and Saint* (*Dangfu Yu Shengnu*) directed by the Taiwan-based drama patriarch Tian Chen made its debut. 此句大意是：中国出品的影片第一次为戛纳所接受是在 1959 年， 当时由中国台湾戏剧界泰斗田琛所执导的影片《荡妇与圣女》初次登上了戛纳的舞台。

3. **Palme d'Or ("Golden Palm"):** 金棕榈奖

    It is the highest prize given to a competing film at the Cannes Film Festival. It was introduced in 1955 by the organizing committee. From 1939 to 1954, the highest prize had been called the Grand Prix du Festival International du Film. From 1964 to 1974 it was replaced again by the Grand Prix du Festival.

4. **new martial arts:** 新武侠

5. **Technical Jury Prize:** 戛纳电影节最高技术委员会奖

6. **The Grand Jury Prize:** 戛纳电影节评委会特别大奖

7. **Best Foreign Language Film:** 最佳外语片

8. **Chinese martial arts:** 中国武术文化

9. **costume drama:** 古装戏

    A costume drama is a period piece in which elaborate costumes, sets and properties are featured in order to capture the ambience of a particular era.

10. **feature films:** 剧情片

11. star-studded：明星荟萃的

12. avant-garde：先锋派的(艺术)

●**Reading Comprehension**

1. Directions: *Choose the best answer to each of the following questions.*

1) Which Chinese film won the Technical Jury Prize in Cannes?

   A. *Shanghai Triad.*

   B. *Crouching Tiger, Hidden Dragon.*

   C. *To live.*

   D. *Sha Nu.*

2) In the late 1980s, the world viewed Chinese films in a new light for the following reasons EXCEPT _____ .

   A. the fifth generation of Chinese directors began to be known by the world

   B. techniques and styles of Western cinematography had been used in Chinese films

   C. audiences were fed up with Hong Kong and Taiwan films

   D. the original "Chinese" narrative was welcomed by viewers

3) Which Chinese film won the Golden Palm in The Cannes Film Festival?

   A. *The Emperor and the Assassin.*   B. *Devils on the Doorstep.*

   C. *Farewell My Concubine.*   D. *Millennium Mambo.*

4) According to the article, which of the following is true?

   A. Gong Li won the Best Actor Award for the film Ju Dou and captured many foreign hearts.

   B. *Not One Less* is one of Zhang Yimou's films competing at the Cannes Film Festival.

   C. In other film festivals except Cannes, Ge You might have little chance of winning the prize for best actor.

   D. Zhang Yimou, as a "professional award-winner", has always been warmly welcomed by the Cannes Film Festival.

5) For Cannes, the top priority is _____ .

   A. heavy investment   B. remarkable filmic skill

   C. shining film stars   D. individuality

2. Directions: *Read the following statements carefully, and decide whether they are true (T) or false (F) according to the text.*

_____ 1) Since 1939, the Cannes Film Festival has become a yearly event.

_____ 2) It was not until 1959 that the first Chinese film competed in the Cannes Film Festival and won the prestigious Palme d'Or.

_____ 3) In 1975, because of *Sha Nu*, the Technical Jury Prize winner, Chinese martial arts began to be known to the world.

_____ 4) After *The Early Spring*, many Chinese mainland films have been selected by organizing committee to compete at the Film Festival.

_____ 5) By the late 1980s, Chinese films began combining the techniques and styles of Western cinematography with the original "Chinese" narrative.

_____ 6) Cannes favored Chen Kaige for both his impressionistic landscape and realistic dark film plot.

_____ 7) As a "professional award-winner", Zhang Yimou's films have won the Cannes film prizes three times.

_____ 8) Chinese comedy clown actor Ge You won the Best Actor Award at Cannes for his uniqueness in performance.

_____ 9) Gong Li became the most popular Chinese actress at Cannes for her five competition films and won the best actress award.

_____ 10) The avant-garde and original nature of the Cannes are attracting more Chinese directors to display their remarkable filmic skill and talent for story telling at the festival.

Part Three

Topic-related Activities

1. Congratulations, You Win the Oscar Award

Step One

Directions: *Work in groups of 4 or 5 and act out a scene of a Chinese film or an English film and let other students guess what film it is.*

Step Two

Directions: *Choose one of the students from each group as the judge and evaluate the performance of each group based on the criteria provided by the teacher. The group which has got most points will be awarded the "best group of the performance".*

Suggested criteria: 1) Language (fluency and correctness) (3 points)

2) Content (3points)

3) Cooperation of the group members (2 points)

4) Interaction with the audience (2 point)

Total points: (10 points)

Step Three

Directions: *After all the groups finish their performance, students (in the whole class) can choose their favorite actor (or actress) by writing down their names on the paper, and finally the one who is at the top of the list will be the winner of the award.*

Step Four

Directions: *Winners may have 45 seconds to deliver an acceptance speech.*

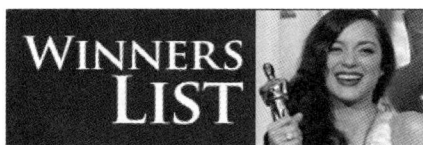

2. Movie Posters

Directions: *Work in groups to guess the name of the movie based on movie posters.*

3. A Matching Game

Directions: *Please work in pairs and match the movies in Column A with its translation in Column B.*

Group I

Column A	Column B
1) *Gone with the Wind*	a. 《阿甘正传》
2) *Frikey Friday*	b. 《黑客帝国》
3) *Forrest Gump*	c. 《辣妈辣妹》
4) *Legend of Fall*	d 《虎胆龙威》
5) *Dead Poets' Society*	e 《春风化雨》
6) *Die Hard*	f 《生命因你而动听》
7) *Mr Holland's Opus*	g 《刺激 1995》
8) *Matrix*	h 《情归巴黎》
9) *Sabrina*	I 《燃情岁月》
10) *Shawshank's Redemption*	j. 《乱世佳人》

Group I

Column A	Column B
1) 《英雄》	a. *Peacock*
2) 《三峡好人》	b. *Chungking Express*
3) 《我的父亲母亲》	c. *Still Life*
4) 《十七岁单车》	d. *Shang Hai Dreams*
5) 《孔雀》	e. *Tuyas Marriage*
6) 《可可西里》	f. *Beijing Bicycle*
7) 《青红》	g. *Hero*
8) 《重庆森林》	h. *Li Chun*
9) 《图雅的婚事》	i. *Mountain Patrol*
10) 《立春》	j. *The Road Home*

4. Case Study

The film *The Treatment,* directed by Zheng Xiaolong, who is known for his TV series, "Beijingers in New York", tells a compelling story of the culture clash between East and West. Set in the American mid-west, the movie centres on a young Chinese couple who immigrate to St Louis to pursue their American Dream. They have a bright young son, who they are raising to become a full-fledged American. DaTong and his wife are very well educated and understand that the only chance for the son to succeed in America, is to speak English without an accent. They even go so far as to ask the kid to use a fork and knife instead of chopsticks, even when they are eating Chinese style food.

One day, when Da Tong's father finds that his grandson is sick, he performs the traditional Chinese treatment, called Gua Sha, on his grandson. Though painless, the treatment leaves bright red marks on the skin, which are interpreted by the kid's teacher as welts. Soon the Child Welfare Agency is accusing the family of the child abuse and neglect, and transfers the kid to a foster home. Numerous court hearings ensue, followed by lots of overwrought melodrama. It seems that Da Tong's American dream is being sheltered because of the treatment. This film was screened at the 2001 Cannes Film Festival.

Note: Gua Sha is a treatment in traditional oriental medicine in which a wooden board repeatedly slides across the patient's acupuncture/acupressure/massage points. It works in similar principles to those of acupuncture/acupressure/massage. This method would inevitably leave bruise on the skin.

Questions

1. What is the cultural clash reflected in the movie? What is the reason for the clash?
2. Could you list any other features of Chinese culture that is not accepted by the Americans?
   Could you list any features of American culture that is not accepted by the Chinese people?

Other films that reflect cultural conflict

   1) *Crash*

   2) *Joy Luck Club*

   3) 《喜宴》

Part Four

Topic-related Information

1. Introduction to the World's Most Prestigious International Film Festivals

The Cannes Film Festival, founded in 1939, is one of the world's oldest, most influential and prestigious film festivals alongside Venice and Berlin. The private festival is held annually (usually in the month of May) in the resort town of Cannes, in the south of France. The most prestigious award given out at Cannes is the Palme d'Or ("Golden Palm") for the best film.

法国戛纳国际电影节：创办于 1939 年，每年 5 月 10 日至 21 日，最高奖为金棕榈奖。

The Berlin International Film Festival, also called the Berlinale, is one of the world's leading film festivals and most reputable media events held in Berlin, Germany. Founded in 1951, the festival has been celebrated annually in February since 1978. With 230,000 tickets sold and over 430,000 admissions, it is considered the largest publicly-attended film festival worldwide. Up to 400 films are shown in several sections, representing a comprehensive array of the cinematic world. Around twenty films compete for the awards called the Golden and Silver Bears.

德国柏林国际电影节：创办于 1951 年，每年 2 月 7 日至 18 日，最高奖为金熊奖。

The Venice Film Festival is the oldest film festival in the world. It began in 1932, since then has taken place every year in late August or early September on the island of the Lido, Venice, Italy. It is one of the world's most prestigious film festivals and is part of the Venice Biennale, a major biennial exhibition and festival for contemporary art. The festival's principal awards are the Leone d'Oro (Golden Lion), which is awarded to the best film screened at the festival, and the Coppa Volpi (Volpi Cup), which is awarded to the best actor and actress.

意大利威尼斯国际电影节：创办于 1931 年，每年 8 月 30 日至 9 月 9 日，最高奖为金狮奖。

The Montreal World Film Festival (WFF) is one of Canada's oldest international film festivals and the only competitive film festival in North America accredited by the FIAPF(国际电影制片人协会). A prestigious competitive event, it is open to films by established filmmakers as well as beginners. Launched with the support of national cinematography institutions, the festival is open to fiction feature length films, as well as documentaries and short films. The Festival's top prize is the Grand Prize of the Americas.

蒙特利尔国际电影节：创办于 1977 年，每年 8 月 25 日至 9 月 4 日，最高奖为美洲大奖。

The Karlovy Vary International Film Festival is a film festival held annually in July in Karlovy Vary (Carlsbad), Czech Republic (捷克共和国). Because of its success in the past few years the Karlovy Vary festival has become one of the most significant film events in Central and Eastern Europe, Crystal Globe for the best feature film.

卡罗维法利国际电影节：创办于 1946 年，每年 7 月 5 日至 15 日，最高奖为水晶球奖。

The Shanghai International Film Festival, abbreviated SIFF, is one of the largest film festivals in East Asia. The first festival was held from October 7 to 14, 1993, and was held biennially until 2001. In 2003 there was no festival. It has recently begun to gain an international reputation, after it was listed as one of the "A" Festivals by FIAPF. It awards several "Golden Cup" Awards ("Jin Jue" or 金爵) for best film, best director, best actor/actress, and other categories, as well as a "Special Jury Award."

中国上海国际电影节：创办于 1993 年，今年起每年 6 月上旬，最高奖为金爵奖。

2. Film Genres

Film Genres are various forms or identifiable types of films that have similar, or instantly-recognizable patterns, filmic techniques or conventions that include one or more of the following: settings, content and subject matter, themes, period, plot, central narrative events, motifs, styles, structures, situations, recurring icons, characterizations, and stars. Many films straddle several film genres.

The main film genres include: action/adventure, comedy, crime/gangster, drama, epics/historical, horror, musicals, science fiction, war, and westerns. By the end of the silent era, many of the main genres were established: the western, the horror film, comedies, and action-adventure films. Musicals were inaugurated with the era of the Talkies, and the genre of science-fiction films wasn't generally popularized until the 1950s. There are also identifiable sub-classes of the larger film genre, with their own distinctive subject matter, style, formulas, and iconography. Some of them are major sub-genres, such as film noir, romance films and melodramas.

1) Action/adventure films usually include high energy, physical stunts and chases, designed for pure audience escapism. The James Bond series is a typical example. A major sub-genre is the disaster film. Adventure films are usually exciting stories, with new experiences or exotic locales, very similar to or often paired with the action film genre. A good example in this field is *Expendables* (2010).

2) Comedies are light-hearted, designed to amuse and provoke laughter by exaggerating the situation, the language, action, and characters. There are various forms of comedy through cinematic history, including slapstick, screwball, spoofs and parodies, and more. *Roman Holiday* (1953), *Notting Hill* (1999) and *Sleepless in Seattle* (1993), etc. are typical examples in this field.

3) Crime/ gangster films are developed around the sinister actions of criminals or mobsters and their conflict with law, competitive colleague, or a rival gang. Headline-grabbing situations, real-life gangsters, or crime reports have often been used in crime films. See films like *Gangs of New York* (2002), and you will get to know some features of this type.

4) Dramas are serious presentations or stories with settings or life situations that portray realistic characters in conflict with either themselves, others, or forces of nature. A dramatic film shows us human beings at their best, their worst, and everything in-between. Dramatic themes often include current issues, societal problems, or injustices. Dramatic films are probably the largest film genre because many other genres have developed from it, such as crime films, melodramas, epics (historical dramas), biopics (biographical dramas), etc. *The Social Network* (2010) is within this field.

5) Epics often involve a historical or imagined event, legendary figure, cast in extravagant setting and accompanied sweeping musical score. Epics include costume dramas, historical dramas, war film epics, etc. They are often expensive to produce, like *The Lord of the Rings* (2001, 2002, 2003) and *Avatar* (2009).

6) Horror films are designed to cause dread and alarm, invoke our hidden worst fears, and captivate and entertain us at the same time. Whatever dark, primitive, and revolting traits that simultaneously attract and repel us are featured in the horror genre. They are often combined with science fiction. The typical examples in this type will be *Halloween* (1978), *Alien* (1979), *Scream* (1996), and *Saw 7* (2010), etc.

7) Musical/dance films are cinematic forms that emphasize full-scale song and dance routines or the films that are centered on combinations of music, dance, song or choreography. Musicals highlight various musical artists or dancing stars, with lyrics that support the story line, often with an alternative, escapist vision of reality—a search for love, success, wealth and popularity. Like, *Chicago* (2002), *Nine* (2009) are examples here.

8) Science fiction films are usually imaginative, with distant planets, impossible quests, improbable settings, futuristic technology, inexplicable forces, etc. Commonly, sci-fi films express society's anxiety about technology and attempt to figure out the future. *Inception* (2010) is within this field.

9) War films acknowledge the horror and heartbreak of war, letting the actual combat fighting provide the primary plot or background for the action of the film, such as *Hur Locker* (2008). War films are often paired with other genres, and they often take a denunciatory approach toward warfare.

10) Western films are the major defining genre of the American film industry, a nostalgic eulogy to the early days of the expansive, untamed American frontier (the borderline between civilization and wilderness). They have also been called the horse opera or the cowboy picture. Over time, westerns have changed a lot. A typical example of this type is *Unforgiven* (1992).

Hyperlinks

[1] Resources for posters

http://www.movieposter.com/

http://www.cyber-cinema.com/

[2] Resources for Oscar Acceptance Speech

http://quotations.about.com/od/movieandtvquote/a/oscars3.htm

References

[1] http://www.filmsite.org/films.html

[2] Sean Smith, Allison Samuels. Colorblind at Last? *Newsweek*[J], Feb. 12th, 2007

[3] http://french.10thnpc.org.cn/english/features/film/84968.htm

[4] Belinda Luscombe. Who Killed the Love Story? *Time*[J], Aug. 9th, 2007

Unit 12

Travel and Transportation

Part One

Lead-in

As the traveler who has once been from home is wiser than he who has never left his own doorstep, a knowledge of one other culture should sharpen our ability to scrutinize more steadily, to appreciate more lovingly, our own.

—Margaret Mead (America)

离开家乡的旅行者要比没离开过家门半步的人聪明，所以来自异国的文化能使我们更敏锐地审视两种文化的差异，最终更加欣赏我们自己的文化。

——玛格丽特·米德（美国）

We know already that over history, most people traveled to satisfy basic needs for survival. Some people traveled for fun, some traveled just out of curiosity, and others traveled for the purpose of conducting trade. In the modern life, travel plays an extremely important role. We can see different views, feel relaxed and broaden our horizons by travel.

Part Two

Reading Passages

In-Class Reading

Warm-up questions:

1. Among all the places you have ever been to, which place impresses you most?

2. What plans have you ever made before you travel?

Dealing with the Daily Tourist Grind

1   If you expect to see the best of Paris in just a few days, you'd better have a good game plan or the Eiffel Tower[1] is going to slip through the cracks in your schedule, and you'll leave town without the joy of climbing the world's most famous TV antenna.

2   I've drawn up some killer itineraries[2] for tackling major cities in 1-3 days (and countries in 1-2 weeks, all of Europe in 2-3 weeks), but you can just as easily plan your own time. After all, how do I know what you're interested in? However, before you plan your daily agenda, you need to be aware of the **quirks** of European hours and days of operation.

Making the Most of Mondays, Sundays, & Mornings

3   Monday is the day that over half the museums in Europe are closed (although Paris prefers Tuesday). Also expect **meager** happenings on Sunday, the traditional day of rest for many businesses, including sights—although many sights may be open Sunday morning.

4   How do you deal with Sundays and Mondays? First, make sure the Monday rule applies to the cities and towns you want to visit by checking your guidebook for open hours and closed days.

5   Next, when drawing up your trip itinerary, be sure Monday (or whatever day everything's closed) is not the only day (or one of your only two days) in a city or town filled with museums. Plan to do about half as much on Sundays as you would on a weekday.

6   Most importantly, find the sights and restaurants in town that are open on Mondays or on Sunday afternoons and save them for those times when everything else will be closed.

7   After you've planned out how to deal with the Sunday and Monday situation, remember that the first rule of getting the most out of your daily sightseeing is to get up early. Be at the most popular sights when the doors open, and you'll beat the lines. I'm about as far as you can get from a morning person, but I routinely get up at 6:30 a.m. when traveling.

8   Besides, especially in summer and in southern Europe, the sun can be **broiling** by midday, and you'll want to retreat to lunch and perhaps a nap to recharge your touring batteries. Speaking of a nap...

The Midday Siesta

9   You know how you naturally get sleepy in the middle of the afternoon? Well, Mediterranean countries[3] have always kept **attuned** to the **biorhythms** that American culture tries to ignore, and they've found a way to work around the body's internal clock. It's called the siesta (riposo in Italy).

10   Italy, Spain, Portugal, and Greece traditionally observe an early afternoon shutdown that begins at noon to 1:30 p.m. and runs until 2:30 to 4 p.m. Museums, most churches, shops, businesses—just about everything except restaurants—lower the shutters and lock the doors so that **proprietors** can either go home (or head to a local **trattoria**) for a long lunch and perhaps a **snooze** during the day's hottest hours.

11   At first this break can be very annoying, especially if you're on a tight sightseeing schedule, but after a while you get used to it. Learn to take the siesta and **revel** in it. If your time is short, make sure you know which sights (often churches) will be open during siesta and save them to visit at that time.

12   Sadly, the United States' economic influence is slowly forcing the rest of the world to live and work according to our **hectic**, stressful, non-stop schedule. Increasingly, businesses in larger cities are staying open through the middle of the day, and people are taking smaller, quicker lunches and bigger dinners (which any nutritionist will tell you is a trend in the wrong direction). It's good news for shoppers, but bad news for the general pace and quality of life.

Drawing Up a Daily Itinerary

13   You've been so careful planning every other aspect of your trip; don't leave the sightseeing to chance. I've seen too many people arrive at the doors of the museum or church that was to be the highlight of their trip only to find that it's closed that day. And they're leaving tomorrow.

14   You shouldn't **micromanage** your entire vacation, but it doesn't hurt to do a little advance planning to make sure you manage to squeeze in at least what's most important to you.

15   After being shut out of my share of sights by not reading the fine print ahead of time, I've come up with a **fail-safe** method for creating daily agendas. I happily ignore my schedules as often as I follow them, but at least the process of drawing them up alerts me to the odd hours of special sights.

16   The following steps may seem like a chore, but they take less than 30 minutes on the train on

your way into town (or in your hotel room on the night before you arrive).

17   Some people prefer to go with the flow and see stuff as they come across it, and that's perfectly fine. But if missing St. Peter's[4] will ruin your trip, this bit of advance paperwork can be a **godsend**.

18   Although this section deals mainly with sights, don't forget to look for, and mark, any restaurant or activity that you want to be sure you hit. **Virtually** all restaurants close at least one day of the week; if you're in town for two days, make sure you're not going to miss that great-sounding trattoria. Other "extras" to check the hours on include day trips as well as cultural events (for example, does the opera perform every night? When are the soccer matches?).

＊Write all the sights you want to see down the left side of a piece of paper. Next to each, write the open hours, and then make a third column showing the day(s) each is closed. Underline any opening or closing hour that's exceptional (say, if something closes at 6 p.m. instead of the town's usual 4 or 5 p.m.; underline the "6 p.m." part). For outstanding exceptions (wow, it closes at 7:30 p.m.), double-underline. Do the same for any unusual closed day. Mark places that stay open through siesta. If any sight has particularly restricted hours or days, put a box around it.

＊Below the list of sights, make a list of day trips and other activities you want to fit in (leather shopping in Florence, a tour of the sewers in Paris, a pub crawl in London[5]).

＊Take a second piece of paper and make blank daily schedules for each day you'll be in town, with each page marked with a day of the week. Put in headings for Morning (leave five to six lines), Lunch (one line), Afternoon (five to six lines), Dinner (a line), and Evening (two to three lines).

＊Use the hours-at-a-glance sheet you made in step 1 to fill in your daily itinerary chart smartly. Stick the earliest-opening sights first thing in the morning, the late-closing ones at the end of the day, and open-nonstop sights into the siesta hours just after lunch (in Mediterranean Europe).

＊Fill in the later morning and earlier afternoon with the sights that keep more standard hours. Write on the schedule a time to arrive at each sight and when you need to leave in order to get to the next one. Schedule things that aren't as important to you in between things that are.[6] That way, if you find yourself running short on time, you can cut sights out and still not miss the best stuff. Do this with a map in front of you, and budget time to get between sights. Don't pack the schedule too tightly, and don't forget to write in things like "**gelato** break."

＊Stuff the itinerary in your pocket when you go out for the day. Cross things off as you see them, and if you misjudged time and miss something, circle it so you can rearrange your afternoon or next day's schedule to fit it in.

＊Don't over-schedule yourself. Build in one day each week for relaxation and **decompression**, or for getting the laundry done, or to **cushion** your plans against **impromptu** day trips or festivals. Do the same for each day, leaving a bit of "free" time in there for waiting in the ticket line at the train station, heading to the post office to mail postcards, going shopping, or just sitting at an outdoor cafe table to sip a cappuccino.

New Words and Expressions

grind	n.	hard monotonous routine work 艰苦的工作
itinerary	n.	a guidebook for travelers 旅程，旅行指南，游记
siesta	n.	a nap in the early afternoon (especially in hot countries)午睡，晌觉
quirk	n.	a strange attitude or habit 怪癖
meager	a.	deficient in amount or quality or extent 贫乏的
broiling	a.	extremely hot 炽热的，酷热的，似烧的
attune	v.	adjust or accustom to; bring into harmony with 调，使……合调，使……相合
biorhythm	n.	a periodic physiological or behavioral change that is controlled by a biological clock 生物节律
proprietor	n.	someone who owns a business 所有者，经营者
trattoria	n.	饮食店(较大众化的餐厅，多为家庭式经营者，用餐时可省略前菜及甜点)
snooze	n.	sleeping for a short period of time (usually not in bed) 打盹
revel	n.	unrestrained merrymaking 作乐，狂欢
hectic	a.	marked by intense agitation or emotion 兴奋的；繁忙的
micromanage	v.	微管理
fail-safe	a.	guaranteed not to fail 自动防故障的
godsend	n.	a sudden happening that brings good fortune 天赐之物，意外获得的幸运
virtually	ad.	almost; very nearly 几乎；实际上
gelato	n.	(意大利语)冰淇淋
decompression	n.	relieving pressure 解压
cushion	v.	protect from impact 加垫褥，使缓冲
impromptu	a.	with little or no preparation or forethought 即席的，即兴的

Notes

1. **Eiffel Tower:** The symbol of Paris, Eiffel Tower was built in 1887 to commemorate the 100th anniversary of the French Revolution. It is named after its designer, Eiffel. The 320-meter-high tower is a hollow steel framed structure and shoots straight up to the clouds. It weighs 9000 tons. More than 200,000,000 people have visited the tower since its construction, making it the most

visited paid monument in the world. Including the 24 meters antenna, the structure is 324 meters high (since 2000), which is equivalent to about 81 levels in a conventional building.

2. killer itineraries: itineraries that will be very useful (to check these itineraries, refer to www.reidsguides.com)

3. **Mediterranean countries:** Twenty-one modern states have a coastline on the Mediterranean Sea. They are: Europe (from west to east): Spain, France, Monaco, Italy, Malta, Slovenia, Croatia, Bosnia and Herzegovina, Montenegro, Albania, Greece, Turkey; Asia (from north to south): Turkey, Cyprus, Syria, Lebanon, Israel, Egypt; Africa (from east to west): Egypt, Libya, Tunisia, Algeria and Morocco. Here they refer to European Mediterranean countries.

4. **St. Peter's:** 圣彼得大教堂 (罗马基督教的中心教堂，欧洲天主教徒的朝圣地与梵蒂冈罗马教皇的教廷，位于梵蒂冈，是全世界第一大教堂)

   The Papal Basilica of Saint Peter, officially known in Italian as the Basilica Papale di San Pietro in Vaticano and commonly known as St. Peter's Basilica, is located within the Vatican City. St. Peter's has the largest interior of any Christian church in the world, holding 60,000 people. It is regarded as one of the holiest Christian sites and has been described as "holding a unique position in the Christian world" and as "the greatest of all churches of Christendom". In Catholic tradition, it is the burial site of its namesake Saint Peter, who was one of the twelve apostles of Jesus and, according to tradition, first Bishop of Rome and therefore first in the line of the papal succession.

5. **the sewers in Paris, a pub crawl in London:** They are both one of the most famous parts of the cities. The sewers in Paris refer to sewer system of Paris, also known as the Paris Sewer Museum. In 1850, the Prefect for the Seine, Baron Haussmann and the engineer Eugéne Belgrand, designed the present Parisian sewer and water supply networks. Thus was built, more than a century ago, a double water supply network (one for drinking water and one for non drinking water) and a sewer network which was 600 km long in 1878. Tours of the sewage system have been popular since the 1800s and are currently conducted at the sewers. Visitors are able to walk upon raised walkways directly above the sewage itself. The basic premise of the pub crawl is to visit a succession of pubs, rather than spending the entire evening or day in a single establishment. The simplest pub crawl idea is to visit a number of pubs in a given area, for example Soho, or Holborn. London offers an excellent choice of themes for your pub crawl.

6. schedule things that aren't as important to you in between things that are: 在重要事情中间安排一般重要的事情(指安排参观景点的顺序)

●**Reading Comprehension**

1. Directions: *Discuss the following questions with your classmates.*

　　1) According to the author's plan, how long do people need to spend in visiting two countries?

　　2) As the author indicated in the article, the visitors need to be aware of the quirks of European

hours and days of operation. What are those quirks?

3) How will you deal with Sundays and Mondays when visiting European countries?

4) Why did the author suggest finding the sights and restaurants in town that are open on Mondays or on Sundays?

5) In Paragraph 7, the author said, "Be at the most popular sights when the doors open, and you'll beat the lines." What does "beat the line" mean?

6) What is the author's suggestion for the period of shutdown time?

7) What can tourists do if they find themselves running short on time?

8) Do you think this article is practical for you when you are making a travel plan? What do you usually do before travel?

2. Directions: *Read the following statements carefully, and decide whether they are true (T) or false (F) according to the text.*

_____ 1) People usually don't go to the museums in Paris on Mondays because over half the museums are closed.

_____ 2) In order to get the most out of your daily sightseeing, you need to get up early.

_____ 3) The midday siesta means nap.

_____ 4) In Italy, Spain, Portugal and Greece, traditionally everything will shut down at noon.

_____ 5) According to the nutritionists, it is quite good for people to take smaller, quicker lunches and bigger dinners.

_____ 6) The author in the article advised tourists to pack the schedule as tightly as possible so as to see the most of the sightseeing.

●Discussion

The most popular time to travel may not be the best, or provide the most memorable trip, and by and large the "tourist season" is not the one you want. Paris in January? Lovely. Athens in August? Forget about it!

Picking your time can be as important as picking your place—do you plan to hit the grape harvest, or ride into town during the annual folk festival or the start of opera season?

Sure, a trip to Europe will probably be fantastic at any time, but do a little homework and you can make it happen at precisely the right time to have the time of your life.

1. What is the most important part about traveling according to your understanding?

2. What is your attitude to travel? Is it beneficial or time-consuming? Discuss with your classmates.

After-Class Reading

Passage One

Warm-up questions:

1. In what ways can we get around in a big city like Beijing?

2. Which means of transportation do you prefer when traveling in an unfamiliar city? Support your idea with specific reasons.

Getting Around

Metrorail[1]

1   Almost every sight worth seeing in Washington can be reached by Metrorail, the city's clean, often-efficient subway system. There are five color-coded lines, and each train's direction is determined by its destination. For example, an Orange Line train to Vienna is traveling west, while those heading for New Carrolton are going east. Lights flash on the edge of the platform when a train is approaching the station. Before boarding, look at the maps and signposts on the train platform, and double-check the direction and color of the train, noted on the screens at the top of each car.

2   Fares vary by the length of your journey and time of day; on weekdays, you'll pay more from 5 to 9:30 a.m., 3 to 7 p.m. and 2 to 3 a.m. The minimum fare is $1.35 one way, rising to a maximum of $2.35 outside of rush hour. If you plan on hitting a number of sites, it's probably more cost-effective to buy a one-day pass ($6.50), which allows unlimited travel after 9:30 a.m. weekdays and all-day on weekends and holidays. Farecards can be purchased from machines in each station. Keep your card handy, as you'll need it each time you enter and exit a station.

3   The Metro runs until midnight Sunday through Thursday and until 3 a.m. on Friday and Saturday nights. Signs with times for last trains are posted inside each station, above the main kiosk[2]. While it's not widely advertised, bathrooms are available for customers who find themselves in dire straits[3]—just ask the kiosk attendant.

Taxis

4   Unlike seemingly every other city in the western world, taxi cabs in Washington don't use meters to determine your fare. Instead, it's a complicated zone system that confuses and

confounds[4] residents as often as visitors. (If you're in Virginia or Maryland, cabs use the traditional meter system.)

5　You'll find a map in the back seat of every cab. Note that the map is not oriented north-south, as you might expect. The fare is determined by the address where you hailed the cab and the address of your destination—you pay for the number of zones you travel through, not the mileage.

6　This method has its benefits—including no surcharge for waiting in traffic and that drivers can take a longer route to get around jams—but it's often downright confusing for those unfamiliar with Washington geography and is exploited by unscrupulous[5] drivers. (If you're unsure of how much a ride should cost, check the D.C. Government's Taxicab Fare Calculator.)

7　For an average one-zone trip downtown, expect to pay a basic rate of $6.50 for the first passenger, but extra fees can quickly add up: $1.50 for each additional passenger, a $1 rush hour surcharge for travel between 7 and 9:30 a.m. and 4 and 6:30 p.m.

8　When choosing a cab in Washington, make sure the driver's photo and license number is posted on the passenger's side and that there's a map in the back seat. If you don't see either, find another taxi.

Metrobus[6]

9　Washington's Metrobus system covers much more of the city than the Metro system, but can be more daunting[7] for new users. Bus stops frequently list route numbers and letters but not their destinations or schedules, while buses show only their destination, not their route.

10　With a little planning through, things become easier. Detailed bus maps are available from Metro's Web site, www.wmata.com, or the Metro sales office at the Metro Center station. Individual stations usually have maps for bus routes that run through that neighborhood. Check for the large route maps at downtown bus kiosks to see which bus goes your way.

11　Fares are $1.25 for most journeys (35 cents if you're transferring from Metrorail and grabbed a transfer slip before boarding a train), and you can ask the driver for a transfer that will allow you to board another Metrobus for free during a two-hour time limit.

D.C. Circulator[8]

12　The newest method of public transportation is this visitor-friendly bus, which runs two routes: East and West from Union Station to Georgetown, and north and south from the Convention Center to the Waterfront. Fares are $1 for adults, 50 cents for seniors and the disabled, and free with a transfer from a Metrobus or another Circulator bus.

Old Town Trolley[9] and Tourmobile[10]

13   These two popular companies offer guided tours of the sites, but are especially useful because they allow visitors to shuttle between museums and monuments, hopping on and off whenever the mood strikes once a one-day ticket has been purchased.[11] Old Town Trolley, which ventures into Georgetown, Dupont Circle and upper Northwest as well as covering the Mall, costs $28 for adults and $14 for children. Tourmobile sticks to the monumental core and Arlington Cemetery, and costs $20 for adults and $10 for children.

Parking

14   A simple piece of advice: Avoid driving and parking downtown. Washington's traffic is among the worst in the nation, and the congested streets, rush-hour restrictions and frequent backups are maddening enough for the folks who deal with them on a daily basis.[12] It's hard to find street parking near the Mall—impossible during major events—and there are few parking garages nearby.

15   Some residential neighborhoods (Woodley Park, Georgetown, Foggy Bottom) have street parking without meters, but there are plenty of restrictions for nonresidents, such as a two-hour limit between 7 a.m. and 6:30 p.m. Most allow unlimited parking on weekends, though.

16   If you're driving to Washington from outside the area, you can park at terminal Metro stations, where parking is free on weekends. Vienna, Shady Grove, Greenbelt and New Carrollton all have large lots. Parking during the week, though, requires the use of a SmarTrip card[13], which you can buy inside the station.

Getting to and from the Airports

17   All three local airports—Washington Dulles International, Ronald Reagan Washington National and Baltimore/Washington International—can be reached by public transportation, taxi or private shuttle services. Reagan National is on Metro's Blue and Yellow lines, and BWI is serviced by Amtrak[14] and commuter[15] trains that stop at Union Station.

Union Station

18   The hub for Amtrak service, Union Station is located on Capitol Hill, a stone's throw from the Capitol, and connects directly to Metro's Red Line.

—Fritz Hahn

Proper Names

Vienna	维也纳(镇) (位于弗吉尼亚州)
New Carrolton	新卡罗敦(位于马里兰州)
Georgetown	乔治城
Dupont Circle	杜邦圆环
the Mall	摩尔区(博物馆大道)
Arlington Cemetery	阿灵顿国家公墓
Woodley Park	伍德里公园
Foggy Bottom	雾谷(美国国务院的谑称)
Shady Grove	雪迪格罗夫(位于马里兰州)
Greenbelt	格林贝尔(位于马里兰州)
Washington Dulles International	华盛顿—杜勒斯国际机场
Ronald Reagan Washington National	里根华盛顿国家机场
Baltimore / Washington International	巴尔的摩—华盛顿国际机场
Union Station	联合车站
Capitol Hill (the Capitol)	国会山

Notes

1. **Metrorail:** 华盛顿都会区捷运系统(Washington Metrorail)，一般简称华盛顿地铁，为美国第二繁忙的城市轨道交通系统，仅次于纽约地铁，于 1976 年开始营运。

2. kiosk: (车站、广场等处的)书报摊，音乐台，广告亭，公共电话间，问讯处

3. dire straits: a state of extreme distress 此处 "customers who find themselves in dire straits"指那些需要用洗手间的乘客。

4. confound: 混淆，使混同，使混乱；使惊慌失措，使迷惑

5. unscrupulous: 不择手段的，无所不为的；肆无忌惮的，寡廉鲜耻的

6. **Metrobus:** 和地铁同属首都圈交通局营运的巴士称为 Metrobus，是从地铁站前往稍远的乔治城等地。

7. daunting: 使人畏缩的

8. **D. C. Circulator:** 特区环线大巴

9. **Old Town Trolley:** 旧城巴士。搭乘宛如老式路面电车般的巴士环绕各主要观光景点，司机兼导游用英语为游客解说。环绕一圈约 2 小时 15 分钟，由联合车站出发，沿路可任意上下车。

10. **Tourmobile:** 观光巴士，车票有效期 1 天，不限次数任意上下车，全年行驶。以国家大草坪为中心，前往国会大厦、史密苏尼博物馆、林肯纪念堂、阿灵顿墓园等主要历史纪念地、政府机构等都很方便。

11. They allow visitors to shuttle between museums and monuments, hopping on and off whenever

the mood strikes once a one-day ticket has been purchased. 此句意为：旧城巴士和观光巴士便于乘客穿梭于各个博物馆和纪念馆之间，而且乘客只要购买一张一日通的车票就可以随兴上下车。

12. Washington's traffic is among the worst in the nation, and the congested streets, rush-hour restrictions and frequent backups are maddening enough for the folks who deal with them on a daily basis. 此句意为：华盛顿是美国交通最糟糕的城市之一。其拥挤不堪的街道、高峰期的交通管制和经常性的交通堵塞足以把每天与之打交道的人们逼疯。

13. **SmarTrip card:** 智慧旅卡(应用于华盛顿地区捷运系统)

14. **Amtrak:** 美国国家铁路客运公司 Amtrak 的列车开往美国的 500 多个目的地。该公司运营跨大陆的长途列车，以及沿东北走廊的商务目的地之间的便利列车服务。

15. commuter：［美］长期票通勤旅客；经常来往于两地之间的人

●**Reading Comprehension**

1. Directions: *Discuss the following questions with your classmates.*

1) What determines the amount of money passengers have to pay for their journey with Metrorail?

2) What would be the most cost-effective way if visitors plan to visit more than one site in Washington?

3) What is needed when passengers enter and exit a station according to Paragraph 2?

4) What exactly determines the fare you have to pay to the taxi driver?

5) How much money do two passengers have to pay for a one-zone trip downtown by taxi in rush hours?

6) What will enable passengers to board another Metrobus for free during a two-hour time limit?

2. Directions: *Complete the following sentences with the information you get from the passage. Notice that the blanks are supposed to be filled with either a single word or a phrase or even a sentence.*

1) There are five color-coded lines in Metrorail to different destinations. Passengers should _____ the maps and signposts on the train platform before boarding, and _____ the direction and color of the train, noted on the screens at the top of each car.

2) Passengers pay _____ from 5 to 9:30 a.m., 3 to 7 p.m. and 2 to 3 a.m. on week days by Metrorail.

3) There are machines in each station from which Farecards can be _____. Keep your card _____, as you'll need it each time you enter and exit a station.

4) Taxi cabs in Washington don't use meters to determine your fare and a _____ is employed instead. The fare is determined by both the address _____ and the address _____.

5) The D.C. Government's Taxicab Fare Calculator might prove helpful for visitors who are not sure of _____.

6) Compared with the Metro system, Washington's Metrobus system _____.

7) _____, the newest method of public transportation is a _____ bus service.

8) Washington's traffic is among the _____ in the nation, and the folks tend to be driven mad by _____.

Passage Two

Warm-up questions:

1. Can you figure out any advantages of travelling by train over travelling by air?

2. Do you know anything special about travelling by train in Europe?

The Complete Rail Guide to Europe

1   How will you get to the sun this summer? Most people will grit their teeth and fly. It's grim but at least it's quick. Well, it's quick if you disregard the airport-parking nightmare, the two-hour check-in, the snaking queues at security, the flight delays and the long wait at the luggage carousel. As air travel becomes increasingly unpleasant, many people are taking the train. Not just for cheeky weekend breaks to Paris and Brussels, but all the way to southern France, Spain and Italy.

2   Why? For a start, trains are getting a lot faster, with several new high-speed rail links coming into operation this year. In addition, the experience is altogether more civilized than flying: services are more reliable, security is more relaxed, check-in time is shorter and you don't have to scramble to get a seat, or pay extra to take a suitcase.

3   Then there's the undeniable romance of train travel, and the knowledge that you're as green as the fields swooshing past your window.[1] In France, where intercity trains all use nuclear-powered electricity, your carbon footprint is virtually nonexistent.

4   But how do you start planning a rail-borne holiday—and how far can it take you? Here's our guide to where you can go, how to book, and how to get the best fares.

Eurostar[2]

5   It's arguably the most civilized way to leave the country, and, on top of that, Eurostar is fast, easy and—if you know how to work the system—inexpensive. The key to bagging a bargain is to buy tickets as soon as they are released, 120 days before your last day of travel.

6   Standard returns start at £59 to Paris and £55 to Lille. Brussels costs £59, although this includes onward travel to any station in Belgium (Bruges and Antwerp are favorites). Book online (www.eurostar.co.uk) and you will avoid the £5 supplement to use the call centre (0870 518 6186).

7   You can buy a ticket from Eurostar to almost anywhere in France, usually involving a change of train in Lille or Paris. Of the two hubs, Lille is easier and often entails no more than a change of

platforms. Return fares from London are good value: for £79 you can get as far as Poitiers or Dijon; for £89, Limoges or Clermont Ferrand; for £99, Bordeaux or La Rochelle; and for £109, Avignon or Nice.

8   Your chances of securing these lowest fares will be improved if you avoid bank holidays, Bastille Day[3] and this year's Rugby World Cup[4] (September 7 to October 20). If you're flexible on dates, you can search the Eurostar website for the days showing the lowest fares (click on "Latest Deals", then "On a Budget?").

9   Waterloo[5] to Paris currently takes 2 hours and 35 minutes, with Lille 1 hour and 40 minutes away. When Eurostar moves to its new home at St Pancras on November 14, these times will drop to 2 hours and 15 minutes and 1 hour and 20 minutes respectively. From the new Ebbsfleet International station, near the M25[6] in Kent, Lille will be just 70 minutes away.

10   Eurostar offers three classes: standard, leisure select and business. Although leisure select and business are priced very differently—the former costs from £139, rising to £405, for a return to Paris; the latter is a flat £450—the seats are identical. The main difference is that the business ticket is fully flexible and refundable; leisure select is not. Business also buys you lounge access, a dedicated carriage, a 10-minute check-in rather than the regular half-hour, and—on morning departures —the option of an express breakfast.

11   The move to St Pancras promises other significant benefits: improved punctuality (because the entire journey to France will be on dedicated high-speed rails); and through-ticketing[7] from any train station in the UK. At a stroke, the benefits of speedy rail connections to Europe will be available to millions of people in the Midlands and north of England. You just have to wait until November.

Explore France

12   Although Eurostar lets you book travel throughout France, there is a snag: SNCF[8] has a booking window of 90 days, compared with Eurostar's 120 days. This means if you travel at peak times and wait until the opening of the 90-day window, you can miss out on the lowest cross-Channel fares.

13   The trick is to book your Eurostar tickets 120 days in advance, then book onward connections 30 days later with Rail Europe (0870 830 4862, http://www.raileurope.co.uk/) or European Rail (020 7387 0444, http://www.europeanrail.com/).

14   SNCF's lowest intercity fares—known as Prem's[9]—offer up to 75% off standard rates. For instance, Paris to Nice by TGV[10] can be had for just £19 each way, reduced from £78.50. Go first class and you can pay just £33.50, down from £108.50. These fares are understandably popular, so it pays to get in at the start of the 90-day window.

15   Another bargain is the new low-cost, high-speed IDTGV service that runs between Paris and the south of France—Marseilles, Bordeaux, Montpellier, Aix-en-Provence, Nice and Toulouse. It has one-way fares from £13.50.

16   These can only be booked online (http://www.idtgv.com/), up to 120 days in advance (perfect for combining with Eurostar). When you book you will be offered a choice of carriages: IDzen, if you want quiet (no mobile phones or children under 12), or IDzap, if you prefer to chat, play your iPod or rent a PSP games console.

17   The big news this summer is the opening of TGV Est on June 10, which will slash journey times to eastern France and on to Germany and Switzerland. The new 200mph trains will have coaches designed by Christian Lacroix, with comfortable seating and extra legroom. There will be 16 return departures a day between Paris and Strasbourg, taking 2 hours and 20 minutes. Currently, the journey takes 4 hours.

18   Travellers to Alsace, Champagne and Lorraine will also benefit. Paris to Reims will take 45 minutes, down from 1 hour and 35 minutes. TGV Est services will run out of Gare de L'Est[11]. Details: http://www.tgvesteuropeen.com/.

Go Dutch

19   Travel to Holland by train is relatively easy, with a quick change at Brussels. But the length of the journey—currently 5 hours between London and Amsterdam—means that many travellers opt to fly instead. That may change on December 8, when the Dutch unveil their own new high-speed rail line, cutting journey times to destinations across Holland. London to Amsterdam will take just 3 hours and 36 minutes (plus 20 minutes to switch platforms in Brussels).

20   And, of course, rather than arriving at Schiphol airport[12], 11 miles outside Amsterdam, the train takes you to Central Station, slap bang in the centre of the city. With return fares from £69, there really will be no excuse for flying. Book with Eurostar, Rail Europe or European Rail.

SPAIN AND ITALY

21   Go much further than the south of France and you're talking about an overnight trip—but that's no bad thing. Sleeper-train travel combines old-fashioned romance with 21st-century timesaving. Not only do you avoid the whole miserable airport experience, you also arrive bright and early in the centre of a city with what amounts to an extra day's holiday. (This assumes, of course, that you can sleep on trains. Top tip: pack earplugs.)

22   The best place to pick up European overnight services is Paris. Take Eurostar over in the morning, drop your bags at left luggage[13], then head off for lunch and some sightseeing before

hopping on board the evening sleeper.

23   One of the most useful trains is the Elipsos[14], which runs from Paris Austerlitz[15] to Madrid and Barcelona, both journeys taking about 12 hours. The train offers a range of accommodation, including Grand Class, where you get a cabin with shower and a three-course dinner with wine. If you book 90 days in advance with Rail Europe, you may be able to pick up a Prem's fare, from £50 each way including a couchette in a four-berth compartment.

24   From Paris Bercy[16], the high-speed Artesia runs overnight services into Rome (14 hours), and Venice and Turin (13 hours). Prem's fares are also available 90 days in advance, making it possible to get to Venice in a six-berth couchette for just £19 each way. Rome, Florence and Parma start at £26. (Note: there are no left-luggage facilities at Bercy station. Stash your bags at Gare du Nord instead.)

InterRailing

25   Once the preserve of soap-swerving students[17], InterRail[18] passes now have no upper age limits. This year, for the first time, you can also buy a single-country pass or upgrade to first class.

26   Fares are still weighted towards young people.[19] If you are under 26, you are classified as a "youth" and qualify for a reduction of about 35% on adult fares. Youths can't, however, buy first-class passes, which is a relief for the rest of us.

27   InterRail prices are the same year-round, so they really come into their own during the summer months. Single-country passes are valid for a month, for either three, four, six or eight days of travel during that period. Europe-wide passes are available for five days' travel within a 10-day period, 10 days' travel within a 22-day period, 22 continuous days or one month's unlimited travel.

28   Prices vary between countries. France, Germany, Norway and Sweden are the priciest, at £197 for six days' travel (youths £128), while Turkey and Bulgaria are among the least expensive, at £73 (youths £47). InterRail pass-holders also qualify for a 50% discount on Channel crossings with SeaFrance (0870 571 1711, http://www.seafrance.com/). Book with Rail Europe (0870 830 4862, http://www.raileurope.co.uk/).

What about Home?

29   TRAIN TRAVEL in the UK is rarely romantic, with one notable exception: the Caledonian Sleeper. Running six nights a week between London Euston and a slew of cities across Scotland, it provides comfortable beds, convenient overnight travel times and one-way fares from as low as £19.

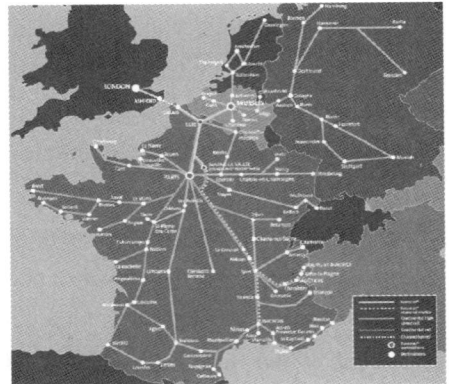

30 Bookings are taken up to 12 weeks in advance, with new batches of tickets released on a weekly basis. There is no service on Saturday nights. You can book with First ScotRail (0845 755 0033, http://www.firstgroup.com/).

31 For other long-distance train travel in the UK, contact National Rail Enquiries (0845 748 4950, http://www.nationalrail.co.uk/). The best deals are usually on advance fares.[20] These are inflexible —only valid on the date and time stated, with a single operating company.

—Mark Hodson

Notes

1. Then there's the undeniable romance of train travel, and the knowledge that you're as green as the fields swooshing past your window. 该句大意为： 乘火车很浪漫，也很环保。句子中的 "green" 一语双关，既指田野的颜色，更指没有污染。

2. **Eurostar:** 欧洲之星。英、法、比利时三国铁路部门联营的客运服务。列车车速达 300 km/h。列车连接伦敦的滑铁卢车站和巴黎的北火车站(Gare du Nord)。不到 3 小时, Eurostar 带您从伦敦市中心出发，抵达巴黎市中心。伦敦到布鲁塞尔更只需 2 小时 20 分。

3. **Bastille Day:** 法国革命纪念日

    Bastille Day (July 14th) is a National holiday in France. It is very much like Independence Day in the United States because it is a celebration of the beginning of a new form of government.

4. **Rugby World Cup:** 橄榄球世界杯

5. Waterloo: 指位于英国伦敦的滑铁卢火车站

6. the M25: 伦敦周围的环形高速公路

7. **through-ticket:** 直通客票, 联运客票

8. SNCF: [法] Société Nationale des Chemins de Fer 法国国营铁路公司

9. **Prem's:** 特价票

10. **TGV:** Train a Grande Vitesse 巴黎至里昂间高速火车

11. Gare de L'Est: 巴黎东火车站

12. Schiphol airport: 阿姆斯特丹斯希普霍尔机场

13. **left luggage:** 行李寄存

14. Elipsos: 一种夜火车

15. Paris Austerlitz: 巴黎奥斯特利茨站

16. Paris Bercy: 巴黎贝西火车站

17. soap-swerving students: 自由往返的学生

18. **InterRail pass:** 欧洲火车联票

19. Fares are still weighted towards young people. 此句意为：对年青人，票价依然还是有优惠的。

20. The best deals are usually on advance fares. 此句意为：提前预付票款往往能得到最多的优惠。

Proper Names

Paris	巴黎 (法国首都)
Brussels	布鲁塞尔 (比利时首都)
France	法国
Spain	西班牙
Italy	意大利
Lille	里尔 (法国北部城市)
Belgium	比利时
Bruges	布鲁日 (比利时西北部城市)
Antwerp	安特卫普 (比利时北部一城市)
Poitiers	普瓦捷 (法国一城市)
Dijon	第戎 (法国东部城市)
Nice	尼斯 (法国东南部城市，在戛纳东北的地中海沿岸)
Clermont Ferrand	克莱蒙费朗 (法国一城市)
Bordeaux	波尔多市 (位于法国西南的一个港口城市)
La Rochelle	拉罗谢尔 (法国一城市)
Avignon	阿维尼翁 (法国东南部城市)
Limoges	里摩日 (法中西部城市)
St Pancras	圣潘克勒斯国际火车站
Kent	肯特郡(英国东南部州名)
Marseilles	马赛 (法国东南部一城市)
Toulouse	图卢兹 (法国南部城市)
Aix-en-Provence	艾克斯 (法国一城市)
Montpellier	蒙彼利埃 (法国南部的一个城市)
Switzerland	瑞士
Strasbourg	斯特拉斯堡 (法国东北部城市)
Alsace	阿尔萨斯 (法国东北部一地名)
Champagne	香巴尼 (法国东北部一历史地区)
Lorraine	洛林 (法国东北部一地区)
Reims	兰斯 (法国东北部城市)
Holland	荷兰
Amsterdam	阿姆斯特丹 (荷兰首都)
Barcelona	巴塞罗那 (西班牙东北部临地中海的一个城市)
Madrid	马德里 (西班牙首都)
Parma	帕尔马 (意大利北部城市)
Venice	威尼斯 (意大利东北部的一个城市)
Turin	都灵 (意大利西北部城市)

Florence	佛罗伦萨 (意大利都市名)
Rome	罗马 (意大利首都)
Bulgaria	保加利亚
Norway	挪威
Sweden	瑞典
Turkey	土耳其
Germany	德国

● **Reading Comprehension**

1. Directions: *Discuss the following questions with your classmates.*

1) How do you understand the words "cheeky weekend" in Para. 1?

2) Why more and more people come to prefer to take trains rather than fly?

3) What does "bagging a bargain" (in Para. 5) mean?

4) What does the word "flat" in the sentence "the latter is a flat £450" (in Para. 10) mean?

5) What is the difference between the leisure select class and business class of Eurostar?

6) What are IDzen and IDzap? And what's the difference between them?

2. Make a plan of traveling through Europe

Directions: *First figure out the cities in Europe that you are eager to visit; Then make the best journey plan by referring to the information offered in the passage, and if possible, calculate the total fares of your journey. Last, share your journey plan with others and ask for advice for improvement.*

Part Three

Topic-related Activities

1. Guessing Game

Directions: *Students are supposed to figure out which city it is within 5 seconds according to the description or clues provided by the teacher.*

1) The city is not the capital of the U.S., but its financial center and that of the entire world to some extent.

2) The city enjoys a reputation for perfume and Eiffel Tower.

3) The city of water.

4) The cradle of western civilization.

5) The city where Hollywood stars are created.

6) The city has an opera house with glittering white shell-shaped roofs.

7) The city where Big Ben is located.

8) A German city which is famous for beer and holds a beer festival annually.

9) The city of cars in the U.S.

10) The city of watch and clock.

2. Where Are They?

Look at the pictures carefully and find out where they are.

1) List as many scenic spots as you can in this city. If you can not spell the names correctly, please refer to the Internet or other references.

2) Suppose you are a guide, can you arrange a suitable line for the tourists to visit in each place?

3. A Matching Game

(1) Match the countries with their capitals

1) Switzerland		A. Budapest
2) Norway		B. Rome
3) Finland		C. Amsterdam
4) Hungary		D. Madrid
5) Holland		E. Oslo
6) Denmark		F. Paris
7) France		G. Stockholm

8) Spain   H. Copenhagen

9) Sweden   I. Helsinki

10) Italy   J. Bern

(2) Match the following 10 Views of the West Lake with their English names and memorize them

苏堤春晓	Lingering Snow on the Broken Bridge
曲院风荷	Autumn Moon over the Calm Lake
平湖秋月	Twin Peaks Piercing Clouds
断桥残雪	Spring Dawn at Su Causeway
柳浪闻莺	Three Pools Mirroring the Moon
花港观鱼	Evening Bell at Nanping Hill
雷峰夕照	Orioles Singing in the Willows
双峰插云	Viewing Fish at Flower Harbor
南屏晚钟	Sunset Glow at Leifeng Pagoda
三潭印月	Lotus in the Breeze at Crooked Courtyard

4. Case Study

Whether you go to the beaches of the Mediterranean or the old landscape of the Arctic, how you travel can have a huge impact on the environment.

1) Make tourism and conservation compatible—the money you spend on your trip helps determine the development and direction of tourism. Use your money to support reputable, conservation-minded tour operators and suppliers.

2) Visit parks and nature reserves—Get any necessary permits before visiting nature reserves or other protected areas. Leave these areas as you find them and do not disturb the wildlife there.

3) View and photograph wildlife from a distance and remember that in the optimal wildlife viewing experience, the animal never knows you are there. Suppress the natural temptation to move too close and respect signs of distress such as alarm calls and distraction displays. Respect the environment, stay on trails during hikes, do not remove plants or feed animals, and never litter. At the sea do not take any corals, shells, dried fish, starfish, sea-fans and other marine souvenirs—removal can seriously disrupt ecosystems. Navigation in reef water needs special care—do not anchor on reefs which can be easily damaged.

4) Reduce your air travel. When you travel to your holiday destination by plane you are contributing to significant emissions of climate change causing carbon dioxide. Take vacations nearer to home, or get there by other forms of transport such as train, bus or boat. If you have to fly, consider buying carbon offsets[1] to compensate for the emissions caused by your flight.

5) Reduce your car use—choose other ways to get around like trains, buses or bikes. Share taxis and take shuttles to and from the airport. Encourage drivers to turn off their engines when they're parked, or stuck in traffic.

6) Conserve water—take showers rather than baths, and use a refillable water container, sterilizing water when necessary, rather than buying bottled water.

7) Limit energy use, including your use of air conditioning and hot water. Turn off all lights and taps when you leave hotel rooms.

8) Minimize your use of personal care products and detergents to wash linen, and reuse your hotel towels and bed-linen[2]. Dispose of sanitary waste[3] properly—or you might just find them on the beach next time you visit.

9) Choose lodgings that have effective waste treatment systems, that are energy efficient, and that use environmentally friendly energy sources such as solar energy or hydroelectric power.

10) Say "No" to bad souvenirs. Some souvenirs could end up costing a lot more than you paid for them. Think twice before you buy any products made from any endangered species, including animal furs and body parts, tortoise-shell, ivory, or coral—they could be illegal.

Notes

1. carbon offset: 所谓的 "碳平衡"，就是算出使用的交通工具、电器等排出的二氧化碳量，然后再捐款给种树或支持再生能源的组织，来抵消或平衡所产生的碳。
2. bed-linen: 被单和枕套
3. sanitary waste: 生活废物(如厕所丢弃的卫生纸等)

Questions

1) According to the ten items related to travel, which ones do you think are not sufficiently done by Chinese?
2) If you travel abroad, which item will be a barrier to you?
3) Imagine, if you were a foreigner traveling in China, which part would be most difficult for you to adapt to?

Part Four

Topic-related Information

1. Eurostar

Eurostar is a high-speed train service in Western Europe connecting London and Kent in the United Kingdom, with Paris and Lille in France, and Brussels in Belgium. In addition, there are limited services from London to Disneyland Resort Paris (Gare de Marne-la-Vallée—Chessy) and seasonal destinations in France. Trains cross the English Channel through the Channel Tunnel.

The service is operated by 18-carriage Class 373 trains at up to 300 km/h (186 mph) on a network of high-speed lines. Since Eurostar began in 1994, new lines have been built in Belgium (HSL1) and Southern England (High Speed 1) to the same standard as the LGV Nord line originally used in France, reducing journey times. The two-stage High Speed 1 project was completed on 14 November 2007, when the London terminus of Eurostar transferred from Waterloo International to St Pancras International station.

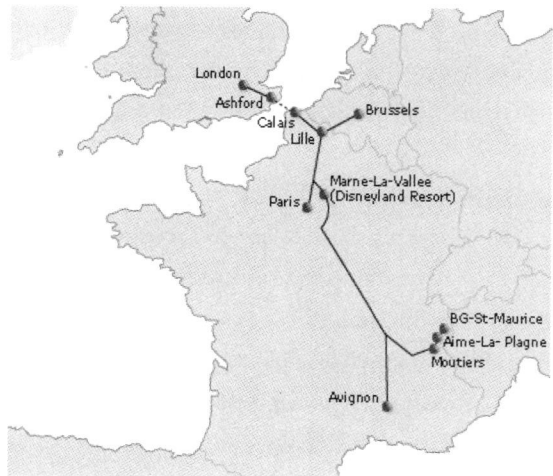

2. Bank Holidays

In England, Bank Holidays refer to: New Year's Day, Easter Monday, May Day (not necessarily 1 May, it is the 2nd of May), Spring and Late Summer Holidays at the end of May and August respectively, and Boxing Day. There are also two common law holidays on Good Friday and Christmas Day. And 30th of April is called Spring Bank.

In Scotland, bank holidays are: New Year's Day, January 2, Good Friday, Easter Monday, May Day (not necessarily 1 May), Spring and Summer Holidays at the end of May and the beginning of August respectively, Christmas Day and Boxing Day.

In Northern Ireland, bank holidays are: New Year's Day, St. Patrick's Day (17 March), Easter Monday, May Day (not necessarily 1 May), Spring and Late Summer Holidays at the end of May and August respectively, and Boxing Day. There are also two common law holidays on Good Friday and Christmas Day and a public holiday on the anniversary of the Battle of the Boyne (12 July).

3. The Orient-Express

Orient-Express runs luxury trains between London and Venice from March to November, with side trips to Prague, Budapest, Istanbul and—new this year—Cracow and Warsaw.

The adventure begins at 11 a.m. on Platform 2, London Victoria, where you board the British Pullman to Folkestone. After crossing the Channel by Eurotunnel (on a coach), you switch to the Venice Simplon-Orient-Express, which gets you to Paris by 9 p.m., followed by breakfast in the Swiss Alps, finally reaching Venice just after 6 p.m.

London to Venice costs £1,430 pp, based on two sharing a compartment, with all meals included (but not a shower—this train is old-school posh, and old-school doesn't include bathing facilities). You can also book a single leg of the journey, such as London-Paris. Because London-Paris-Venice is so popular, fares are rarely discounted, but it is sometimes possible to get seasonal reductions of up to 25% on less busy routes, such as Venice-Budapest.

4. Train Car

It matters which train car you sit in when travelling in Europe, because not all the cars in your train may be going to the same destination. Long-distance European trains often split up en-route and head in different directions. Make sure you select a car going to your destination. Check the car's clearly marked origin city and destination city before boarding.

You must also choose between 1st and 2nd class, and between smoking and non-smoking.

All of the above choices are mapped out on a train plan. This plan is usually displayed next to the printed schedules on the track from which your train will depart. This plan tells you exactly where to stand on the platform given the above choices.

If you have a reservation, sit in the car and seats that you reserved.

5. E-ticket

The e-ticket is the electronic image of a common paper ticket. It's a recording of some electronic numbers. Currently, it's the most advanced passenger ticket format, providing great convenience via electronic ticket reservation, payment, and boarding procedure while reducing greatly the airline cost. It's a much better choice than the common passenger ticket.

The e-ticket doesn't have to be delivered to you. When you have purchased one, you can get on board via valid certificate and your trip sheet ID. It will take no more than 10 minutes to apply through the phone or on the net for a date modification. Special prices promoted by airlines especially for e-tickets will help you to save cost.

6. Mileage Plus

Frequent flier programs started in their current form in 1981. United began one week after American Airlines started the first program. United's program is called Mileage Plus.

Airlines who are part of the Star Alliance, such as Air Canada, Lufthansa, Singapore Airlines, and others participate in a program enabling passengers on these airlines to receive Mileage Plus credits.

Miles earned do not expire, provided that any miles are earned or redeemed at least once every 18 months.

Elite level membership, which has added benefits over the standard level membership, is a feature that was not initially part of the program.

Premier Associate (3P) is a new elite level created in 2006 that can be gifted by elite members as a reward for reaching certain plateaus. Privileges are much like Premier members and get access to Economy Plus seating, but does not include the 500-mile e-upgrades or the 25% mileage bonus on flown miles.

Premier (2P) members, who accumulate at least 25,000 Elite Qualifying Miles (EQM) or fly 30 segments, are offered priority boarding, free access to Economy Plus seating, upgrade privileges from any fare, complementary 500-mile e-upgrades and a 25% mileage bonus on flown miles. In 2005, 535,000 members of Mileage Plus qualified for Premier status.

Premier Executive (1P) members fly at least 50,000 EQM or 60 segments, and receive all Premier benefits plus a 100% mileage bonus, higher upgrade priority, access to exit row seating in advance of flight, and lounge access when traveling internationally on any Star Alliance member airline the same day. In 2005, 239,000 members of Mileage Plus qualified for Premier Executive status.

1K (also known as Premier Executive 1K) members fly at least 100,000 EQMs or 100 segments, and receive all Premier Executive benefits plus six free System-wide Upgrades good for a one-class upgrade anywhere United flies, along with the ability to earn confirmed regional upgrades valid across United's North and Latin American route system. 1K passengers are sometimes granted accommodations and meals during flight delays and irregular operations caused by weather or air traffic control. In 2005, 46,000 members of Mileage Plus qualified for 1K status.

Global Services, while not officially part of the Mileage Plus program, is an invitation-only program to recognize United's most valued high-yield customers. Full invitation criteria are not made public by United; re-qualification for current UGS members could be attained by flying 50,000 full-fare miles in a calendar year, according to company letter to members. Benefits complement and expand upon those offered to 1K passengers, including: higher priority for upgrades and front-of-line access in premium security lines. Global Services members are able to upgrade award flights using miles, system-wide upgrades, confirmed regional upgrades and 500 mile upgrade certificates. In 2005, 18,000 members of Mileage Plus qualified for Global Services membership.

Million Miles and Beyond is a program offered to Mileage Plus members who have flown one million miles or more on United Airlines during their lifetime. These customers permanently receive the benefits of Premier Executive members.

Hyperlinks

[1] http://www.travelandleisure.com/cityguides/new-york-city

[2] http://www.visiteurope.com/

[3] http://www.transitionsabroad.com/

[4] http://www.raileurope.com/train-faq/

[5] http://www.hostelbookers.com/article/

[6] http://howtotravelamerica.com/

[7] http://www.chinatraveldepot.com/

[8] http://www.travelforum.org/

References

[1] http://www.reidsguides.com/

[2] http://www.reidsguides.com/t_ss/t_ss_planning.html

[3] Fritz Hahn. Getting Around. *Washington Post*, October 25, 2005

[4] Mark Hodson. The Complete Rail Guide to Europe. *The Sunday Time*, April 22nd, 2007

[5] http://www.panda.org/how_you_can_help/at_home/travel/index.cfm

[6] http://en.wikipedia.org/wiki/History_of_the_New_York_City_Subway

[7] http://www.united.com/page/article/0,8566,1176,00.html?navSource=mileageplus&linkTitle=13partnerguide

图书在版编目（CIP）数据

实用跨文化交流教程:英文 / 李果红主编. —杭
州:浙江大学出版社,2011.2(2016.7重印)
　ISBN 978-7-308-08155-9

　Ⅰ.①实…　Ⅱ.①李…　Ⅲ.①文化交流－教材－英文
Ⅳ.①G115

　中国版本图书馆 CIP 数据核字（2010）第 233301 号

实用跨文化交流教程

李果红　　主编

责任编辑	诸葛勤
封面设计	刘依群
出版发行	浙江大学出版社
	（杭州市天目山路 148 号　邮政编码 310007）
	（网址:http://www.zjupress.com)
排　　版	杭州中大图文设计有限公司
印　　刷	杭州丰源印刷有限公司
开　　本	787mm×1092mm　1/16
印　　张	18.5
字　　数	556 千
版 印 次	2011 年 2 月第 1 版　2016 年 7 月第 3 次印刷
书　　号	ISBN 978-7-308-08155-9
定　　价	39.00 元